State Politics in Zimbabwe

Written under the auspices of the
Center of International Studies, Princeton University

State
Politics in
Zimbabwe

Jeffrey Herbst

Perspectives on Southern Africa, 45

University of California Press

BERKELEY   LOS ANGELES   OXFORD

University of California Press
Berkeley and Los Angeles, California

University of California Press, Ltd.
Oxford, England

First published in 1990
in Zimbabwe by University of Zimbabwe Publications
and in the United States of America by the University of California Press

Library of Congress Cataloguing-in-Publication Data

Herbst, Jeffrey Ira.
    State politics in Zimbabwe.

    (Perspectives on Southern Africa ; 45)
    Includes bibliographical references.
    1. Zimbabwe—Politics and government.   2. Agriculture and state—
Zimbabwe.   3. Industry and state—Zimbabwe.
I. Title.   II. Series.
JQ2922.H47   1990   361.6'1'096894   89-20393
ISBN 0-520-06818-1

Typeset at the University of Zimbabwe
Printed in the United States of America
9 8 7 6 5 4 3 2 1

PERSPECTIVES ON SOUTHERN AFRICA

For my parents

Contents

List of Tables

List of Figures

Acknowledgements

States can be autonomous but researchers never are. I could never have conducted this study without the encouragement, financial support, and friendship of institutions and individuals on two continents. This study began as a dissertation for the Department of Political Science at Yale University. At Yale, I was supported by a Yale University Fellowship and a National Resources Fellowship. I am especially grateful to Bill Foltz for his wisdom, friendship, and camaraderie during my time at Yale. It was in large part due to him that I found graduate school to be, surprisingly enough, an enjoyable experience. I am also grateful to Jim Scott for his advice and help. Yale's Department of Political Science provided a proper intellectual home and I wish to express my thanks to many including Miles Kahler (now at the University of California, San Diego), Tom Biersteker (now at the University of Southern California), Barney Rubin (now at the US Institute for Peace) and David Apter. I also benefited greatly from participation in the Southern Africa Research Program under the direction of Leonard Thompson. SARP provided an exciting atmosphere in which to study Southern Africa and I benefited from a SARP seminar on an early version of Chapter 1 and another on Chapter 9. I am also grateful for a SARP summer grant which allowed me to begin research on this project.

A Fulbright Scholarship administered by the Institute of International Education funded my stay in Zimbabwe, and I, following countless others, can only marvel at the wisdom of this programme of cross-cultural exchange. I am grateful to Bob Dahlsky of the United States Information Agency and Walter Jackson of the Institute of International Eduction for their friendly assistance.

A large number of individuals were extraordinarily generous in their help during my trip to Zimbabwe. I must first thank Zimbabwe's Ambassador to the United States, the Hon. Edmund R. H. Garwe, for his early assistance. At the University of Zimbabwe, I am grateful to the Registrar, Mr R. D. D. Blair for his help, especially in housing. I benefited greatly from the use of all of the University's facilities and am grateful to the many who helped me unstintingly. A special word of thanks to Mr Jacob C. Kufa and Miss Caroline MacNaughtan, librarians at the University of Zimbabwe, for their help and good humour in the face of what must have seemed like an endless torrent of questions.

My debt to the Department of Political and Administrative Studies, where I was a Fulbright Research Associate for eighteen months, can never be repaid. I am especially grateful to my friends and colleagues, Dr Rukudzo Murapa, Prof. Hasu Patel, Mr Chakanyuka Karase, Dr Elias Mukonoweshuro, Dr Solomon Nkiwane, and Ms Joyce Shava for their friendship and assistance. Visitors to the Department, including Marcia Burdette and Carol Thompson (now at the University of Southern California), also provided assistance at different stages of my project. Others at the University of Zimbabwe, including Brigid Strachan, Des Gasper, Prof. A. M. Hawkins (Dean of the Faculty of Commerce) and Rob Davies, provided help and were encouraging.

Access to the facilities of the National Archives of Zimbabwe and the Zimbabwe Institute of Development Studies was of great value to me. I am also grateful to the librarians at the Ministry of Information, Posts and Telecommunications for their assistance.

My debt to the literally hundreds of Zimbabweans who answered questions during interviews, dug through old files for facts, and provided directions for further research cannot be overemphasized. They must remain anonymous but without their help I could not have finished this project. Most of the interviews cited here were conducted during 1986 and 1987, with a few more being done in 1988.

While writing and revising the text, I have benefited greatly from sharing ideas with others. I am grateful first to the Commercial Farmers Union, Roger Riddell, Melanie Ross, Kate Truscott and Rene Loewenson for access to their unpublished material. I was helped greatly by the chance to present an early version of Chapter 5 to a seminar sponsored by the Department of Political and Administrative Studies of the University of Zimbabwe and to another arranged by the Department of Political and Administrative Studies of the University of Botswana. An earlier version of Chapter 7 was presented as part of the Seminar on Southern African Responses to Imperialism sponsored by the University of Zimbabwe. The students of the Public Policy course in the University of Zimbabwe's Master of Business Administration programme also deserve my heartfelt thanks for allowing me to present five of my chapters for discussion in class. In Zimbabwe and in the United States I benefited from comments on my work by Marcia Burdette, Des Gasper, Robert Bates, Kate MaKuen, Roger C. Riddell, Paul R. Thomas, Alan Whiteside and Jennifer Widner.

At Princeton University I completed the process of changing the dissertation into a book. A Pew Foundation Grant to Princeton's Center of

International Studies allowed me to return to Zimbabwe to gather more material. I am also grateful to Forrest Colburn and John Waterbury for their valuable comments while I revised the work and for Michael Stoner's assistance with the charts. My greatest thanks go to Henry Bienen who as teacher, colleague and friend has always been a source of encouragement and support.

I owe a debt of gratitude to Roger Stringer of University of Zimbabwe Publications for his meticulous help in editing the manuscript and in compiling the index.

A somewhat different version of Chapter 5 was originally published in *Comparative Politics* (1988), XX, 265–88, © City University of New York.

A Note on Names and Units

It is a measure of the conflict throughout Zimbabwe's history that even the name of the country should be contentious. In order to minimize confusion, I refer to the country as 'Southern Rhodesia' or simply 'Rhodesia' for the years between 1890 and 1963, 'Rhodesia' for the period between 1963 and 1980, and 'Zimbabwe' for the post-Independence era beginning in 1980. Although those, including myself, who supported the liberation struggle referred to the country as Zimbabwe throughout the UDI period, it is easier to use the more traditional practices when writing about different periods of the country's history. This usage also serves to indicate who controlled the state at any particular point in time. I have, therefore, also used the colonial names for places when referring to them in the pre-1980 period although I have usually also given the current names.

Many Zimbabwean ministries have also changed names in the years since Independence. In all cases where the change was minor, I have simply used the then current name of the Ministry. For example, the Ministry of Local Government and Town Planning became the Ministry of Local Government, Urban and Rural Development and I make no special note of this type of change. However, to avoid confusion I refer in Chapter 5 to the Ministry of Agriculture throughout, even though in 1985 this Ministry merged with the Ministry of Lands, Resettlement and Rural Development to become the Ministry of Lands, Agriculture and Rural Resettlement. Zimbabwe changed from a Westminster style of government to an executive Presidency in 1988. I therefore refer to 'Prime Minister' Mugabe for the period 1980–1988 and to 'President' Mugabe after 1988.

Unless otherwise indicated, all monetary figures in this study are given in Zimbabwe dollars. The fluctuations of the Zimbabwe dollar made it impossible to convert the figures into meaningful US dollar equivalents. For the reader's benefit, Table I provides approximate exchange rates for the post-Independence period. Metric measurements, including the decimal comma, are used thoughout the book.

Table I

APPROXIMATE EXCHANGE RATE VALUES, 1980–1989

Year	US dollars	Pounds sterling
	(Per Zimbabwe dollar)	
1980	1,59	0,66
1981	1,39	0,73
1982	1,09	0,67
1983	0,90	0,62
1984	0,67	0,57
1985	0,61	0,42
1986	0,59	0,41
1987	0,59	0,40
1988	0,52	0,29
1989	0,46	0,29

Sources: Zimbabwe, *Annual Economic Review of Zimbabwe, 1986* (Harare, Ministry of Finance, Economic Planning and Development, 1987), 15; *Europa Yearbook 1987* (London, Europa Publications, 1987), 3209; *Wall Street Journal*, 3 Jan. 1989, C12; RAL Merchant Bank, *Quarterly Guide the the Economy* (Mar., June, Sept. and Dec. 1989).

Abbreviations

AMA	Agricultural Marketing Authority
BSA Company	British South Africa Company
CFU	Commercial Farmers Union
CMB	Cotton Marketing Board
CZI	Confederation of Zimbabwe Industries
DC	District Council
EMCOZ	Employers Confederation of Zimbabwe
FIC	Foreign Investment Committee
GAPWUZ	General Agricultural and Plantation Workers Union of Zimbabwe
GMB	Grain Marketing Board
IMF	International Monetary Fund
MECC	Ministerial Economic Co-ordinating Committee
MMCZ	Minerals Marketing Corporation of Zimbabwe
NFAZ	National Farmers Association of Zimbabwe
OPIC	Overseas Private Investment Corporation
PDL	Poverty Datum Line
PF-ZAPU	Patriotic Front – Zimbabwe African People's Union
PMD	Provincial Medical Director
RC	Rural Council
RF	Rhodesian Front
RNFU	Rhodesian National Farmers Union
SADCC	Southern African Development Co-ordination Conference
TTL	Tribal Trust Land
UDI	Unilateral Declaration of Independence
VIDCO	Village Development Committee
WADCO	Ward Development Committee
ZANU(PF)	Zimbabwe African National Union (Patriotic Front)
ZCTU	Zimbabwe Congress of Trade Unions
ZNFU	Zimbabwe National Farmers Union

ZIMBABWE

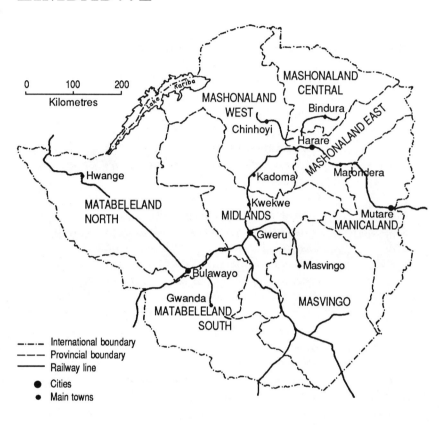

SOUTHERN
AFRICA

Chapter One

Choice and African Politics

At the core of African politics is an enigma. The achievement of political independence was exceptionally important because it gave African leaders formal control of the state apparatus. However, African states are extremely vulnerable because they are disorganized and poor, and because they face societal groups that have the potential to mobilize large numbers of people or great economic resources — for example, ethnic movements and multinational corporations, respectively — in order to pressure leaders on major distributive issues. Therefore, twenty-five years after most African countries received their independence, the extent to which government decisions are made according to the preferences of leaders and the extent to which the state has lost its autonomy to societal groups in the political conflict over resources is still unclear. The problem of volition in African politics is not merely an academic issue: the question of how insulated the state is from societal groups is also crucial to international organizations, such as the World Bank, or developed countries, such as the United States, which recommend programmes of economic reform to African leaders. In addition, Africans who contemplate the potential of existing institutions to transform their societies must understand the limits of the state to act as an agent of change.

The urgency of understanding the autonomy of the African state is heightened by the crucial role that the state plays. While the state in Africa may have relatively few resources, it generally operates in an environment that is so materially deprived that the sphere outside the public sector is even poorer and provides few, if any, opportunities for economic advancement.[1] Therefore, as Richard Hodder-Williams explains, the state

---

[1] Of the 42 countries listed by the World Bank as 'low income', nearly two-thirds are African. Average per capita income throughout the continent is only US$300, World Bank, *World Development Report, 1989* (New York, Oxford Univ. Press, 1989), 164–5.

dominates the job market, is deeply involved in most economic activities and commands control over an extremely wide range of goods and services as well as badges of status. The lack of a developed indigenous private sector, of entrenched pressure groups and of secondary organizations results in the 'monopolistic' state.[2]

The African state's ability — by virtue of its institutional presence and, sometimes, sheer physical force — to control many new sources of wealth guarantees that the private economic realm will not become significantly more important in the near future. For instance, foreign aid, one of the most lucrative income streams in an African nation, is almost always funnelled through the state apparatus.

The state's unrivalled position in the economy automatically leads to its pre-eminent political role. Henry Bienen notes:

Employment in the modern sector in Africa is often employment by government. Control of the state apparatus brings the ability to reward and to coerce. Private wealth is scattered in most countries, and power and status frequently stem from a place in or access to the state apparatus. Elites in Africa derive their power from control of the state, not from private property or private large-scale organizations.[3]

Furthermore, those élites in power will have every incentive to increase the size and importance of the state at the expense of the private sector in order to broaden their own powers and prevent independent bases of authority from developing.[4]

In addition to the economic rewards, the urgency of controlling the state is heightened by the winner-take-all nature of most state structures in Africa. With the major exception of Nigeria, African states have not devolved power away from the centre of the state in order that those who lose out in the battle for the institutional apex can still have some kind of political reward. The political arena beyond the core of the state is almost non-existent; correspondingly, the battle for absolute control of the state

[2] R. Hodder-Williams, *An Introduction to the Politics of Tropical Africa* (London, Allen and Unwin, 1984), 95.

[3] H. Bienen, 'State and revolution: The work of Amilcar Cabral', *Journal of Modern African Studies* (1977), XV, 555. See also H. Goulbourne, 'Some problems of analysis of the political in backward capitalist social formations', in his *Politics and the State in the Third World* (London, Macmillan, 1979), 27.

[4] This point is made persuasively by C. Young and T. Turner, *The Rise and Decline of the Zairian State* (Madison, Univ. of Wisconsin Press, 1985), 31–2.

is the central political drama in Africa. For instance, Robert Mugabe's victory in the 1980 Zimbabwe elections gave him and his party complete control over the entire country, including the two Matabeleland provinces where only ten per cent of the electorate, at most, voted for ZANU(PF).[5] Zimbabwe has tried to decentralize by creating the posts of Provincial Governor, but, in the manner of most African states, the Governors are appointed by the President rather than elected.

The Ambiguity of State Autonomy

In trying to explain how the state carries out its important role in Africa, many scholars would agree with Theda Skocpol that the state is potentially autonomous from societal influence.[6] Unfortunately, most studies have not been able to go beyond the affirmation of the potential of autonomy to the far more important problem of predicting when and under what conditions state leaders will actually be free from outside pressure. For instance, Martin Ougaard, writing from a Marxist orientation, can highlight only the ambiguity of the conflict over resources in poor countries:

In situations of conflicting interests between the dominating classes there is no consistent pattern of prevalence of the special interests of any one class. Rather the prevailing interests will vary from time to time and from political issue to political issue, depending on the class struggle.[7]

Similarly, Robert Jackson and Carl Rosberg, who argue that examining the different styles of personal rule is the key to understanding African politics, are unable to describe the 'political space' available to leaders; they simply state that leaders are no longer autonomous when their power ends:

Personal rule is a system of relations linking rulers not with the 'public' or even

[5] *The Herald* [Harare], 9 July 1985.

[6] T. Skocpol, *States and Social Revolutions: A Comparative Analysis of France, Russia and China* (Cambridge, Cambridge Univ. Press, 1979), 29.

[7] M. Ougaard, 'Some remarks concerning peripheral capitalism and the peripheral state', *Science and Society* (1982–3), XLVI, 402. See also E. Hinzen, 'External dependence and structural underdevelopment in Liberia', in E. Hinzen and R. Kappel (eds.), *Dependence, Underdevelopment and Persistent Conflict: On the Political Economy of Liberia* (Bremen, Ubersee Museum, 1980), 328, and J. Samoff, 'Class, class conflict and the state in Africa', *Political Science Quarterly* (1982), XCVII, 126.

with the ruled (at least not directly), but with patrons, associates, clients, supporters, and rivals, who constitute the 'system'. If personal rulers are restrained, it is
by the limits of their personal authority and power and by the authority and
power of patrons, associates, clients, supporters, and, of course, rivals.[8]

Finally, Thomas M. Callaghy, writing from a position heavily influenced
by corporatist thinking, provides another example of the uncertainty that
abounds concerning volition in the African state:

The model African state is conceived here as an organization of domination
controlled with varying degrees of efficacy by a ruling group or class that
competes for power and compliance, for sovereignty, with other political, economic and social organizations both internally and externally. It is a partly
autonomous, partly dependent structure of control in which a dominant group
seeks to cope with constraints and uncertainty, to manage its dependence on all
groups, internally and externally, in its search for sovereignty.[9]

Indeed, Callaghy claims that theoretical statements concerning volition
are impossible: 'The degree of autonomy, both internal and external, must
be empirically investigated in each case and over time, not dogmatically
denied or proclaimed.'[10] While Callaghy is right to stress the nuances of
each country, the proper role of theory should be to provide the investig-
ator with guidelines so that every study does not have to start from
scratch and, instead, can begin to address more complex issues.
    There are many reasons why a comprehensive understanding of state
autonomy has not yet been developed. Firstly, most studies have not
focused explicitly on the question of volition within the state, examining
instead the dynamics of societal groups such as peasants, ethnic groups,
or multinational corporations. Secondly, those theories that have tried to
examine the African state explicitly have attempted to theorize at a very
general level, making implicit assumptions about state autonomy instead of making it an object of investigation. This tendency has been most
noticeable when attempts are made to construct entire theories of African
politics that relegate the dynamics of actual government to simple generalizations. For instance, Colin Leys, in his study of the political economy
of Kenya, called the African state simply a 'sort of sub-committee' of the

---

[8] R. H. Jackson and C. G. Rosberg, *Personal Rule in Black Africa* (Berkeley and Los
Angeles, Univ. of California Press, 1982), 19.

[9] T. M. Callaghy, *The State–Society Struggle: Zaire in Comparative Perspective* (New York,
Columbia Univ. Press, 1984), 32.

[10] Ibid., 33.

international bourgeoisie.[11] Although Leys had the courage to repudiate
his view once better information on Kenya became available,[12] the imperative felt by many scholars to develop grand theories of African
politics has, ironically, been at the expense of detailed investigations —
investigations which could lead to a better understanding of state decision-making and thus of the interaction between state and society.
Indeed, some who have attempted to construct grand theories of African
politics have later felt the need to go back and do more empirical research.
For instance, Issa G. Shivji admits that 'in understanding the states in neo-
colonies much work yet remains to be done at the level of concrete
analysis. Without this it is not possible to theorize, especially on the state
forms in these countries.'[13]

Unfortunately, without a very good understanding of how specific
decisions are made within the state, it is impossible to theorize constructively about state autonomy because we do not have enough information
on how insulated the leaders are from societal pressures.[14] Indeed, there
have been so few studies of actual government decisions in Africa that
Richard Higgot contends that we cannot make useful generalizations
about the operations of the state:

The major pitfall that needs to be avoided in the attempts by students of African
politics to build up some kind of generalized hypotheses around the nature of the
state in post-colonial societies is the danger inherent in the creation of one or
possibly two abstract models of the 'state-in-general'. . . . It would seem methodo-
logically absurd to make generalizations about the post-colonial state of which
our data and knowledge in individual cases is almost always inferior to that which
we possess about the state in advanced industrial societies, but around which we
are far less ready to make similar sweeping generalizations.[15]

This failure to study actual state operations and to examine the
question of volition explicitly is unfortunate, because state autonomy

[11] C. Leys, *Underdevelopment in Kenya: The Political Economy of Neo-colonialism* (Berkeley
and Los Angeles, Univ. of California Press; London, Heinemann, 1975), 10.

[12] See C. Leys, 'Capital accumulation, class formation and dependency: The significance of the Kenyan case', in R. Miliband and J. Saville (eds.), *The Socialist Register 1978*
(London, Merlin Press, 1978), 250–3.

[13] I. G. Shivji, 'The state in the dominated social formations of Africa: Some theoretical
issues', *International Social Science Journal* (1980), XXXII, 740.

[14] R. A. Dahl, 'A critique of the ruling elite model', *American Political Science Review*
(1958), LII, 466.

[15] R. A. Higgot, 'The state in Africa', in T. Shaw and O. Aluko (eds.), *Africa Projected:
From Recession to Renaissance by the Year 2000?* (London, Macmillan, 1985), 22.

provides us with an important analytical tool for studying politics. State autonomy limits the analytical field; if we have an understanding of state autonomy, then we know where to look to understand the resolution of conflicts over resources. If the state is autonomous, then issues such as leadership style and the preferences of civil servants are obviously very important. If, on the other hand, the state is not autonomous, another set of issues — including those such as interest-group strategy and the dynamics of societal groups (such as ethnic movements) — immediately become crucial areas for study. Without such a limiting device, there is the very real prospect that many investigations of African politics will never focus on the crucial problems because there are simply too many institutions and actors to examine.

Indeed, the absence of a theory of autonomy in the African state has probably been an important contributor to the malaise over the present understanding of African politics. Goran Hyden provides the best statement of this problem:

Everybody following African politics over the last two decades will probably agree that the various attempts to conceptualize and understand it have been rather disappointing. It has been difficult to come to the roots of the phenomenon and consequently there is not yet any theory, or theories of African politics that have gained wide currency. The search for adequate interpretations continues.[16]

Therefore, careful scholars, such as Thomas J. Biersteker, are now reluctant to make any kind of generalization from case studies because past theories failed when they tried to be relevant to 'every other country and potentially relevant policy area'.[17] Others have admitted defeat. In the most comprehensive review of the literature on the African state to date, John Lonsdale concludes: 'Africa's observers equally will doubtless be condemned for ever to remain nomads of the intellect in search of a new paradigm.'[18]

In order to exploit fully the usefulness of the concept of state autonomy, this study will investigate the state's freedom to act on two levels: the structural level and the situational level. Structural autonomy concerns the conflict over the political rules of the game in a given area. It indicates whether the *factors responsible for state decisions concerning the*

[16] G. Hyden, *No Shortcuts to Progress* (London, Heinemann, 1983), 33.

[17] T. J. Biersteker, *Multinationals, the State and Control of the Nigerian Economy* (Princeton, Princeton Univ. Press, 1987), 286.

[18] J. Lonsdale, 'States and social processes in Africa: An historiographical survey', *African Studies Review* (1981), XXIV, 206.

design of institutions are found within the state or among societal groups. An explicit examination of the freedom of states to design the institutions which determine basic allocation decisions is especially important in Africa because there is likely to be far more conflict over the rules of the political game in new states than in established polities.

However, most distributional conflicts actually occur within the context of established institutions. Therefore, another level of state autonomy, concerning the everyday struggle between government and interest groups *within* the established rules, must be examined in order to understand state autonomy fully. This concept may be called 'situational autonomy' because it indicates whether the *factors responsible for specific allocation decisions* are found within the state or among societal groups. It is important to understand situational autonomy, even after structural autonomy has been investigated, because a state can be autonomous at the structural level yet not be autonomous at the situational level, and vice versa.

The Locus of Decision-making within the State

We can limit the analytic field further if we are able to develop a theory which can guide us as to where within the state we should look if the state is autonomous. Even small African states are complex organizations; if we know where within the state to look for political conflicts, we can further focus investigations of the decision-making process. Developing a theory of the locus of decision-making is particularly important in Africa because of the problem of the party. The Western concept of party puts it outside the state: parties are, at most, groups of people who occupy the state for certain periods of time. However, in Africa and elsewhere in the Third World, some parties have evolved to such an extent that they must be considered part of the resource-allocation process. For instance, in 1984 Robert Mugabe claimed that the ruling party, ZANU(PF),

[is] more important than the government, and . . . the Central Committee is above the Cabinet because Ministers derive their power from ZANU(PF). . . . In the future there will be no separation of the party from state organs, because after the national congress in August, government programmes will be based on the resolutions of the ZANU(PF) Central Committee.[19]

[19] ZBC News, Radio 1, 1.15 p.m., 18 Feb. 1984, cited in 'Mugabe says party more important than government', *Foreign Broadcast Information Service: Daily Report: Near East and Africa* [Washington, United States Dept. of Commerce], 22 Feb. 1984, U11.

In some other African countries, too, the party is clearly part of the structure that allocates resources. The Tanzanian constitution, for instance, devolves specific state powers to the party, while analysts have found it impossible to disentangle the party from the state in Algeria.[20] On the other hand, the party is not significantly involved in state decisions in other African nations.[21] A doctrinal theoretical statement, therefore, suggesting that the party is or is not part of the resource-allocation process will clearly not do: the very real variation between African states must be considered.

An Alternative Approach: Zimbabwe as a Case Study

Because it is so important that concepts are developed that will indicate how to better examine the politics of conflict in Africa, and because research up to now has not succeeded in developing these concepts, a new approach to the African state is necessary. Specifically, we need a perspective which focuses first on the actual operations of the state. How the procedures, settings and agents of the state operate in actual allocation decisions must be reasonably well understood before further theorizing on the state can begin. Without such an empirical foundation, any theory of state operation can only be vague to the point of uselessness. Once this analytical foundation is in place, it will be possible to theorize constructively about state autonomy and the locus of decision-making; or, as Michael G. Schatzberg has put it, 'interactions between state and civil society should be the object of empirical inquiry before they become the subject of deductive theorizing'.[22]

This study uses Zimbabwe as a case study for the development of middle-level propositions about state allocation decisions. Zimbabwe has great value as a subject for study for several reasons. Firstly, the Zimbabwean state is representative of many states in Africa because it is intimately involved in every aspect of the economy. The state's role is further heightened in Zimbabwe because part of the political agenda of

---

[20] For Tanzania, see A. K. L. J. Mlimuka and P. J. A. M. Kabudi, 'The state and the party', in I. G. Shivji (ed.), *The State and the Working People in Tanzania* (Dakar, CODESRIA, 1985), esp. 57 and 83. For Algeria, see J. Leca and J-C. Vatin, *L'Algérie politique: Institution et régime* (Paris, Presses de la Fondation Nationale des Sciences Politiques, 1975), 41.

[21] See, for instance, I. Scott, 'Party and administration under the one-party state', in W. Tordoff (ed.), *Administration in Zambia* (Manchester, Manchester Univ. Press, 1980), 139–61.

[22] M. G. Schaztberg, *The Dialectics of Oppression in Zaire* (Bloomington, Indiana Univ. Press, 1988), 142.

the new leadership focuses on using the state as the primary instrument for correcting the racial inequalities of the past. Therefore, The government decision-making process itself has been an important issue in the country, and the role of institutions and different interest groups has been highlighted.

Secondly, Zimbabwe is an excellent case for a study of government decision-making because its newness and the recent radical change of regimes negates the 'non-issue' problem. One of the most significant criticisms of projects which focus on government decisions was made by Peter Bachrach and Morton S. Baratz in their article, 'Two faces of power'.[23] They argued that to study only actual decisions was misleading, because many issues are effectively placed off the political agenda because of 'the dominant values and the political myths, rituals and institutions which tend to favour the vested interests of one or more groups, relative to others'.[24]

However, the non-issue problem becomes much less significant in Zimbabwe because the youth of the nation and the leadership's dedication to radical change make it possible to investigate decisions made even in the first days of Independence. In Chapter 3, for example, I examine how the conflict between the Black government and the White farmers over land lost salience from Independence onward. In most other African countries, the passage of time and changes in personnel make it impossible to thoroughly investigate early decisions that serve to institutionalize the myths and practices that Bachrach and Baratz speak of. Zimbabwe is, therefore, a much better case to study than countries which have retained the same pattern of political economy for so long that it is no longer clear why certain practices, beliefs, or even whole systems, have been adopted.

Finally, owing to its recent transition from a White, minority-ruled regime to a Black government, Zimbabwe is important in itself because it immediately became a very significant country in Africa. Given its history, Zimbabwe will also be examined for lessons on the pressures that will be faced by future non-racial governments in Namibia and South Africa.

Even so, care must still be taken when embarking on a middle-level examination of Zimbabwe's politics. There is a danger of withdrawing too far from theory and simply gathering facts that will not lead to any

[23] P. Bachrach and M. S. Baratz, 'Two faces of power', *American Political Science Review* (1962), LVI, 947–52.

[24] Ibid., 950.

kind of generalizable statement. Therefore, in my examination of government decisions in the case studies, the focus is on the role of institutions, issue-areas and the structure of interest groups because a thorough investigation using these three features, which are common to all political conflicts, allows generalizations to be made about state autonomy and the locus of decision-making.

Institutions are important because even new African states, where state structures are poorly established, will usually have a decisive impact on the pattern of allocation decisions. Donald Rothchild and Robert L. Curry note that 'institutions are a major factor in the policy-making process because of the central role they play in enabling the decision elite to manage the strange emanations from their environment'.[25] Not only do institutions govern conflict, but, as the case studies will demonstrate, there is also a substantial amount of conflict over the design of the institutions themselves. Indeed, the conflict over the structure of decision-making is particularly severe in Africa because most of the states are very young and because there are few countries where a consensus has developed concerning the structure of decision-making. Therefore, this study will pay special attention to the degree of autonomy that the state has in designing the structures that govern allocation decisions.

The issue-area itself also has the potential to have a decisive impact on the evolution of state autonomy.[26] There is no reason to believe that either the possession of power or the process of decision-making is the same across all types of issue-areas. Yet most writers on African politics choose to examine different issue-areas in order (at most) to validate their contention that a certain group or individual is powerful, rather than asking whether the structure and context of the issue-area itself has an effect on the players and rules of the political game. Accordingly, a wide variety of issue-areas have been included in this examination of state allocation decisions in Zimbabwe.

Finally, the ability of interest groups to influence and control state decision-making obviously varies. Understanding the way in which differences in the characteristics of interest groups affect the decision-making process is, therefore, clearly essential to a sophisticated perspective on the allocation process within states. For instance, Dennis H. Wrong notes:

[25] D. Rothchild and R. L. Curry, *Scarcity, Choice and Public Policy in Middle Africa* (Berkeley and Los Angeles, Univ. of California Press, 1978), 38.

[26] On the necessity of studying different issue-areas, see F. W. Frey, 'On issues and nonissues in the study of power', *American Political Science Review* (1971), LXV, 1086-7.

Much theorizing about politics is an attempt to answer the question 'Who gets mobilized?' Or who, that is, what groups, communities, or social categories succeeded in creating and maintaining collective resources for political ends? Who become the major contenders in the arena of political competition and conflict? Conversely, which potential or possible groups do not become contenders because they fail to create and maintain collective resources?[27]

The importance of different interest groups has long been recognized and, fortunately, Zimbabwe provides dramatic contrasts in organizations that seek to influence the state.

In order to use these analytical concepts to maximum advantage, it is obviously important to study a wide variety of issues so that differences in institutions, issue-areas and interest groups can be understood. Therefore, the core of the book is a series of seven case studies of government decision-making in Zimbabwe. Chapters 3 and 4 investigate the development of the most important issue in Zimbabwe: the distribution of land. In the land question there are a variety of interest groups, representing White farmers and Black peasants, that seek to gain resources for their constituencies. Land also has certain special characteristics as a political good that makes it especially worthwhile for study. Chapter 5 studies the setting of agricultural producer prices in order to examine how White and Black agricultural producers co-operate in order to gain favourable allocation decisions from the government. A study of the setting of agricultural producer prices is also valuable because the new regime has retained almost the entire institutional structure developed by the previous White governments and has tried to modify these institutions to serve its own ends.

I examine in Chapters 6 and 7 how the Zimbabwe government responds to pressures from foreign actors. Chapter 6 looks at the development of general foreign-investment policies, while Chapter 7 analyses the conflict between the new regime and foreign mining companies over the government's decision to take over all marketing of the nation's minerals from multinational mining companies. The conflicts between the foreign actors and the Zimbabwe government are particularly interesting because, in both areas, new institutional structures have been created; the issue-area, too, plays a significant role in the eventual allocation of resources.

Chapter 8 investigates the delivery of health care to see whether interest groups organized on the basis of ethnicity or class can influence

[27] D. H. Wrong, *Power: Its Forms, Bases and Abuses* (New York, Harper and Row, 1980), 146.

the distribution of a political good. Once again, old and new government structures play an important role in the evolution of health politics. Finally, Chapter 9 examines government policy on the establishment and implementation of a national minimum wage. The government's health and wage policies are important because they focus on the domestic conflicts between powerful (and White-dominated) business interests and nominally-weak groups such as commercial farm-workers and labour unions, to which the government has made a political commitment.

While these cases cover a broad range of institutions, issue-areas and interests groups, they do leave out many other important issues in Zimbabwe. The idiosyncrasies of Zimbabwe meant that it was impossible to conduct research in certain areas. Nor can one study cover every issue. However, the sample of issues presented provides broad enough coverage to enable concrete generalizations to be made about the decision-making process.[28]

Conclusion

Much of the theorizing about Third World politics seeks to step beyond our cognitive limits. Grand theories of politics are developed and then, as further investigation reveals the dangerous simplifications and vagueness of those constructs, they are slowly rejected. As students of politics move like Lonsdale's nomads from paradigm to paradigm, malaise sets in because no theory seems to 'work'. It is the departure point of this study that it is possible to theorize constructively about politics in Africa and other areas of the Third World if our very real cognitive limits are taken into account. Instead of reaching for grand theories which seek to explain everything and end up doing very little, we should search out middle-level issues such as state autonomy and the locus of decision-making, which can shed light on important political phenomena. It may be that, some day, these middle-level propositions will be developed into grand theory; in the meantime they can be valuable in themselves because they lead to concrete and verifiable predictions about crucial political questions.

[28] A good argument for the necessity of research adapting to local conditions can be found in G. Kitching, 'Local political studies in Tanzania and the wider context', *African Affairs* (1972), LXXI, 282–92.

Chapter Two

Prelude to Independence: The Political Inheritance

A new era did begin in Zimbabwe with Independence in 1980, but the political and economic inheritance of the past determines many of the constraints and opportunities facing the new leaders. An examination of the dynamics of White rule between 1890 and 1980 is therefore important because the new government has consciously tried to build on the strengths of the past while changing the inherently discriminatory parts of the economic and political system. To a great extent, the politics of independent Zimbabwe centre on coming to terms with the vestiges of the past.

Early Years to 1923

In 1890 the Pioneer Column, financed by Cecil Rhodes, moved north from South Africa into the territory that would eventually become Zimbabwe in search of a mineral strike on the scale of that on the Witwatersrand. Rhodes had earlier established the British South Africa (BSA) Company to spearhead the development of the territory. The early settlers were interested mainly in exploring for gold or setting up basic services, such as stores, for the miners. At first, the settlers paid at least lip-service to living peacefully with the African population. However, after crushing the 1896–7 revolt, the Whites acted as conquerors and began to move Blacks away from the best farming land to newly created tribal Reserves, although the Whites were still dependent on food supplies from the Blacks in the early years because White agriculture was as yet un-developed.[1] It soon became apparent, however, that Southern Rhodesia, while possessing significant resources, would not yield the kind of

---

[1] V. Machingaidze, 'Company rule and agricultural development: The case of the BSA Company in Southern Rhodesia, 1908–1923', in *The Societies of Southern Africa in the 19th and 20th Centuries: Volume 9* (London, Univ. of London, Institute of Commonwealth Studies, Collected Seminar Papers 24, 1981), 50.

mineral wealth found in the Transvaal. The settlers therefore began to diversify their economic activities and started to move specifically into agriculture.

Although the settlers' early failure to find large mineral deposits and their subsequent decision to stay on but move into other industries, notably farming, are often regarded as aspects of early colonial history that can now be safely ignored, they are absolutely crucial to understanding the entire history of the country. The absence of mineral resources on the scale of South Africa's meant that Southern Rhodesia would never have a large enough White population to introduce the kind of institutionalized separation of the races that was to become known as apartheid in South Africa. However, because there was a significant settler population which was able to initiate many diverse economic enterprises, a White political community developed in Rhodesia which had its own interests, independent of any outside controlling power, be it the BSA Company, South Africa, or Great Britain. The presence of a White community in sufficient numbers with its own interests and with the political acumen to express its preferences made Southern Rhodesia radically different from most other colonies in Africa (Kenya, Algeria, and the Portuguese colonies of Southern Africa are clear exceptions) where the colonists were primarily government officials carrying out the interests of the colonial power.

However, the presence of a significant White population also meant that Rhodesia could never have followed the easy process of decolonization that occurred in the rest of Africa. Unlike in most colonies, where Independence simply meant that the Whites would be transferred to other foreign-service positions by the colonial government, an easy transfer of power was not possible in Rhodesia because the settlers were too entrenched and too numerous to simply 'disappear'. It was the size of Rhodesia's White population — too small for grand apartheid but too large for an easy exit — that accounted for the peculiar twists and particular tragedies in the country's history.

The unusual political position of the settlers soon became apparent in their relations with the BSA Company. There was an almost immediate conflict between the White settlers and the Company when the White farmers and merchants complained that the Company was interested only in mineral exploitation and not in the economic development of the entire colony. These complaints — not unlike those made today by independent African governments — became significant because the

Company, as it repeatedly failed to find significant gold deposits, was forced to rely more and more on the economic activities of the Whites to make its investment profitable. The Company's increasing reliance on settler activity, particularly agriculture, provided the Whites with more leverage against the Company until they eventually achieved the superior political position.[2] Finally, after years of political skirmishing with the settlers, adverse legal decisions and commercial failure, the Company was forced to end its administrative role in 1922.

The British government then gave the settlers the choice in a referendum of becoming part of South Africa or gaining the status of self-governing colony. The BSA Company wanted the Whites to become part of South Africa; Lewis Gann and Michael Gelfand explain that

monied men [and the Company] distrusted the backveld farmers and 'bush lawyers' within the ranks of the Responsible Government Association, and dreaded the idea of a semi-bankrupt settlers' government at Salisbury, which might tamper with mining and railway investments, or put up local taxes to finance lavish public expenditures and provide jobs for pals.[3]

The BSA Company favoured amalgamation with South Africa because the Union under Jan Smuts was seen as a strong guarantor of British commercial interests. However, the settlers, who were mainly British, feared that they would fall under the domination of Afrikaners if they were to join their southern neighbours, so they ignored the wishes of the Company and voted for self government.[4]

The settlers' decision to go against the wishes of the Company that founded the colony was a good example of the ambiguous relationship that would continue for the next fifty-seven years between the Whites and foreign capital. Almost inevitably, given the origins of the colony, foreign investment would play a crucial role in the economic development of Rhodesia and foreign capital would be perceived as a pillar of White strength. The settlers, therefore, could hardly be hostile to foreign capital. However, they also realized that their interests and those of foreign capital would not always coincide. Ian Phimister captures these contradictory impulses well:

[2] C. Leys, *European Politics in Southern Rhodesia* (Oxford, Clarendon, 1959), 8.

[3] L. H. Gann and M. Gelfand, *Huggins of Rhodesia* (London, Allen and Unwin, 1964), 59. The similarity between the fears expressed by domestic and foreign companies in 1922 and at Independence in 1980 is obvious.

[4] Ibid., 60.

For several decades after the occupation of Mashonaland and Matabeleland, members of the settler bourgeoisie were clearer about what they were not than what they were. Contemptuous of the speculative land companies which 'locked up' much of the countryside, and opposed to the monopolistic power wielded by the railway trust, they claimed that they were neither passing adventurers nor slaves of the Chartered Company. By the outbreak of war in 1914, growing numbers suspected that they wanted no part of South Africa either.... 'Rhodesia for the Rhodesians', proclaimed [Sir Charles] Coghlan at the conclusion of the campaign for Responsible Government, 'and Rhodesia for the Empire'.[5]

The conflict between the settlers and the BSA Company was an early indication that the Whites were prepared to assert their own interests in their relationship with foreign capital and that the state would be the settlers' primary instrument of protection. In many ways, the history of Rhodesia from the removal of the BSA Company through the state efforts to 'Rhodesianize' the economy to the Unilateral Declaration of Independence (UDI) can be read as a continual effort to strengthen the position of Whites *vis-à-vis* foreign interests by gradually building up the state apparatus.

Slow Consolidation: 1923–1945

Southern Rhodesia's peculiar self-governing status, unique among British colonies, both reflected and encouraged the White community's distinctive politics. After the 1922 referendum, the British government maintained the extremely low profile it had taken in the colony during Company rule.[6] Additionally, while the British formally reserved a legislative veto on all government measures affecting the African population, supervision by the colonial power did not seriously impinge on the settlers' political autonomy.[7] In practice, the British government did not make use of the channels available to it to influence Southern Rhodesian policy generally or the settlers' specific policies towards Africans. Not once in the colonial history of Rhodesia did the British government formally use its powers to veto a Rhodesian race policy.[8] Anthony Verrier

---

[5] I. R. Phimister, *An Economic and Social History of Zimbabwe: 1890–1948: Capital Accumulation and Class Struggle* (London, Longman, 1988), 180.

[6] L. W. Bowman, *Politics in Rhodesia: White Power in an African State* (Cambridge, Harvard Univ. Press, 1973), 6.

[7] C. Palley, *The Constitutional History and Law of Southern Rhodesia 1880–1965 with Special Reference to Imperial Control* (Oxford, Clarendon, 1966), 270.

[8] D. J. Murray, *The Governmental System in Southern Rhodesia* (Oxford, Clarendon, 1970), 7.

is correct to note that 'the Dominion Office did not, collectively, care what happened to Southern Rhodesia'.[9]

The Early Economy

The most important economic developments in the years immediately after the achievement of self-governing status were in the area of agriculture. With the settlers' decision to move into farming, forced removal of Africans from rich farm areas to tribal Reserves, many with poor-quality land, became an essential aspect of the development of the colony. By 1910, 23,4 per cent of the land had been appropriated by the Whites, and 26 per cent had been declared Native Reserves, later to become known as Tribal Trust Lands (TTLs).[10] The Land Apportionment Act of 1930 legalized the division of the country's land, and prohibited members of either racial group from owning land in areas assigned to the other. By the time of the Land Apportionment Act, 50,8 per cent of the total land had been declared 'European', while 30 per cent had been reserved for the African population. The 'herding' of Africans into overcrowded Reserves and blatantly discriminatory policies against African farmers, designed to protect fledgling White farmers from competition, meant that 'by the end of the 1930s, the agricultural economy of the Shona and the Ndebele, like that of the Kikuyu and most South African peoples, had been destroyed'.[11] Not surprisingly, since control over land was essential to the Whites' achieving economic and political dominance, the colonists' appropriation of the land became the most important African grievance against the settlers.

The over-population in the Reserves and the consequent lack of economic opportunities for peasant farmers turned the TTLs into excellent labour reserves for the White economy. The TTLs served this function because African families, who had previously moved to new land when agricultural productivity began to fall, were now tied to one piece of land that inevitably became less productive with constant use. Faced with decreases in the land's productivity, an increasing number of Africans

[9] A. Verrier, *The Road to Zimbabwe* (London, Cape, 1986), 36.

[10] All statistics on land divisions are from J. W. Harbeson, 'Land and Rural Development in Independent Zimbabwe: A Preliminary Assessment' (Harare, United States Agency for International Development, 1981, mimeo.), 5.

[11] R. H. Palmer, 'The agricultural history of Rhodesia', in R. H. Palmer and Q. N. Parsons (eds.), *The Roots of Rural Poverty in Central and Southern Africa* (London, Heinemann, 1977), 243.

had no choice but to seek income from formal employment to supplement lower returns from agriculture.[12] In addition, the high taxes imposed by the Rhodesians reinforced the necessity for Africans to provide labour for European industries. The system worked so well that in the 1930s Southern Rhodesian businesses were said to be enjoying 'the cheapest Black labour probably in the British Empire'.[13]

The State

In the years immediately after the attainment of self-rule, the Whites also began to construct a highly interventionist state to further their interests. The size of the state, even in the first years of the colony, reflected the settlers' determination to develop a local institutional presence. By 1923, the settler government employed 2 000 Whites in six administrative offices, even though only 33 000 settlers lived in the entire colony. Given that there were only 1 500 administrators at the height of colonial rule in Nigeria (a country with a much larger population),[14] the size of the early state is impressive.

The main motivation for strengthening the colonial state was the insecurity of the settlers in the face of a hostile environment. The colonists — with their aspirations to build a country like South Africa but lacking its wealth and a White population of similar size — had to look toward the state early on for protection against economic competition from Africans, and they used the state to place the Africans in a permanently disadvantaged position. For instance, when the Industrial Conciliation Act of 1934 was passed, the government explicitly excluded Africans from the definition of 'employee'.[15] In addition, in the 1930s the government systematically strengthened the labour reserve system by preventing Africans from moving into 'prospecting and mining, and from competing on even terms in beef production' as well as erecting barriers that excluded Blacks from the domestic maize market.[16] Correspondingly,

---

[12] G. Arrighi, The Political Economy of Rhodesia (The Hague, Mouton, 1967), 31–2.

[13] I. R. Phimister, 'Zimbabwe: The path of capitalist development', in D. Birmingham and P. M. Martin (eds.), History of Central Africa (New York and London, Longman, 2 vols., 1983), II, 280.

[14] M. Bratton, 'The public service in Zimbabwe', Political Science Quarterly (1980), XCV, 445.

[15] Leys, European Politics in Southern Rhodesia, 30.

[16] Ibid., 33.

these provisions and other discriminatory practices developed or condoned by the state guaranteed that White wages would always be high because the labour supply had been artificially restricted.

The small economic base of the colony also meant that it was extremely vulnerable to changes in the world economy. The Whites therefore used the state as a buffer against the threatening international environment. Especially after the Great Depression dramatically illustrated the economic vulnerability of the settlers, the White state began to

regulate control and eventually more systematically orchestrate economic policy. For this it needed to exercise power usable in a wide range of spheres. Interventionist legislation was thus set in motion and applied in the determination of prices (e.g. over maize), quotas, balances in the tobacco market, subsidies (e.g. to small-worker gold mines), employment (through labour-intensive public works schemes), tariffs and administrative protections, and new taxes over previously protected revenue sources.[17]

The setting of agricultural prices is a good example of state intervention to protect insecure Whites. Although the farmers were the pillar of settler power, many of them were about to be forced off the land during the 1930s because of extremely poor prices. The government therefore intervened and began to set the maize price and subsidize the farmers so that they would be able to stay on the land. Most of the maize farmers who remained on the land through the Great Depression were, in fact, kept going by subsidies and 'by being given a virtual monopoly of the domestic foodstuffs market at the expense of African producers'.[18]

In addition to using controls and subsidies, the state moved aggressively to develop public enterprises in areas that it deemed vital to the colony but unattractive to private investors. By 1945 state enterprises included electrical power stations, the Cold Storage Commission's abattoirs, the Rhodesian Iron and Steel Corporation's foundries and the Sugar Industry Board's Triangle estate.[19] The significance, and success, of these interventions is clear: more than forty years later, some of the state-initiated enterprises, notably the Cold Storage Commission and the Iron and Steel Corporation, are among the largest manufacturing enterprises

[17] D. G. Clarke, *Foreign Companies and International Investment in Zimbabwe* (Gwelo, Mambo Press, 1980), 21.

[18] Leys, *European Politics in Southern Rhodesia*, 15.

[19] Ibid., 16.

in the country. Table II demonstrates the growing importance of manufacturing industries during this period.

The development of an economic system based on private enterprise
coexisting with a highly interventionist state led to a particular type of
interest-group politics that came to characterize White Rhodesian politics. The crucial role of the state in what were becoming relatively

Table II

CONTRIBUTIONS TO NATIONAL INCOME, 1924–1943 *

| Year | Percentage contribution | | | |
	Agriculture	Mining	Manufacturing	Services
1924	16,1	29,5	9,4	45
1928	18,5	22,2	14,2	45
1932	14,0	27,8	10,2	48
1936	10,9	29,8	14,3	45
1940	14,5	24,7	14,8	46
1943	15,4	19,1	16,5	49

* These statistics were developed before the United Nations system of national
accounts was formulated. They are, therefore, not directly comparable with the figures
cited below on the structure of the gross domestic product.

Source: Southern Rhodesia, *Report of the Committee of Enquiry into the Protection of
Secondary Industries* (Salisbury, Govt. Printer, 1946), 14.

prosperous industries meant that business had to develop formal lobbying groups in order to try to influence policy decisions. It is not a
coincidence, for instance, that the two lobbying groups in Southern
Rhodesia representing the most important industries in the country, the
Chamber of Mines and the Rhodesian National Farmers Union (RNFU),
were created in 1939 and 1942, respectively, when the importance of the
state's allocation decisions to the fortunes of individuals and industries
was becoming clear to all. These lobbying organizations had tremendous
influence on the state:

White farming, mining, labour and, later, industrial interests had much more
direct channels for influence than a periodic say through elections or rubbing
shoulders with officials at the club. Their representative bodies . . . were not only
well organized and able to articulate their members' interests but [were] also

brought into consultative roles. More crucially, the host of parastatal bodies ... co-opted farmers, mine representatives and others businessmen on to their sector's specialist bodies.[20]

Similarly, Leys noted that pressure groups worked in Southern Rhodesia as they did elsewhere, but that they could 'exercise their power through channels officially dug for the purpose'.[21]

At the same time, electoral politics among the voting (i.e. White) population was relatively less important compared with interest-group lobbying. The fact that Rhodesia, unlike South Africa, lacked significant ethnic or class divisions within its White population greatly reduced the drive for electoral competition. There were ideological splits in the White population, but they were not significant enough to generate real elect-oral conflict.[22] In addition, most Whites conceived of the central conflict in their country as being between Blacks and Whites, so the numerically insignificant White population tended to unite against the perceived Black threat rather than look for divisions among themselves.[23] Therefore,

of eight general elections down to and including Garfield Todd's victory in 1954 (by exactly the same margin as Coghlan's [the first Prime Minister]), the govern-ment party under whatever name won six [elections] with a majority of not less than fourteen in the Legislative Assembly, i.e. not less than twenty-two seats or 73 per cent of the total. Only once did the opposition actually win ... Rhodesia had in effect throughout these years [1930s to 1950s] a one-party system . . .[24]

This pattern of electoral politics was to continue without interruption to the end of White rule.

Growth and Consolidation: 1945–1965

The settlers' real economic opportunity came with the Second World War and the economic explosion that accompanied and succeeded the war. The war effort vastly increased the demand for Rhodesian chrome and

[20] L. Cliffe, 'Zimbabwe's political inheritance', in C. Stoneman (ed.), Zimbabwe's Inherit-ance (Harare, College Press; New York, St Martin's Press, 1981), 12.

[21] Leys, European Politics in Southern Rhodesia, 71.

[22] Some of the divisions in the White community are described by I. Hancock, White Liberals, Moderates and Radicals in Rhodesia (New York, St Martin's Press; London, Croom Helm, 1984).

[23] Leys, European Politics in Southern Rhodesia, 88.

[24] R. Blake, A History of Rhodesia (London, Eyre Methuen, 1977), 194–5.

asbestos, and the large military presence in the colony led to substantial gains in domestic manufacturing. The post-war boom sustained the demand for Rhodesia's raw materials, and immigration of Whites to the colony after 1945 from Britain and South Africa (due to the victory of the Nationalist Party in 1948) had the effect of strengthening the White community. In 1941 there were 69 000 Whites in the colony; by 1954 there were 158 000.[25] The colony averaged a real (after inflation) growth rate of over 10 per cent per annum and the real Gross Domestic Product of the colony almost doubled between 1947 and 1953 (see Table III). As it had from the very beginning of the colony, foreign investment played a major role in financing economic growth. Stoneman estimates that seventy to seventy-five per cent of investment in the colony between the end of the Second World War and 1953 was foreign.[26]

The State

During this period, the state intervened even more in the economy in order to secure the interests of the Whites. For instance, in the early 1950s the government enacted comprehensive price controls over large parts of the economy.[27] In addition, White farmers were the beneficiaries of a government system that set prices for many of their crops and guaranteed the purchase of those crops when they were marketed. Similarly, manufacturing industries, which could take advantage of import substitution promoted by high tariffs and of the inexpensive labour provided by the labour reserve system, were protected from the vagaries of the market. Therefore, despite frequent declarations of their belief in capitalism, the settlers by the 1950s were clearly developing a system best described as 'Socialism-for-the-Whites'. In this system the state sought to provide an economic life for Whites that was basically shock-free with a near guarantee of an extraordinarily high standard of living. Even in the early 1950s, each White household had, on average, two African servants, and the number of automobiles per capita (one for every four Whites) was almost as high as for the United States.[28]

[25] Southern Rhodesia, *Yearbook of Southern Rhodesia, 1952* (Salisbury, Central Statistical Office, 1952), 131, and Rhodesia, *Monthly Digest of Statistics: January 1973* (Salisbury, Central Statistical Office, 1973), 3.

[26] C. Stoneman, 'Foreign capital and the prospects for Zimbabwe', *World Development* (1976), IV, 33.

[27] Arrighi, *The Political Economy of Rhodesia*, 40.

[28] Leys, *European Politics in Southern Rhodesia*, 85.

Table III

STRUCTURE AND GROWTH OF THE RHODESIAN ECONOMY, 1947–1979

Year	Sectoral distribution of GDP (%)			Real growth of the economy (%)
	Agriculture	Mining	Manufacturing	
1947	n.a.	8,9	13,4	14,64
1948	26,9	10,0	13,0	12,26
1949	23,6	10,0	13,6	8,38
1950	23,4	9,9	14,7	10,77
1951	n.a.	9,4	17,1	7,31
1952	n.a.	10,5	16,0	9,69
1953	n.a.	9,1	15,3	8,05
1954	22,8	8,6	14,6	n.a.
1955	21,3	8,4	14,4	8,85
1956	21,8	7,9	14,2	8,74
1957	19,8	7.4	15,0	9,14
1958	18,7	7,1	15,6	1,18
1959	19,2	6,5	15,8	3,37
1960	18,8	6,8	16,9	3,24
1961	21,7	6,4	16,8	2,35
1962	21,0	5,7	17,5	–0,45
1963	20,9	5,1	17,4	1,85
1964	20,5	5,9	18,3	2,04
1965	17,0	7,1	19,7	3,90
1966	19,6	6,6	17,9	–2,12
1967	20,2	6,2	18,9	7,41
1968	15,4	6,2	20,1	1,87
1969	17,9	6,7	19,6	15,66
1970	15,2	6,8	22,4	2,18
1971	16,1	5,8	20,2	8,77
1972	16,5	5,4	20,9	8,46
1973	13,8	6,7	22,1	3,00
1974	16,9	7,3	22,6	6,44
1975	16,2	6,6	22,4	–3,63
1976	16,2	7,0	22,2	–1,04
1977	15,2	6,8	20,9	–11,90
1978	12,4	6,6	21,8	0,73
1979	11,5	8,0	22,1	3,84

Sources: C. Stoneman, 'Foreign capital and the prospects for Zimbabwe', *World Development* (1976), IV, 30 for 1947–71, and Zimbabwe, *National Income and Expenditure Report* (Harare, Central Statistical Office, 1985), 6 for 1972–9. Deflators for real growth rate from Southern Rhodesia, *Economic and Statistical Bulletin of Southern Rhodesia: April 1953* (Salisbury, Central African Statistical Office, 1953), 37, and Rhodesia, *Monthly Digest of Statistics: January 1976* (Salisbury, Central Statistical Office, 1976), 15.

While the state was building its Socialism-for-the-Whites system, the African population was experiencing continual economic decline. Most of the economic problems faced by the Blacks were caused by the rising population in the Reserves and the resultant decreasing productivity of the land. The Native Production and Trade Commission estimated as early as 1945 that thirty-eight of the Reserves were being used at a rate at least 50 per cent above their carrying capacities and that nine of them were overused by at least 150 per cent.[29] Humphrey Wightwick, an MP in the 1950s, accurately summed up the importance of the land division for the country's entire economic and political system: 'To the South of us we have a country which practises a thing called apartheid. Here, in Southern Rhodesia we do not speak Afrikaans, so we pronounce it Land Apportionment Act.'[30]

Federation

The state and the economy of the Whites was further strengthened during the ten years between 1953 and 1963 when Southern Rhodesia belonged, together with Northern Rhodesia (now Zambia) and Nyasaland (now Malawi), to the Federation of Rhodesia and Nyasaland. Federation was a boon to the White economy because it solved the classic problem faced by a small country which is beginning to industrialize: how to capture a market that is big enough for economies of scale to be achieved and at the same time protect enterprises from low-cost competition which could kill industrial development in its infancy. The Federation was a brilliant solution to these problems because it gave the colony assured markets in both Northern Rhodesia and Nyasaland and access to finance from Northern Rhodesia's Copperbelt.[31]

The granting of independence to Zambia and Malawi in the early 1960s caused the dissolution of the Federation and a major crisis in Rhodesia. As independence dawned on the rest of the continent, the problem of a settler community that was simply too large and too entrenched to be ignored or bribed came to the fore.[32] Just before the

---

[29] Cited in H. V. Moyana, *The Political Economy of Land in Zimbabwe* (Gweru, Mambo Press, 1984), 85.

[30] Quoted in M. L. Rifkind, 'The Politics of Land in Rhodesia' (Edinburgh, Univ. of Edinburgh, M.Sc. thesis, 1968), 212.

[31] Stoneman, 'Foreign capital and the prospects for Zimbabwe', 40.

[32] L. Cokorinos, 'The political economy of state and party formation in Zimbabwe', in M. G. Schatzberg (ed.), *The Political Economy of Zimbabwe* (New York, Praeger, 1984), 27.

Federation was dissolved, the Whites received a constitution from Britain which removed even the ineffective clauses which had previously given Her Majesty's Government a veto over policies affecting Africans.[33] The removal of the clauses was simply an acknowledgement of the almost total autonomy the Rhodesians had gained since the beginning of self-rule.

However, Great Britain was not willing to grant formal independence unless the colony's government had at least some aspirations toward majority rule. The Whites rejected even these minimal conditions and chose the Rhodesian Front (RF) headed first by Winston Field and then by Ian Smith, a man absolutely dedicated to continued White rule, to lead them. Smith soon became aware that he would not obtain Rhodesia's independence from Britain on his own terms and therefore unilaterally declared the country independent on 11 November 1965. The declaration immediately led to international ostracism and comprehensive sanctions — at first, voluntary, later mandatory — against Rhodesia. While many people viewed UDI as mass hysteria inflamed by one man, the declaration, seen in the context of Rhodesian history described here, was simply another, albeit dramatic, step that the White state took to protect the settlers against the international pressures that threatened their domestic position.

The UDI Years: 1965–1980
The fifteen years of UDI and international sanctions that began in 1965 were, above all else, symbolic of the Whites' determination to pursue their own interests unyieldingly. A more dramatic contrast to the situation in most African colonies, which the settlers usually left after little or no protest, would be hard to find. W. H. H. Nicolle, the Permanent Secretary for Internal Affairs during UDI, presented an extreme but representative example of the settlers' defiant view of the outside world:

I think, in many respects, we in Rhodesia have been extremely fortunate that for certain reasons we have become involved in a situation commonly known as UDI and in consequence we reaped the reward of sanctions. . . . The strength of our position soon revealed itself because we became masters in our own house through the good fortunes of sanctions which had so effectively removed the

[33] Bowman, *Politics in Rhodesia*, 40.

villains who had previously manipulated our development and had dictated our progress through the fraudulent device of international capital.[34]

The State

The most concrete symbol of the settlers' defiance was their state. The threatening international economic environment induced by sanctions resulted in a further strengthening of state capabilities because the Whites again needed to be protected against economic uncertainty and danger. The necessity of co-ordinated, economy-wide sanctions-busting efforts led the state to intervene either formally or informally in every sector of the economy on a wide variety of issues, including foreign exchange and White employment.[35] Without hesitation the state also seized new powers in order to combat the external threats the Whites faced. Professor Anthony M. Hawkins reported that the 'exigencies of the post-sanctions situation necessitated the action of what a senior government official called "dictatorial powers" in the interests of "both financial and political security" '.[36] It was relatively easy for the state to intervene further in the economy because of the institutional arrangements that had already been established while building the Socialism-for-the-Whites system and because of the expectation on the part of the White population that protection from the threatening environment could be achieved through the expansion of the state.

The necessity of conducting a brutal civil war from the early 1970s against the Black nationalist guerrillas further extended the reach of the state, because not only the economy but the lives of the White population and a significant portion of the Black population had to be co-ordinated by the state. Indeed, even in 1979, after fighting the war for many years, evading international sanctions for fourteen years, and suffering from deep economic depression, the state still demonstrated substantial ability to project authority. For instance, up to half a million people were placed in 'protected villages' by the Rhodesian state during the 1970s in an attempt to end the popular support for the guerrillas.[37]

Apart from using actual war-fighting measures, the state was also able

[34] W. H. H. Nicolle, 'The development of the subsistence sector in Rhodesia', *Rhodesian Journal of Economics* (1971), V, iv, 2.

[35] Bowman, *Politics in Rhodesia*, 116.

[36] A. M. Hawkins, *Economic Growth, Structural Change and Economic Policy in Rhodesia, 1965–1975* (Salisbury, Whitsun Foundation, 1976), 24.

[37] Cliffe, 'Zimbabwe's political inheritance', 27.

to keep the Black population locked into the colonial economy during the UDI years. As always in Rhodesia, agricultural policy was the area of state action that most affected the African population. One official with lengthy experience in the Ministry of Agriculture described the government's stance between 1965 and 1980: 'Agricultural policy was always a weapon of the Smith government. It had an absolutely clear policy of forcing people to grow just enough to be malnourished and prevented them from doing anything more.' By the mid-1970s White agriculture was supplying the TTLs with a substantial proportion of food staples.[38] Therefore, the state had almost completely reversed the agricultural supply situation at the beginning of the century when White settlers were dependent on Africans for food supplies.

In the 1960s, in tandem with the emergence of a strong state, there came, for the first time in Rhodesia's history, a strong party. Continuing Rhodesia's tradition of one-party politics, the Rhodesian Front won all fifty seats in the decisive 1965 elections.[39] The RF was a strong, well-co-ordinated party that was, in many ways, the centre of decision-making in the Smith government. Larry Bowman, writing a decade after the establishment of the RF, argued that 'every important decision made in Rhodesia since December 1962 has been hammered out first within the closed confines of the Rhodesian Front'.[40] Indeed, the RF was able to remain the dominant political organization in Rhodesia until 1980, repeatedly overwhelming all White opposition groups.

African Opposition and Guerrilla Warfare

The particular pattern of state growth in Rhodesia also had an effect on the development of opposition to the White government. Internal Black opposition to Rhodesian racial practices had been continual since the establishment of the colony, and organized opposition had developed a visible, if highly limited, presence by the mid-1950s. However, systematic repression by successive White governments prevented this opposition from becoming a powerful force. By the late 1950s open meetings in the TTLs were banned, a person could be imprisoned for making a statement that would 'undermine the authority' of any government officer, the government was given the power to ban any organization 'likely to raise

[38] M. Bratton, 'Settler state, guerrilla war and underdevelopment in Rhodesia', *Rural Africana* (1979), IV–V, 118.

[39] Bowman, *Politics in Rhodesia*, 82.   [40] Ibid., 109.

disaffection among the inhabitants of Southern Rhodesia', preventive detention of up to five years was possible for anyone 'concerned in any activities which in the opinion of Governor [were] potentially dangerous to public safety or public order', police could search property without a warrant, and publications could be banned.[41] The declaration of the state of emergency in conjunction with UDI formally eliminated the possibility of a significant internal African political presence because the government could do by decree anything that it did not already have sufficient legal powers to do.[42]

African opposition in the early years of UDI, therefore, was in disarray. Protest inside the country against the Smith regime was impossible, and the hope that the international sanctions imposed on Rhodesia would result in an easy transfer of power to the African majority delayed the development of an armed opposition. It was only after Rhodesia's competence in evading sanctions, and the world's lack of seriousness in enforcing the penalties it had enacted, became apparent that the futility of waiting for the UN-imposed sanctions to work became clear to all.

The nationalist movement was also hindered by a serious split in the leadership, which eventually led to the creation of two, sometimes competing, parties, each with its own army. Joshua Nkomo's Zimbabwe African People's Union (ZAPU) was the successor organization outside the country to a large number of internal organizations that had been successively banned by the Rhodesians throughout the 1950s. However, even though Nkomo was the undisputed champion of Zimbabwe nationalism, differences over how to confront the Rhodesians led to a split in the leadership in 1963. The breakaway group, eventually to be led by Robert Mugabe, formed the Zimbabwe African National Union (ZANU).

The split in the nationalist camps soon came to reflect (and aggravate) the ethnic division in the country, because ZANU was perceived by the African population to represent the Shona (who account for 80 per cent of the population) while ZAPU was seen as the party of the Ndebele (17 per cent of the population).[43] While the Shona–Ndebele conflict is really quite

---

[41] Ibid., 58–9.   [42] Ibid., 59.

[43] John Day has argued that tribal considerations are of secondary importance in understanding the divisions in the nationalist camp compared to the role of patron–client relationships. However, he ignores the fact that the nationalist groups, while perhaps not initially based on tribal divisions, came to be seen by others as representing either the Shona or Ndebele, see J. Day, 'The insignificance of tribe in the African politics of Zimbabwe Rhodesia', in W. H. Morris-Jones (ed.), *From Rhodesia to Zimbabwe: Behind and beyond Lancaster House* (London, Cass, 1980), 85–109.

a recent phenomenon,[44] the division did have a debilitating effect on the nationalist struggle. ZANU was also riven with intra-Shona divisions that led to deep suspicions between competing subgroups.[45] The two parties did pledge to unite in the late 1970s and formed the Patriotic Front (PF), but the two organizations never actually merged. The addendum of 'PF' to ZANU's and ZAPU's official names (thus 'ZANU(PF)' and 'PF-ZAPU') was the only remnant of this short marriage of convenience until the parties finally united at the end of 1987.

The armed struggle began slowly, and it was not until 1975 that the nationalist armies developed a significant military presence in Rhodesia. In that year the Frelimo victory in Mozambique allowed ZANU to open a second front, allowing guerrillas to infiltrate into Rhodesia through the Eastern Highlands. However, neither nationalist party ever developed the kind of control over an area that Frelimo did in parts of Mozambique during its long struggle against the Portuguese.[46] This was probably because of the Rhodesians' greater competence in fighting a guerrilla war, and because there are fewer areas in Zimbabwe that would have been remote enough to allow the easy establishment of a guerrilla government.

The Lancaster House Agreement and Peace

By 1979, the war, economic difficulties and White emigration forced the Smith government to seek a negotiated settlement. The Black nationalist forces also decided to seek peace through negotiations because their leaders realized that a complete military victory would cost thousands of African lives and result in large-scale destruction of the country's infra-structure and industry. The leaders of other Southern African countries, which were being severely affected by the war, also pressed them to negotiate. With the aid of the then British Foreign Secretary, Lord Carrington, the two sides eventually agreed to the constitution drawn up at

[44] See D. N. Beach, *War and Politics in Zimbabwe 1840–1900* (Gweru, Mambo Press, 1986), 14–15.

[45] For instance, when Rhodesian security agents killed ZANU leader Herbert Chitepo, the murder was attributed by nationalists and their supporters to rivalries between different Shona sub-groups, see Zambia, *Report of the Special International Commission on the Assassination of Herbert Witshire Chitepo* (Lusaka, Govt. Printer, 1976), 44. The fact the Rhodesians were actually responsible for Chitepo's death is admitted by Ken Flower, the former head of Rhodesian intelligence, in his *Serving secretly* (Harare, Quest; London, Murray, 1987), 147.

[46] On Frelimo operations in liberated areas, see B. Munslow, *Mozambique: The Revolution and Its Origins* (New York and London, Longman, 1983), 92–7.

Lancaster House in late 1979.[47] In return for procedural safeguards —
including a provision against the seizure or property, notably land,
special clauses to prevent a change in the constitution for seven years after
Independence, and twenty per cent of the seats in Parliament (even
though they comprised only two to three per cent of the population) — the
Whites agreed to a Black government on the Westminster model with a
titular President and a Prime Minister representing the majority party in
Parliament. The British, under the last Colonial Governor, Lord Soames,
regained control of the colony for several months and managed to enforce
a cease-fire and hold elections which were widely considered to be free
and fair. Robert Mugabe and ZANU(PF) won an overwhelming victory
over Nkomo's PF-ZAPU and several other parties in an election that was
decided mainly along ethnic lines.

The Political and Economic Endowment at Independence

The State

The particular way in which Blacks achieved majority rule in Zimbabwe
had important implications for post-Independence politics. In 1980,
ZANU(PF) did not gain control over a weak colonial state that had been
hurriedly improved for Independence and on which they could quickly
put their imprimatur (the typical scenario for countries that gained their
independence in the 1960s). Nor did the guerrillas win an outright victory
as Frelimo had done in Mozambique, where the old state collapsed
creating a vacuum into which new government structures and practices
could be placed. Instead, the Black government took over a bruised, but
not defeated, settler state which contained powerful anachronistic elements that were hostile to the political project of the new regime.

A good example of the opportunities and problems faced by the
Zimbabwean government, as well as a crucial aspect of state politics in
itself, is the civil service. In 1980 there were 40 000 civil servants, of whom
approximately 29 000 were Black. However, almost all of these were
teachers or clerical assistants. Of the 10 570 'Established Officers' only
3 368 were Black, and no Blacks held positions above the senior administrative level.[48] As a result,

---

[47] The negotiations are described well by J. Davidow, *A Peace in Southern Africa: The
Lancaster House Conference on Rhodesia, 1979* (Boulder, Westview, 1984).

[48] *The Herald,* 18 Apr. 1985.

at Independence, the ZANU(PF) leadership constituted a thin veneer atop a largely untransformed state apparatus. The Cabinet found itself in a fragile position because institutions wholly or partly controlled by groups of dubious loyalty were interposed between the leadership and its popular base.[49]

The government moved slowly at first and chose not to force Whites out — both because of its general policy of reconciliation and because it wanted to take advantage of the White civil servants' experience. Instead, the new regime adopted the more time-consuming tactic of expanding the civil service to allow more Blacks in and waited for the White civil servants to retire or resign. The civil service was therefore increased from 40 000 to 80 000 people (the vast majority of the increase was accounted for by teachers) to allow Blacks to move into the state apparatus even while Whites still held many of the most significant positions. By 1983, owing to the departure of Whites and the increase in the number of positions, 86 per cent of the Established Officers were Black.[50]

However, Africanization of the state did not of itself guarantee the new leaders control of the state. Indeed, senior government officials constantly express concern that civil servants may 'hijack' policy and perhaps even become an 'invisible Cabinet'.[51] Herbert Ushewokunze, the former Minister of Transport, has gone so far as to argue that Ministers must become 'Super Permanent Secretaries' because they cannot trust civil servants to implement government policy.[52]

Ideology

The new regime's incomplete control of the state was aggravated by its failure to develop a comprehensive ideology. As Barry Munslow notes,

[49] M. Bratton, 'Development in Zimbabwe: Strategy and tactics', *Journal of Modern African Studies* (1981), XIX, 452.

[50] R. Murapa, 'Race and the public service in Zimbabwe, 1890–1983', in Schatzberg (ed.), *The Political Economy of Zimbabwe*, 72.

[51] These fears are expressed in Zimbabwe, *Report on the Seminar on the Roles of Ministers and Senior Civil Servants in Policy-Making, Implementation and Review in the Government of Zimbabwe* (Harare, Public Service Commission, 1982), 16.

[52] In Zimbabwe, the Permanent Secretary is the highest ranking civil servant in each ministry. Minister Ushewokunze is quoted in Zimbabwe, *Air Zimbabwe Corporation: Interim Report of the Committee of Inquiry into Parastatals* [Chairman: L. G. Smith] (Harare, Govt. Printer, 1986), 8.

although the party [ZANU(PF)] had fought a long liberation struggle, in certain
ways along similar lines to those in Vietnam, China and Mozambique, one crucial
distinction was that no permanent alternative agriculture productive system had
been established in liberated zones. . . . In this sense, outside the externally-based
transit and refugee camps, little experience of organizing any production, let
alone socialist production, has been gained by the party.[53]

There was a visible commitment to socialism, but socialism was primarily
an ideology of opposition. Socialism was used to explain what the Blacks
were fighting against and to make it easier for the nationalist armies to
receive support — especially in the form of arms but also in the form of
sanctuary and diplomatic backing — from communist countries and
radical Third World states. Also, the ideology developed by the Zimbabweans during the years of exile could not be considered to be a clear
political programme which would be implemented upon the achievement of power, particularly because the nationalists had assumed that
they would win an outright military victory rather than come to power
within the structure of a negotiated agreement that severely constrained
their freedom of action.

The development of a comprehensive ideological blueprint was also
made difficult by the colony's advanced economic development. The
Black leaders knew that Rhodesia's highly sophisticated agricultural,
mining and manufacturing sectors, if run competently, could provide
tremendous resources which could be used for the benefit of the impov-
erished Black population. Especially after witnessing the effects of the
sudden imposition of Frelimo's revolutionary policies in Mozambique,
Zimbabwe's future leaders became aware that the nationalization and
economic upheaval demanded by Mozambique-style socialism, and by
much of their own rhetoric, would cause a flight of the White population
and create economic chaos that would threaten the viability of strategic
sectors of the economy. It was, therefore, clear to the Zimbabweans what
they could not do. However, because their prime objective had been to
win the armed struggle, they never developed a comprehensive ideology
which would explain how the benefits available from a largely unchanged colonial economy could be used systematically to help the Black
population.

At Independence, therefore, the regime did not have many clear

[53] B. Munslow, 'Prospects for the socialist transition of agriculture in Zimbabwe', *World
Development* (1985), XII, 41.

policies to implement. Other than some heuristics inherited from the liberation struggle (such as to eliminate racial discrimination and gain control of the 'commanding heights' of the economy) there were few policy guidelines for concrete actions that the new government could take immediately. For instance, a few days before Independence, Dennis Norman, independent Zimbabwe's first Minister of Agriculture, noted the legacy of operational inexperience and the absence of an ideology that could provide policy guidance: 'For various reasons,' he said, 'this [nation's agricultural policy] has still to be determined'. Among the reasons he cited was the problem that Zimbabwe had

a brand new government in which many of its members had little or no experience in governing. There were also ministries which would be run by people who had little knowledge of the ministries of which they had been placed in charge.[54]

The presence of Norman himself, a White farmer who was the president of the Rhodesian National Farmers Union at the time of his appointment, was a dramatic example of the potential problems faced by a leadership with an uncertain policy agenda that could not fully trust the state apparatus.

The lack of a clear political project also increased the possibility of factional disputes within the national leadership. At Independence there was certainly a 'hard left' element in Zimbabwe's Cabinet, centred around those who had fought the war from the guerrilla bases in Mozambique; at the same time, there was a more technocratic element led by men who had been international civil servants or academics during the war years.[55] Ideological differences, therefore, were reinforced by differences in personal experience and power bases. It is important not to make too much of the divisions in the political leadership because very few, if any, of the leaders can be described simply with a label, and personal positions have clearly evolved over time. Nevertheless, the potential of factional splits within the leadership to play an important part in decision-making was obvious to many at Independence.

[54] *The Herald*, 12 Apr. 1980.

[55] The factions are described by R. T. Libby, 'Development strategies and political divisions within the Zimbabwean state', in Schatzberg (ed.), *The Political Economy of Zimbabwe*, 145–53.

Party Structures

While the guerrillas never had full control over significant parts of
Zimbabwe, it is probably true that the war gave ZANU(PF) and PF-ZAPU
a stronger political presence in the rural areas than most African parties
had at Independence in other countries. David Lan, for instance, noted the
pervasiveness of ZANU(PF) village committees throughout the northern
part of Zimbabwe when he conducted his study of the Dande area on the
Zambezi escarpment.[56] While, given the great degree of regional variation, it is important not to overestimate ZANU(PF)'s local presence in the
countryside (or PF-ZAPU's in Matabeleland), there is no doubt that one
of the parties' inheritances from the guerrilla war was a strong political
base in the rural areas.

Nevertheless, it was uncertain at Independence just what that strong
presence in the rural areas meant as far as actual party leadership was
concerned. ZANU(PF) was relatively strong (for Africa) in the rural areas
and held a near-monopoly on the national leadership, but there was no
middle-level structure. Precisely because the guerrillas were effective as
decentralized, unco-ordinated groups, neither ZANU(PF) nor PF-ZAPU
ever developed a middle-level organizational structure which could
facilitate the upward transmission of demands from the grassroots, or
which could allow policy dictates formulated at the top to be communi-
cated downwards. In addition, their failure to gain sufficient control over
a region to enable them to become the *de facto* government there also
retarded the development of a middle-level cadre with extensive management and administrative experience. This structure, which lacked a
central core, made it uncertain as to how far the national leadership could
depend on the party apparatus as a complement or alternative to the state.

The Economy

In addition to the uncertainty concerning the trustworthiness of the
political institutions, the new government was also unsure about its
control over the economy. Owing to the provisions in the constitution,
and, more importantly, because of the leadership's strategy of gradually
adapting the economy to the needs of the Black population, there were no
dramatic changes in the pattern of ownership in the economy at Independence. The new Black government, therefore, faced the paradox of

[56] D. Lan, *Guns and Rain: Guerrillas and Spirit Mediums in Zimbabwe* (Harare, Zimbabwe
Publishing House; Berkeley and Los Angeles, Univ. of California Press, 1985), 210.

having the opportunity to benefit from an extremely powerful economy
(for Africa) which could provide many resources, while at the same time
being constrained by the fact that this same economy was controlled by
local Whites and multinational corporations whom it could only consider
to be hostile. The new Black government instinctively distrusted the
foreign-controlled companies which played such an important role in the
economy because these companies had collaborated with the Rhodesians
in the evasion of sanctions and their commitment to the country's Black
majority was unclear. In addition, some of these companies were based in
South Africa and were therefore seen by the Zimbabweans as potential
fifth-columnists who could subvert the revolution from within.[57]

The government's uncertainties over the control of the economy were
further aggravated by the country's trade dependence on South Africa.
Rhodesia, because of its geographic position and the dominance of South
Africa in the regional economy, had always had strong economic ties with
its southern neighbour. This dependence was greatly increased during
the UDI years, when Rhodesia was forced to cultivate the South African
market further. Even in 1986, approximately 17 per cent of Zimbabwe's
visible trade was with South Africa and nearly 80 per cent of its external
trade went through the South African transportation system.[58] Given
South Africa's overt hostility to the politics of the new Black regime, its
clear goal of preventing (because of its own domestic concerns) any Black-
ruled country from being considered a success, and its history of destabilization in the region, Zimbabwe's neighbour was clearly willing and able
to seriously disrupt the work of the Mugabe government. As a result, fear
of possible South African actions has affected almost every major policy
decision that the post-Independence government has had to make.

Conclusion

At Zimbabwe's Independence on 18 April 1980, uncertainty pervaded
every aspect of the polity. The new regime was uncertain what its policies
would be, whether it was going to gain control of the state, what the actual

---

[57] Up to a third of total foreign capital stock and a quarter of total capital stock in the
country was controlled by South African companies at Independence, see Clarke, *Foreign
Companies and International Investment in Zimbabwe*, 32. More recent figures are given in
Table XII, p. 114.

[58] R. C. Riddell, 'Regional insecurity clouds economic prospects', *Zimbabwe: An Africa
Economic Digest Special Report* (London, AED, 1986), 4, and Economist Intelligence Unit,
Zimbabwe, 1988–1989 (London, The Unit, 1988), 36.

strength of the party was, and how much influence it had in the economy. There was also grave uncertainty as to what South Africa would do in response to the achievement of Black majority rule in a nation with which it shared a long border. Hundreds of thousands of Africans were trying to return to their homes after years as refugees, and could only wait and see if their sacrifices during the long years of colonial rule and war would be rewarded. The Whites in the country were uncertain whether the new constitution would indeed protect them, or whether there would be some kind of retaliation for war crimes committed during the liberation struggle. Over the last ten years, there has emerged out of this uncertainty a set of sometimes coherent, sometimes contradictory, policies that are the focus of this study. It is important to emphasize how unsettled the country was in 1980 in order to remember that the actions undertaken by the new regime were by no means inevitable. While the new government's choices were certainly limited, the great uncertainty that pervaded the country in 1980 is an indication that it did have a significant degree of freedom in formulating its policies. Examining how governments use their freedom to manœuvre is the key to understanding politics in Zimbabwe and throughout the Third World.

Chapter Three

Conflict over Land:
White Farmers and the Black Government

Land was the central issue during the liberation struggle for Zimbabwe and continues to be the most important domestic issue in the post-Independence period. The appropriation of African land by the European settlers guaranteed White economic dominance and Black poverty during the colonial period, and the inequitable distribution of land in Zimbabwe today is the most dramatic symbol of the enduring structures of an unequal society. The evolution of the government's efforts to address the land question is of great importance because of the peasants' expectations that their long-held grievances will be addressed as the new regime redistributes property formerly held by White farmers. Indeed, there was probably no more controversial question at Independence than how the new regime would be able to resist the influence of the White farmers and implement the promises concerning land that it had made during the liberation struggle.

Agrarian Power in Zimbabwe

The political power of the 4 000, predominantly White, commercial farmers derives from their economic position and their organization.[1] Table IV demonstrates that, although the peasant farmers (also called communal farmers) have made remarkable gains in post-Independence Zimbabwe, White farmers (known as large-scale commercial farmers) still dominate the agricultural sector of the economy. In addition to their overall prominence, White farmers play a key role in the crucial export sector of the economy. For instance, they produce almost all of the country's tobacco, tea, coffee and sugar.[2] In 1984, these crops accounted

---

[1] There is an increasing number of Black farmers who qualify as large-scale commercial farmers. However, this group is still predominantly White, and is perceived as such by the government.

[2] Zimbabwe, *Socio-Economic Review of Zimbabwe, 1980–1985* (Harare, Ministry of Finance, Economic Planning and Development, 1986), 115.

for 34 per cent of total exports.[3] It is unlikely, because of the skill and
capital required, that peasants will soon supplant White farmers in
production of these crops as they have done in the labour-intensive, low-
skill crops such as maize and cotton.[4]

Table IV

COMMERCIAL AND PEASANT AGRICULTURAL PRODUCTION

Year	Percentage contribution to gross agricultural output	
	Commercial farmers *	*Peasant farmers*
1978	84,65	15,35
1979	80,03	19,97
1980	79,48	20,52
1981	74,10	25,90
1982	74,88	25,12
1983	82,18	17,18
1984	78,58	21,42
1985	68,17	31,83

* Includes the small-scale (i.e. Black) farmers. However, subtracting the small-scale
producers' gross output would not significantly affect the relative contributions shown
here.

Sources: Zimbabwe, *Statistical Yearbook, 1987* (Harare, Central Statistical Office, 1987),
144, and Agricultural Marketing Authority, *Economic Review of the Agricultural Industry of
Zimbabwe* (Harare, The Authority, 1987), 3.

The White farmers' economic dominance can be traced back directly
to the inequitable distribution of land. In 1977 the land laws were
amended, and racial classifications were abolished except for the 47 per
cent of the land that was reserved for Africans (now known as Communal
Lands). However, given that few Blacks could afford to buy White farms,
the racial division of the land at Independence was not significantly
different from what it had been a few years before.[5] In addition, there are
considerable inequalities in the quality of the land held. Around Inde-

[3] Zimbabwe, *Annual Economic Review of Zimbabwe, 1986* (Harare, Ministry of Finance,
Economic Planning and Development, 1987), 11.

[4] See Chapter 5.

[5] R. C. Riddell, *The Land Question in Rhodesia* (Gwelo, Mambo Press, 1978), 12 and 33.

pendence, 74 per cent of all peasant land was in areas where droughts are frequent and where even normal levels of rainfall are inadequate for intensive crop production.[6] Similarly, in areas where Blacks were allowed to own land (previously known as African Purchase Areas, but now known as small-scale commercial farming areas), 75 per cent of the land is located in regions where only extensive crop and livestock production, at best, can be conducted.[7] In contrast, the large-scale commercial farm-land is concentrated in good rainfall areas where intensive crop produc-tion is possible.[8] The Communal Lands have a population density of approximately twenty-eight people per square kilometre compared with nine people per square kilometre in formerly White areas,[9] even though the Communal Lands are least able to support intensive cultivation and large concentrations of people. Table V shows the production indices for the different land classifications at Independence.

Table V

LAND AND PRODUCTION INDICES AT INDEPENDENCE

Indicator	Large-scale commercial farms	Small-scale commercial farms	Communal Lands
Average farm size (ha)	2 474	125	23
Value of output ($ millions)	374 (76%)	12 (2%)	109 (21%)
Output per person ($) *	213,8	117,6	31,1
Output per hectare ($)	25,2	11,3	6,7

* Includes all workers on farms.

Source: Personal communication from the Department of Rural Development.

The White farmers are also powerful because they are extremely well organized. Their status as the most powerful and sophisticated political grouping in Rhodesia can be traced back to the passage of the Farmers Licensing Act and the subsequent establishment of the Rhodesian Na-tional Farmers Union (RNFU) in 1942. Owing to the demands of the

[6] Zimbabwe, *Statistical Yearbook, 1987* (Harare, Central Statistical Office, 1987), 138.
[7] Ibid.   [8] Ibid.
[9] Whitsun Foundation, *Land Reform in Zimbabwe* (Harare, The Foundation, 1983), 26.

Second World War, the colonial government needed the farmers' co-operation to be able to increase food production. The farmers were able to use this leverage to have the government pass the Licensing Act which made it mandatory for all commercial farmers to buy a farming licence from the newly formed Union.[10] The Licensing Act was a stroke of organizational brilliance because it eliminated any worries that the Union might have had that it would not get the full support of the farmers, and it gave it an assured source of finance. To this day, the Commercial Farmers Union (CFU), as the RNFU became after Independence, may be the only farmers' union in the world that has a government-enforced closed shop. This closed shop allows the White farmers to undertake research and lobbying exercises of enormous sophistication and expense. The CFU is, for instance, able to support a large staff and a farmer-president who leaves his homestead to work full-time for the Union during his term of office. It is, therefore, no surprise that the RNFU operating from the ten-storey Agriculture House (now occupied by the CFU) had as its motto 'Unity is Strength'.

The Importance of the Land Issue

Land was the central issue in the liberation struggle for Zimbabwe that culminated in the Mugabe government coming to power. One report on the new government's resettlement plans began by noting that

from the very onset of political armed struggle against colonialism, the key issue was land. It was the fight for land which led to the death of tens of thousands of Zimbabweans during the Armed Struggle: true Zimbabwean patriots saw there could be no freedom without the liberation of the land from the colonial settlers.[11]

Similarly, Robert Mugabe stated in ZANU(PF)'s 1980 election manifesto, 'It is not only anti-people but criminal for any government to ignore the acute land hunger in the country, especially when it is realized that 83 per cent of our population live in the rural areas and depend on agriculture for their livelihood.'[12] Furthermore, the President has stated that, because of the importance of land in the lives of the people, 'We can never have

[10] Murray, *The Governmental System in Southern Rhodesia*, 97–8.

[11] 'Settling debts before peasants', *Moto* (Sept. 1983), 17.

[12] Zimbabwe African National Union (Patriotic Front), *ZANU(PF) 1980 Election Manifesto* (Salisbury, ZANU(PF), 1979), 9.

peace in this country unless the peasant population is satisfied in relation to the land issue'.[13]

Land is such an important issue for both economic and cultural reasons. Firstly, the inequitable distribution of land had doomed most peasants to ever-worsening poverty. By 1979, the population of the tribal Reserves exceeded their carrying capacity by approximately two million people.[14] Zimbabwe's major commission of inquiry into incomes and prices, the Riddell Commission, bluntly summarized the economic problems caused by the inequitable distribution of land: 'The most fundamental constraint on raising the incomes of families in the peasant sector to a level that will meet their minimum needs is land shortage.'[15]

It is not enough, however, to stress simply the economic and ecological effects of the settlers' appropriation of the land. The people of Zimbabwe, especially the roughly 80 per cent of the population who are Shona, have a spiritual relationship with the land which was profoundly disrupted by settler colonialism. In a culture in which land is held collectively and in which it is a cardinal principle that no member of the community should be landless,[16] the appropriation of the land by the Whites was more than a severe economic handicap — it was a profound challenge to the very foundation of Shona society. Lan describes the importance of land to the Shona polity:

The single most important duty of the spirit medium is to protect the land. From the grave, from the depths of the forests, from the body of the lion or of their mediums, the *mhondoro* control in perpetuity the land they conquered during their lives. Under the rule of the Whites their land had lost its fertility. Sacred places had been fenced off and ruled out of bounds. The guerrillas offered land as renewed fertility and restored tradition. They offered a Zimbabwe returned to its original and rightful owners.[17]

The land grievances were the driving force behind the liberation struggle; Lan notes: 'The imagery of dispossession, of loss, of landlessness, of

[13] *The Herald*, 29 Oct. 1981.

[14] J. D. Jordan, 'The land question in Zimbabwe', *Zimbabwe Journal of Economics* (1979), I, 134.

[15] Zimbabwe, *Report of the Commission of Inquiry into Incomes, Prices and Conditions of Service* [Chairman: R. C. Riddell] (Harare, Govt. Printer, 1981), 57.

[16] J. G. Mutambara, 'Africans and Land Policies: British Colonial Policy in Zimbabwe, 1890–1965' (Cincinnati, Univ. of Cincinnati, Ph.D. thesis, 1981), 107–8.

[17] Lan, *Guns and Rain*, 148.

longing for the "lost lands" to be restored was a constant pulse in the literature, the oral tradition, and the rhetoric of the nationalist movement'.[18]

Despite the importance of the land issue to the people, the Zimbabwe government was severely restricted in its efforts to redistribute land. The Lancaster House Constitution requires that all land acquired by government be purchased on a 'willing seller–willing buyer' basis, and that owners of any land seized by the government must be compensated in foreign currency. This provision is seen by many analysts as the embodiment of the Whites' political strength because the provision severely limits attempts to right the injustices of the colonial era by demanding that the new government pay for land that was originally stolen. Michael Bratton, for instance, argued that a Zimbabwe dependent on development funds from aid donors to purchase White land will undergo the same process which led to the 'neo-colonization of Kenya'.[19]

In addition, many are sceptical that Zimbabwe will be able to meet the goals set within the constraints of the Lancaster House Constitution because of the political pressure brought to bear by commercial agriculture. One of the few studies of Zimbabwe's land programme argues that

it is the White farmers and the multinational agribusinesses backed up by the terms of the Lancaster House Constitution that are influencing the land acquisition policy more than the peasants. Their economic interests appear to converge with the economic interests of the political elites.[20]

Indeed, the political and economic strength of the commercial farmers makes it improbable that the new government would be able to go against White agrarian interests.

The Evolution of Zimbabwe's Land Programme

Upon gaining power in April 1980, the Mugabe government initiated a programme to resettle 18 000 families on approximately 1,1 million hectares of land at a cost of $60 million.[21] Half of this programme was to be

---

[18] Ibid., 121.

[19] M. Bratton, 'Structural transformation in Zimbabwe: Comparative notes from the neo-colonisation of Kenya', *Journal of Modern African Studies* (1977), XV, 611.

[20] E. M. Chiviya, 'Land Reform in Zimbabwe: Policy and Implementation' (Bloomington, Indiana Univ., Ph.D. thesis, 1982), 173.

[21] B. H. Kinsey, 'Emerging policy issues in Zimbabwe's land resettlement programmes', *Development Policy Review* (1983), I, 170.

Figure 1: EVOLUTION OF THE LAND PROGRAMME

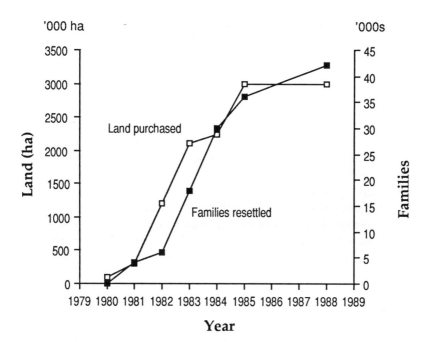

funded by the British government, while Zimbabwe would pay for the remainder. Given the clear inadequacy of this programme in a country where 800 000 peasant families faced severe land pressures, the government soon decided to embark on a much more ambitious programme. In the three-year *Transitional National Development Plan* published in November 1982 and covering the period 1983–5, the new government stated its intention to resettle at least 162 000 peasant families, 'subject to practical financial and economic constraints'.[22] This was an exceedingly ambitious goal because it would have meant resettling approximately 20 per cent of all peasants in the nation. The new programme implied the purchase of nine million hectares (the equivalent of 57 per cent of all White agricultural land before Independence) and an expenditure

[22] Zimbabwe, *Transitional National Development Plan 1982/83–1984/85* (Harare, Ministry of Finance, Economic Planning and Development, 2 vols., 1982), I, 66.

of at least $570 million.[23] Owing to a number of constraints (discussed below) the government has since scaled down the immediate goals of the resettlement programme. In Zimbabwe's *First Five-Year National Development Plan* (covering the years 1986–90) the government set a new goal of resettling 15 000 families during each year of the Plan.[24] The figure of 162 000 families is now seen as the total number of families that should eventually be resettled, although there is a fair amount of confusion within the resettlement bureaucracy over even this goal.

Government resettlement programmes now lag considerably behind the admittedly ambitious targets set by the two National Development Plans. Figure 1 indicates that land acquisition and family resettlement increased impressively during the first three years of Independence. However, because of the severe economic crisis caused by the unprecedented three-year drought between 1982 and 1984, land acquisition and resettlement began to level off after 1983. After good rains in 1985 and 1986, the programme encountered a number of problems, resulting in a slow-down in the total number of people resettled. For example, in the financial year 1986/7, plans were made for only 2 750 families to be resettled instead of the original target of 15 000.[25] By 1988 the government had resettled approximately 42 000 families on approximately 2,6 million hectares of land.[26] Given the interests and power of the White farmers, the important question to ask now is: To what extent has the power of the settlers played a part in the disappointing evolution of the land programme?

Explaining the Evolution of the Land Programme

To truly appreciate the way in which the land programme has evolved, it must be noted that it is fruitless to judge the progress of the resettlement programme by the public goals set for it. These goals were never realistic, and the government made almost no effort to transform stated targets into reality. Conversations with present and former government officials revealed that the figure of 162 000 families, which is now accepted by

[23] Kinsey, 'Emerging policy issues in Zimbabwe's land resettlement programmes', 180–1.

[24] Zimbabwe, *First Five-Year National Development Plan 1986–1990* (Harare, Ministry of Finance, Economic Planning and Development, 2 vols., 1986), I, 28.

[25] Zimbabwe, *Annual Economic Review of Zimbabwe, 1986*, 27.

[26] A. Meldrum, 'The prize-winning peasant farmers', *Africa Report* (Sept.–Oct. 1988), 43.

everyone in Zimbabwe to be the target figure for resettlement, was developed with little reference to government capabilities and the actual situation. A former Ministry of Lands official said in an interview: 'The 162 000 families figure was just a figure produced. No real calculations went into the figure.' The official confirmed that the target had essentially been pulled out of thin air. Similarly, a Ministry of Lands official in the Mashonaland region noted in another interview: 'We were totally mortified by the 162 000 figure. Neither the land nor the money was available for the goal.'

It is even unclear whether the new goal of resettling 15 000 families a year was conceived of as a target that could be translated into an achievable programme. I asked officials involved in the resettlement programme in each of Zimbabwe's eight provinces what the Five-Year Plan's goal of resettling 15 000 families a year implied for their province. The response of one Masvingo Province official was typical: 'I don't know. I have not addressed myself to how many would be resettled here.' Or, as one Manicaland Province official said, 'government resettlement goals are not translated into budgets. The goals from the top bear little resemblance to what actually goes on.'

The National Plans, therefore, can be read as essentially ideological statements from the regime detailing what it would like to do, rather than as blueprints outlining what the government will do. The planning and budgeting — the stuff of government — has never been supplied or even seriously contemplated. Indeed, the best way to understand Zimbabwe's resettlement programme is to ignore the targets stated in the *Transitional National Development Plan* and the *First Five-Year National Development Plan*. Instead, the starting point for an analysis of the land programme should be the original programme of resettling 18 000 families in three years, the only goal that was ever supported with a committed budget and real plans. This programme was completed and resettlement is continuing, though at a slower pace. This is not a surprising outcome, given that governments must run on real budgets and concrete plans, but those who look simply at the societal balance of power miss this perspective. Far from it being derailed, the only land programme that was ever seriously planned is continuing.

Although the programme has not achieved its stated aims, the scope of Zimbabwe's land resettlement programme should not be underestimated. For instance, during the first year and a half of Independence the Zimbabwe government managed to resettle 8 600 families on 520 000 hectares of land. Bill Kinsey, comparing the magnitude of Zimbabwe's land programme to that of Kenya, noted:

In only eighteen months Zimbabwe transferred from White to Black control only ten per cent less land than Kenya had transferred under its small-holder resettlement schemes dating from Independence to the middle of 1976 — a period of more than fifteen years. Indeed, the three year target of 1,1 million hectares for the intensive resettlement programme alone is only seven per cent less than the total of all land transfers (large-scale and small-scale) achieved in Kenya over fifteen years; and more than half of the Kenyan transfers were made by private sale.[27]

Kenya has resettled more people (63 000 families had been resettled by official government programmes up to the end of 1975),[28] but this is due in part to better agro-ecological conditions in Kenya which allow more intensive farming per unit of land. In comparative perspective, Zimbabwe's resettlement programme, conducted by a young government with no experience in this area, must be seen as a substantial achievement.

The Lancaster House Constitution also has to be examined in its proper context if the evolution of the land programme is to be fully appreciated. The Black liberation forces did not win a military victory in 1980. They probably could have won, but outright victory would have taken a further year or more at the very least and would have resulted in thousands of additional deaths among Black combatants and peasants and in the destruction of a large part of the country's infrastructure and its agricultural and industrial base. The land provision of the Lancaster House Constitution was an essential part of any political solution to the war, because the last settler government could not have compromised unless its most important constituency, the White farmers, were at least to some extent reassured about their future. Dr Bernard Chidzero, the Senior Minister of Finance, Economic Planning, and Development, recognized that the constitutional bargain was essential to Zimbabwe's future:

We have a constitution that guarantees property rights. It is as watertight as any constitution you can ever imagine. We cannot therefore expropriate or nationalize without compensation, and if we do, it requires changing the constitution and it

---

[27] B. H. Kinsey, 'Forever gained: Resettlement and land policy in the context of national development in Zimbabwe', in J. D. Y. Peel and T. Ranger (eds.), *Past and Present in Zimbabwe* (Manchester, Manchester Univ. Press, 1983), 102.

[28] A. Hazlewood, 'Kenyan land-transfer programmes and their relevance for Zimbabwe', *Journal of Modern African Studies* (1985), XXIII, 449.

is not very easy to change the constitution. We have accepted the constitution and we live by it. Therefore, we respect property rights.[29]

Those who are cynical about the bargain struck at Lancaster House, especially those who speculate about today's Zimbabwe without the 'willing seller–willing buyer' provisions, are being unrealistic, because without these clauses there would have been much greater damage to the country's entire economy, fundamentally changing the country's economic prospects.

The Lancaster House provision, therefore, represents an essential part of a complex bargain that, while certainly constraining the state actions on land redistribution, was hardly a simple concession to imperialism or an outright sell-out of the Patriotic Front's peasant supporters. In the best of all possible worlds, the injustices of the colonial era would have been corrected immediately. However, Zimbabwe's leaders accurately perceived that Southern Africa in 1980 was a long way from paradise and so they made the best total bargain they could for their supporters.

There is, in fact, no doubt that the method of purchases required by the Lancaster House Constitution has been a major constraint on the land programme. A Department of Rural Development document pointed out that

in the 1982/1983 fiscal year, no adequate provisions were made for purchase of land for 54 000 families. Enough funds were voted for approximately 20 000 families only. . . . For land acquisition to keep up with the vastly increased programme, $4 million has to be spent per month. That kind of money and capacity for land purchase are not available at present.[30]

However, in the early years of the programme, land-acquisition costs amounted to only 44 per cent of the total costs incurred in resettlement.[31] Therefore, even if Zimbabwe had been free of the Lancaster House provisions, funding for the programme would still be a very significant problem and the government would have had great difficulty resettling 162 000 families. The highly sophisticated and technical approach Zimbabwe has taken to resettlement — involving complex geophysical plans,

---

[29] See the interview with Chidzero by A. J. Hughes and M. A. Novicki, 'Interview: Bernard Chidzero', *Africa Report* (May–June 1982), 7.

[30] Zimbabwe, *Intensive Resettlement Programme: Planning and Management Perspectives* (Harare, Department of Rural Development, 1983), 24.

[31] Kinsey, 'Forever gained', 104.

thoroughly demarcated plots, and the construction of roads, schools and clinics for each project — has probably contributed as much to the funding problems of the resettlement programme as land-acquisition costs have. This sophisticated approach will no doubt pay dividends in the future, but it is important to recognize at this stage that the method of land acquisition demanded by the Constitution is hardly the only drain on the resettlement programme.

Obstacles within Government to Resettlement

While the land-acquisition costs are significant, other factors, too, have influenced the pace of the government's current resettlement programme. Firstly, the government simply does not have the organizational expertise to resettle people significantly faster than it did in the first years of Independence. Resettlement in Zimbabwe is an extraordinarily complicated task which involves literally government-wide co-operation. As President Mugabe noted,

you don't resettle people purely to provide them with a home or a piece of land. You resettle them so they can develop in the new environment and develop the land. . . . Then as you resettle them, you must ensure that there are areas that have been marked out for building schools, hospitals, and clinics, and the establishment of growth points, where they will have their little shops. . . . You must have the Ministry of Roads involved in it, and the Ministry of Agriculture for the agricultural inputs. So it is that combination of inputs that has tended to delay the exercise.[32]

For instance, one Department of Rural Development document lists twenty-five ministries, departments, and parastatals which have a role in the resettlement programme.[33]

As an example of one, but the most serious, obstacle, even at the resettlement programme's current pace, the provision of vitally needed water resources for the newly resettled farmers has been difficult for the government to co-ordinate:

At one time, Ministry of Water Resources and Development could only meet about 33 $1/3$ per cent of the water requirements for resettlement but at present the Ministry is falling further behind in meeting the water demands. . . . The 464 boreholes which are in existence will have about 50 per cent of them out of order

---

[32] M. A. Novicki, 'Interview: Robert Mugabe', *Africa Report* (Sept.–Oct. 1982), 8.

[33] Zimbabwe, *Intensive Resettlement Programme: Planning and Management Perspectives*, 5–8.

at any one time because of overuse to draw water for domestic and livestock purposes as a result of the drought. . . . Water is the key to the development of all resettlement schemes and has been the major impediment to the consolidation of these schemes.[34]

In interviews, resettlement officials consistently emphasized the water problem, bemoaning the fact that some peasants have essentially been 'dumped' on newly acquired land while geophysical surveys are conducted to search for the necessary water resources which may or may be there. This is a critical problem, because 91 per cent of the land purchased for resettlement is in areas where it is doubtful that surface water will be adequate for agriculture and living needs.[35] If Zimbabwe could have simply seized well-watered commmercial farming land, the water constraint would not have been nearly as important. However, owing to the Lancaster House settlement, the government was forced to focus much of its resettlement efforts on land that needed a great deal of preparation before it could be farmed. Therefore, the Lancaster House provisions, by effectively requiring the government to buy the land that needed the most work, put tremendous strains on the already weak resettlement bureaucracy.

Apart from its organizational problems, the resettlement bureaucracy has come to realize that the original emphasis on the value of resettlement was overly optimistic, given the constraints imposed by the Lancaster House Constitution. This realization has been prompted by two simple facts which too many people who study Zimbabwe's land problem fail, or refuse, to recognize. Firstly, as a result of population growth alone, Zimbabwe's Communal Lands are producing the equivalent of approximately 40 000 new families each year, and nothing can be done to change this fact in the short to medium term.[36] Thus, even if government had managed the Herculean feat of resettling 162 000 families, in four to six years the communal areas would be facing the same land-pressure problems that were evident in 1980. Secondly, there are already 263 000 farm-workers and their families on White farms, and these people would have to be resettled first (since they have nowhere else to go) if the farms on which they work are acquired by the government.[37] While this

---

[34] Ibid., 25.

[35] *The Herald*, 8 Aug. 1984.

[36] *The Financial Gazette*, 20 Jan. 1984.

[37] For a discussion of commercial farm-workers, see Chapter 8.

problem has yet to become significant, because most of the land that has been used for resettlement was not previously in use, it could begin to have an impact in the near future. Kinsey estimates that the programme to resettle 162 000 families, if fully adopted, might displace as many as 92 000 farm-workers and their families, and these people would have priority over those in the Communal Lands.[38] Therefore, less than half the families to be resettled would actually come from the old tribal Reserves.

The cumulative weight of these two factors has caused what one Ministry of Lands official called a 'sea change' in thinking about resettlement. He said in an interview that there has been a 'creeping collective consciousness that resettlement alone would not be enough'. He explained that

settlers get 35 hectares per family and there is simply not enough to go around. There has been an undeclared shift in policy. The initial prime objective was redistribution, but we made no real significant impact on Communal Lands. We realize that no matter how many people move off we won't have that great an impact.

A Provincial official in Mashonaland also commented on the 'realization that resettlement is not going to solve the problems in the Communal Lands'. Similarly, a Masvingo official said, 'in this part of the world I don't really see resettlement making a major impact'.

The gradual collective reassessment that resettlement will not address the major problems of the Communal Lands has caused a decided, if only partially declared, change in government policy. In the first place, the government de-emphasized the land issue throughout most of the 1980s. Indeed, for most of Zimbabwe's first ten years of Independence it was surprising how little was being said about land redistribution in view of the inherent importance of the issue to the lives of the majority of the population. A Department of Rural Development official noted in an interview that

some politicians have now begun to see the light. They realize that there is neither the land nor the money for the kind of programmes they were suggesting. Land becomes de-emphasized. Politicians see how dangerous their statements were.

Similarly, a Ministry of Lands official remarked in an interview: 'You don't have people standing up in Parliament talking about land — it's not

[38] Kinsey, 'Emerging policy issues in Zimbabwe's land resettlement programmes', 185.

an issue. This is true even though no one suggests that Zimbabwe would go down the drain if lots more commercial farms would be resettled'. An agricultural extension official also agreed: 'The land issue is not dealt with and not discussed. . . . Someone would have to disagree with the entire economic thrust of government to disagree on the land issue. . . . [The land issue] is an issue that has been shelved.' It is important to stress that the land programme is by no means 'dead' or even standing still. However, the expectations about what can be achieved from resettlement, even if the programme proceeds significantly faster than it does now, have been scaled down tremendously.

The lack of emphasis on the land issue is reflected in the decreasing number of stories that have appeared in the daily newspapers concerning resettlement (see Table VI). As the newspapers generally reflect at least

Table VI

NEWSPAPER STORIES ON LAND REDISTRIBUTION *

Year	Stories
1980	76
1981	110
1982	141
1983	119
1984	108
1985	46

* Stories were counted if the major emphasis of the report was on any aspect of land redistribution. Files for some years are incomplete so the figure for the full year was extrapolated from the number of stories in the incomplete file.

Source: Ministry of Information, Posts and Telecommunications's newspaper-clipping files for *The Herald* and *The Sunday Mail.*

the emphasis in government thinking,[39] the land issue's loss of salience in the press is a reflection of the government's realization that resettlement will provide no quick solution to the land problem. The frequency of stories does, in fact, correspond directly to the pace of the resettlement programme detailed in Figure 1. The drop-off in stories after 1982, just when the programme was slowing down, is particularly noticeable.

[39] The daily newspapers are owned by the Mass Media Trust, which is in turn controlled by the government.

In 1989, ZANU(PF)'s search for an issue for the 1990 general election, and the imminent expiration of the Lancaster House Constitution's prohibition on land seizure, gave cause for a new debate over the future of land distribution in Zimbabwe. In President Mugabe's 1989 Heroes' Day address, he pledged renewed stress on the land issue, noting its central importance. At the same time, he pledged to keep the willing seller–willing buyer policy, but said that coercion might be used to make some of the farmers more willing to sell — a seeming contradiction.[40] However, Joshua Nkomo, who was named a Senior Minister in the President's Office after the unity accord between ZANU(PF) and PF-ZAPU was signed, also said in a 1989 speech that the government was well aware that resettlement by itself would not solve the problems of the communal areas and that the government would continue to examine the prospects for reorganization of the Communal Lands.[41]

Instead of focusing entirely on resettlement, government officials have now recognized that the land-use patterns in the communal areas themselves can and should be changed to increase the land's carrying capacity and provide better economic opportunities for peasant farmers. The history of the Communal Lands is a history of more and more people being forced on to the same piece of land with little attention being paid to rational land-use patterns. Therefore, there is great potential for the redevelopment of the Communal Lands. Although the shift to redeveloping the communal areas has received relatively little attention in Zimbabwe, the Five-Year Plan actually calls for a major re-organization of the communal areas to help 20 000 families a year.[42] While this target is as unrealistic as the Plan's goal to resettle 15 000 families a year, the fact that the number of families to be affected by improvements in the communal sector is greater than the number to be resettled reflects a basic change in government thinking. The *Transitional National Development Plan* was much vaguer on the redevelopment of the Communal Lands.

Funding may also be much less of a problem for programmes designed to rehabilitate the communal areas. Redevelopment is generally less expensive than the highly sophisticated technical planning that has to be done when White commercial farms are transformed into new peasant areas. Of course, if Zimbabwe had the alternative of resettling

---

[40] *The Herald*, 12 Aug. 1989 and *The Chronicle*, 29 July 1989.

[41] *The Financial Gazette*, 10 Aug. 1989.

[42] Zimbabwe, *First Five-Year National Development Plan*, I, 28.

peasants on well-watered land owned by Whites, then redeveloping the Communal Lands would not be nearly as economically attractive as it is now. However, in view of the restrictions of the Lancaster House agreement, redeveloping the Communal Lands makes more sense than resettling people on poor land. While only the British were willing to fund land acquisition, many donors are reportedly attracted to the higher benefit per dollar spent that could be garnered by redeveloping the communal areas. A Ministry of Lands official suggested in an interview that 'donors are pushing in the direction the Ministry wants to go'. While resettlement will undoubtedly continue, it is clear that the redevelopment of the Communal Lands will be a major focus of future rural-development efforts.

Absence of Political Conflict

The unexpectedly slow pace of the resettlement programme has meant that, in the main, the government has bought land that was underused or that had been abandoned during the liberation war rather than farms that were in operation. The pattern of buying underused land is reflected in provincial resettlement figures. Of all the families resettled, approximately a third have been settled in Manicaland (on the border with Mozambique) because a large percentage of the farmland in that province was abandoned during the liberation war. In contrast, only a fourteenth of all families resettled have been placed in Mashonaland Central because this area was not substantially affected by the war and because this province, notably the Mazowe Valley, is an area of intensive commercial agricultural production.[43]

There is, in fact, a significant amount of unused or underused land in Zimbabwe that can serve as something of a buffer between White agriculture and the government's resettlement programme. While estimates of unused land vary tremendously, even in the 1970s the RNFU suggested that there were approximately 2,8 million hectares underused.[44] The Whitsun Foundation, in perhaps the most sophisticated study of this issue, used three criteria (population density per square kilometre, planted

[43] *The Herald,* 8 Aug. 1984. Manicaland Province has 14,6 per cent of Zimbabwe's total population, while Mashonaland Central has 7,5 per cent. Population figures from Zimbabwe, *Main Demographic Features of the Population of Zimbabwe: An Advance Report Based on a Ten per cent Sample* (Harare, Central Statistical Office, 1985), 43.

[44] R. C. Riddell, 'Zimbabwe's land problem: The central issue', in Morris-Jones (ed.), *From Rhodesia to Zimbabwe,* 4.

area as a percentage of total area, and hectares per head of cattle, all adjusted for ecological variation) to study land use and concluded that there were 3,8 million hectares of land in eighteen commercial farming areas that qualified as underutilized on *all three* criteria.[45]

The bureaucracy's organizational problems, their evaluation of the resettlement programme, and the presence of underused land has meant that the White commercial farmers have not had to come into conflict with the government over land policies. A former Ministry of Lands official said in an interview: 'In talks with commercial [i.e. White] farmers they never indicate that there is a shortage of land for commercial farming. Commercial farmers are experts at exaggerating but they do not indicate even the slightest problem'. Similarly, Moven Mahachi, then Minister for Lands, Agriculture and Rural Resettlement, began his address to the Commercial Farmers Union annual meeting in 1986 by saying that he did not expect much controversy when discussing land and legislation because 'there are no contentious issues on lands and legislation among government and farmers'.[46] Jim Sinclair, then President of the Commercial Farmers Union, also noted that farmers had not had to pressure the government on the land issue because of problems within the resettlement bureaucracy; he said in 1983: 'if we believed they could do it [resettle 162 000 families], we'd be a lot more worried'.[47] Certainly, as far as the land issue is concerned, there is nothing approaching the co-ordinated pressure tactics that the White farmers orchestrate annually to obtain higher producer prices.[48] However, White farmers may have to resort to these types of tactics in the future if the government should embark on a more radical land programme.

While White agricultural power has not come into direct conflict with the land resettlement programme so far, the White farmers have lost a few skirmishes. In terms of actual land law, commercial farmers were unable to prevent the passage of the Land Acquisition Act in 1985. The Act's most important provision was to give the government the right of first refusal on any rural land that was being offered for sale.[49] This provision gave government substantial control over land supply and may have had an

[45] Whitsun Foundation, *Land Reform in Zimbabwe*, 12.

[46] Author's notes of Commercial Farmers Union Annual Congress, Meikles Hotel, Harare, 31 July 1986.

[47] M. A. Novicki, 'Zimbabwe: The economic outlook', *Africa Report* (Jan.–Feb. 1983), 13.

[48] See Chapter 5.

[49] Zimbabwe, Land Acquisition Act (No. 21 of 1985), section 6.

effect on the price of land. The Act also established a Derelict Lands Board to enable the government to seize abandoned land.[50]

From an observation of more informal government practices, it is also less than clear that White political power is a significant influence on the government's land practices at present. For instance, the Commercial Farmers Union has tried to persuade government to indicate well in advance which farming areas the resettlement bureaucracy intends turning into resettlement areas so that farmers can plan accordingly. Knowing where the resettlement areas will be is important to White farmers because, while they cannot be forced off their land, the government could purchase all the land around them, thereby surrounding their farms with resettlement schemes. Most White farmers find this an unattractive option because of the continued poaching of animals and pastures by peasants, and possibly because they feel threatened by being gradually encircled by Blacks. In addition, as is made clear in Chapter 8, having a critical mass of White farmers is crucial if they are to exercise significant local political power in such areas as roads and health care. However, the government has consistently refused to commit itself to identifying which land it will eventually purchase; one Department of Rural Development official said in an interview,

we just have guidelines. We can't make decisions that far in advance because there are other intervening factors such as the budget.... Government makes a decision [on acquiring land] when land is scarce. The CFU and government will just have to go along and make a decision when the time comes.

The government's refusal to identify in advance the land that they intend to acquire has the effect of reducing the commercial farmers' leverage because they will be forced to make investment decisions while being unsure how long they will actually remain on the land. If White commercial agriculture were really influencing the land programme, the farmers would at least have been able to force the government into saying which land it is going to use for the resettlement programme.

Rather, the White farmers have affected the government's thinking in a more subtle manner. The role that commercial agriculture plays in the economy of Zimbabwe is so daunting that government officials have, of necessity, been quite cautious in tampering with it. Politicians and civil servants who are involved in the resettlement programme are well aware that, in a country still reliant on agriculture and unwilling to be dependent

---

[50] Ibid., section 27.

on South Africa for food supplies, changes in land-tenure patterns can have an absolutely disastrous impact on the nation's future if they are carried out incorrectly. For instance, Minister Enos Nkala, a hard-line ZANU(PF) supporter who was hardly known for his sympathy toward Whites after nearly a decade in prison during the liberation war, said in 1984: 'It would be quite possible to distribute everything we found, but after that, what? The answer to this is too ghastly to contemplate.'[51] Similarly, one former Ministry of Lands official involved in the early planning of the programme said that the bureaucracy was forced to take a cautious view of the resettlement programme because government officials 'feared destroying the agricultural base of the country if commercial land was acquired too quickly'. The risk-averse nature of the bureaucracy was aggravated by the fact that Zimbabwe has yet to develop a vision of how White farmers should participate in the country's economy. Another former official noted in an interview that 'no one has a clear understanding of the role of commercial farms. Mugabe has said that there will be a commercial sector for the next twenty years as long as he has influence; but no one says how large the commercial sector should be'. This attitude, to be expected in a new country undertaking a venture without precedent in the region, was just another factor which has forestalled the need for Whites to begin actively pressuring the government on land reform.

The political power of White farmers, therefore, has been important, but by no means consequential, in the government's land-policy decisions. The power that the farmers exercised was not so much in direct lobbying as in contributing to an atmosphere of risk-aversion by stressing the importance of commercial agriculture. White farmers tried to affect the 'atmospherics' of the land debate by stressing the dangers of drastic change, by giving wide circulation to reports that argued against quick resettlement, and by highlighting the importance of White commercial farming to Zimbabwe. Emphasizing the need for caution was particularly easy in Zimbabwe because the government had decided to err on the side of caution when changing the agrarian system, and because the government still has no long-term vision of how agriculture in Zimbabwe will develop. In addition, the government simply did not have the organizational capability to resettle families at a rate significantly faster than it had

[51] Quoted in C. Gregory, 'The impact of ruling-party ideology on Zimbabwe's post-Independence domestic development', *Journal of Social, Political and Economic Studies* (1987), XII, 139.

been. The White farmers were surprised to find the ship of state going in the general direction that they favoured, and were then faced only with the task of constructing informational buoys so that the government did not go — in their view — off course.

The Absence of Countervailing Pressure

Organizational and technocratic decisions are allowed to dominate Zimbabwe's land policy because peasant farmers are unable to bring significant political pressure on the government. The National Farmers Association of Zimbabwe (NFAZ), the mass organization representing Zimbabwe's 800 000 peasant families, was present only in Fort Victoria (now Masvingo) Province before 1980 and was then basically non-political.[52] To transform a provincial master-farmer organization which gave technical advice into a national organization representing the political interests of several million peasants is naturally extremely difficult. The NFAZ, operating from a three-room office, has, in fact, experienced severe organizational problems in attempting to represent its constituency. A study of the peasant organization noted that

probably one of the biggest problems of the NFAZ is poor communication within its structure. Within the districts there is lack of means of communication in the rural areas, lack of funds available to representatives to enable them to visit the [farmers] clubs in their areas and some representatives are not very active.[53]

The political impact of these organizational problems was summed up by one extension official in an interview:

The peasant farmers aren't really organized to present their views. The channels barely exist for peasant farmers to have a national voice . . . There is no mechanism [for peasant farmers] to actually have an impact on the Ministry of Lands . . . There is no way to translate land pressure into policy.

Similarly, a former CFU official familiar with the NFAZ called it 'a patsy'; he noted that the NFAZ does not have 'the organizational ability to negotiate. . . . It doesn't have real influence.'

---

[52] J. W. Mutimba, 'A Case Study of the Victoria Association of Master Farmers' Clubs with Specific Reference to the Role of Provincial Committees' (Harare, Univ. of Zimbabwe, B.Ed. thesis, 1981), 68.

[53] L. T. Chitsike, 'Agricultural Co-operative Development in Zimbabwe' (Harare, in co-operation with the Friedrich Ebert Stiftung, 1986, mimeo.), 182.

To test further the ability of the NFAZ (in particular) and the communal farmers (in general) to influence policy-makers, I asked several
government officials how information about land pressure was transmitted to them. The following, each from a different official in the
Ministry of Lands, were typical responses:

Land pressure can be seen by movements of people and squatting. The key is
movements of people . . . The NFAZ plays no role.

I can recognize that an area is over-populated or over-grazed from data, including
the 1968 census and personal observation.

Government officials also note land pressure by their Sunday drives around the
communal areas.

While several other government officials echoed these comments, none
mentioned the NFAZ or communal farmers in general as the means by
which reports of land pressure are transmitted to the government. This
inability to influence the government might be less important if communal farmers were able to maintain an active political debate on the
issue, but, as it has been demonstrated in Table VI, the land question was
not prominent for a substantial portion of Zimbabwe's first ten years of
Independence. Even when the debate on land re-emerged in 1989, it
was a result of the leadership's own initiative rather than because of the
increasing prominence of the NFAZ.

There is another Black farmers' union in Zimbabwe, but it, too, does
not have a significant impact on the resettlement programme, although
for very different reasons. The Land Apportionment Act of 1930 that
legalized the division of colony's land did create certain areas known as
African Purchase Areas, which could be bought outright by Blacks.
Today, the average size of these small-scale commercial farms (as they are
now known in Zimbabwe) is between 200 and 250 acres, about a twentieth
of the size of the average large-scale commercial farm. These farms
currently cover 3,8 per cent of the country's land mass, but they hold only
2,5 per cent of its people.[54] The Black producers on these lands, many of
them old-time farmers or former soldiers, formed the Bantu Farmers
Congress in 1925 and, as a parallel to the RNFU, the African Farmers
Union in 1942. The 9 000-strong Black freeholders have now renamed
their organization the Zimbabwe National Farmers Union (ZNFU). From

[54] A. P. Cheater, *Idioms of Accumulation: Rural Development and Class Formation among
Freeholders in Zimbabwe* (Gweru, Mambo Press, 1984), x.

its suite of offices the ZNFU is charged with presenting small-scale farmers' views and demands to the government.

The ZNFU is in a conspicuously poor position to influence the land programme and has essentially no impact on government policy. As outright landowners, the small-scale farmers were sometimes accused of collaborating with the colonial regime during the liberation struggle, and the existence of Black farmers committed publicly to individual ownership has caused some friction with the new socialist government. In addition, the fact that this class of farmers has shown neither the productivity of White farmers nor the remarkable achievements of peasant farmers has led government officials to lecture the Black landowners several times on the need to use their land better.[55]

In fact, after years of silence, the ZNFU has now begun to argue that master farmers and agricultural institute graduates, rather than the communal farmers represented by the NFAZ, should be resettled on land purchased from White farmers. For instance, in a 1987 document, the ZNFU argued,

a study of the current production levels of the different groups of farmers shows that master farmers are capable of significantly out-producing the communal farmers. If government policy was modified to emphasize the bringing of under-utilized land into *full* production then such qualified farmers should, of necessity, be the settlers.[56]

Indeed, Gary Magadzire, the President of the ZNFU, has openly criticized the 162 000 families goal as 'unprofessional' because the wrong people might have been resettled.[57] While there is not an explicit alliance between the ZNFU and the White farmers on land, it is clear that the interests of Black freeholders probably coincide more with those of the White farmers than with those of the communal farmers.

Conclusion

The picture of political influence and state autonomy that emerges from the examination of the political conflict over the national distribution of

---

[55] See, for instance, the speech by Mugabe to Black farmers in which he expressed dismay at inefficiency in farming, *The Herald*, 25 Sept. 1986.

[56] Zimbabwe National Farmers' Union, *Settlement of Qualified Farmers in Resettlement Areas* (Harare, The Union, 1987), 13.

[57] 'Banking on the Black farmer', in Meldrum, 'The prize-winning peasant farmers', 42–3.

land is a complicated one. The Lancaster House Constitution clearly affected the government's land policy, but other factors, such as evolving judgements within the bureaucracy about resettlement, are also extremely important in understanding just how the government has proceeded. The analytic challenge posed by the land issue is to untangle the effects of outside influences such as the Constitution, while attaching appropriate weight to internal factors which have affected the day-to-day evolution of the resettlement programme.

As noted in the introductory chapter, the best way to understand state autonomy in the land area is to examine the state's ability to act on two levels. The first level concerns structural autonomy: the conflict over the political rules of the game in the land area. The Zimbabwe government was clearly not structurally autonomous because detailed provisions guaranteeing White land rights were established by the Lancaster House Constitution. While the concessions on autonomy in the setting of rules over land redistribution may have been sensible from the Zimbabwe government's perspective, there is little doubt that the requirement that government purchase the land has had a major impact on how the resettlement programme proceeds. Indeed, the Lancaster House provisions are a dramatic limitation on the state's autonomy because they impinge on the juridical right of the state to create the rules which will govern political conflicts.

However, although the requirement that the government buy land shaped the nature of politics on the land issue, it by no means resolved all the conflicts to do with land. Therefore, situational autonomy must also be examined: the political conflict that occurs given a certain set of political institutions and rules. At this level the government is autonomous because the factors which determined the way in which the land programme would evolve were within the state. Although the White farmers are politically powerful, organizational problems within the bureaucracy and an ongoing re-evaluation of the exact benefits that Zimbabwe can expect from resettlement have probably been more important at this point in determining the pace of the land-purchase programme than pressure from the CFU. Many of the bureaucracy's problems were caused by the provisions of the Lancaster House Constitution, but the fact was that the political impediments to increased resettlement still resided inside the state. Indeed, the beauty of the Lancaster House agreement from the White farmers' perspective was that it weakened the government in so many ways that the bureaucracy was forced to re-evaluate the benefits of resettlement without significant White political pressure having to be applied. The commercial farmers, therefore, did not have to engage in a potentially divisive debate about the highly sensitive land issue.

Several other factors must still be examined in order to understand why the state was situationally autonomous within the rules set by the Lancaster House Constitution. Firstly, the nature of land redistribution as an issue-area has had a significant impact on the evolving agrarian politics of Zimbabwe. The fact that land resettlement requires a large number of highly technical decisions to be taken over a period of time is the primary factor that has shaped land politics because such an issue is naturally more amenable to control by the bureaucracy than by the national leadership. While a few overarching policy guidelines have been formulated by the national leadership, it is an accumulation of the many decisions that have to be made by the bureaucracy as it undertakes the technical exercise of acquiring land that has largely determined the direction and emphasis of the programme. The national leadership has neither the time nor the ability to control an issue that requires so many complicated judgements. The dominance of the bureaucracy was most clearly demonstrated in the shift in government thinking from an emphasis on pure land resettlement to a programme which includes a strong focus on the redevelopment of the Communal Lands.

Furthermore, the nature of the issue-area had a strong impact on the NFAZ, which lacked the countervailing power to prevent technocratic decision-making from becoming dominant in the land area. Specifically, the NFAZ could not marshall sophisticated arguments which would convince a risk-averse bureaucracy that the government could move faster on land redistribution. Although the NFAZ cannot be considered strong under any circumstances, the type of decision-making in this area plays to the organization's weakness because the NFAZ lacks the technical expertise to provide contrary advice or information on resettlement questions. The NFAZ could not debate with the civil servants on their own terms so they could not engage in the political conflict over the distribution of land.

The fact that the NFAZ is arguing against a mainly Black bureaucracy on the land issue, and not, at the moment, against the White farmers, also weakens the NFAZ because its major strength — the legitimacy it has representing Black peasants — cannot be drawn upon. Since the White–Black conflict on land has become less of an issue than the Black government's own views on resettlement policy, the potential advantage that the NFAZ has in representing a large number of Africans cannot be transformed into a political strength. The government sees itself to be representing the same people that the NFAZ does.

Locus of Decision-making

In this case, the locus of decision-making was clearly at the middle to upper levels of the bureaucracy. Owing to the nature of the issue-area, power flowed towards the central part of government which had responsibility for the day-to-day technical decisions that eventually shaped the land-acquisition programme. It was impossible for Ministers to direct the resettlement programme because competing time demands and their lack of familiarity with the issues prevented them from participating in the many individual decisions which eventually shaped it.

The ruling party, ZANU(PF), does not seem to have been involved at all in making decisions about the overall distribution of land in the country. While there was a widespread belief at Independence that land should be redistributed to the peasants, the new regime did not come to power with any set policies on land distribution, or even with an overall vision of how to limit the role that White farmers would play in the economy. A Ministry of Lands official noted in an interview that 'the party does not come across as important. No plans emanate from it. Politburo sets major goals but government does all the work. The party just has rallies, it doesn't come up with plans or suggestions.'

Too many people have slighted Zimbabwe's land programme for not achieving enough after seven years of Independence. However, taking into account the fact that a completely new bureaucracy had to be created to handle a complicated task, the very real progress made in this issue should be acknowledged. This is especially true when Zimbabwe's land programme is compared to the Kenyan programme. The land programme will continue to make significant strides; however, owing to the bureaucracy's recognition of the real limits to resettlement, redistribution by itself will never be considered a panacea for Zimbabwe's rural ills. Whether the shift to the redevelopment of the Communal Lands will have the expected impact on the peasant areas is unclear, because that aspect of government policy is just beginning to be implemented. Something will have to be done soon to solve the land problem; nothing less than the welfare of the majority of Zimbabweans is at stake.

Chapter Four

Conflict over Land:
Communal Farmers versus Squatters

Almost all the attention in studies on the land question in Zimbabwe has been devoted to the government's attempts to redistribute land from large-scale White farmers to peasants. However, there is another ongoing conflict in the countryside: the battle between squatters and those who have stayed in the old tribal Reserves over who should have access to land that the government has purchased from White farmers. The squatters are thought to be politically weak because of their lack of organization, their inability to influence the government formally at the national level, and because the government has repeatedly declared the squatters' attempts to jump the resettlement queue and seize land to be illegitimate and illegal. In contrast, the peasant farmers who have stayed in the Communal Lands and have waited for the government to redistribute land to them are represented nationally by a formal lobbying organization and are the intended beneficiaries of the resettlement programme. Yet, in most places in Zimbabwe where there are squatters, it is these illegal settlers who have managed to gain control over the resettlement plots.

A review of the tactics of the supposedly weak squatters will lead to an understanding of how they were able to circumvent the resettlement bureaucracy and triumph over those who waited in the overcrowded Communal Lands. The squatters succeeded, in part, through their determination and innovative tactics when confronting the government. However, the squatters' tactics cannot be considered in isolation because two other factors greatly aided their quest for land. Firstly, the particular characteristics of land as a political good, particularly the fact that it can be seized and immediately put to use without further state aid, was important to the illegal settlers' success. Secondly, the initial weakness of the government bureaucracy which had been charged with carrying out the resettlement programme, and the willingness of national politicians to circumvent that bureaucracy on behalf of the illegal settlers, was also crucial to the squatters' ability to gain land at the expense of the intended beneficiaries of the resettlement programme. A study of the issue of land seizures allows an understanding of how even nominally-weak groups can successfully influence government allocation decisions and of how they can use the nature of political goods and institutions to their own advantage.

Communal Farmers and Squatters

The distinction between communal farmers and squatters is necessarily somewhat artificial. Squatters are often former farmers from the Communal Lands and they will often bring their families from the Communal Lands once they have acquired land. However, *politically*, communal farmers and squatters are distinctly different groups, and are perceived as such by the government. The former Deputy Minister of Lands, Mark Dube, noted that the government had a preference to resettle 'people who had waited patiently [rather] than those who preferred to be squatters'.[1] The communal farmers are also represented at a national level by the National Farmers Association of Zimbabwe, which is seen by the government as the legitimate lobbying organization representing peasant farmers and which has also received significant financial support both from the government and from foreign aid organizations. Finally, the Zimbabwe government is perceived by some as being obligated to the peasantry because of the rural population's support of the guerrillas during the war. Chiviya argues, for instance, that

the peasants as an interest group are quite an important component of the government's land acquisition and redistribution programme. It is the peasants who put political elites into power and not the White commercial farmers or multinational enterprises.[2]

In contrast, squatters are in a dramatically different political position. There are some in the government, notably certain members of Cabinet and members of the ruling party, who are sympathetic to the illegal settlers because squatting was encouraged by the liberation armies during the war in order to disrupt White agriculture and because illegal settlement is seen by some as a manifestation of the land problem in the Communal Lands. However, squatting is now officially viewed as an

---

[1] Zimbabwe Information Service, *Press Statement*, 10 Feb. 1983.

[2] Chiviya, 'Land Reform in Zimbabwe', 165.

unacceptable activity, even though there is no doubt that some squatters are poor enough to meet the government's criteria for resettlement.

Squatters are also perceived as politically weak by most observers. By their very nature, illegal settlers consist of small, unco-ordinated groups in widely separated rural areas who have no contact with each other. They have no national representation and, unlike the NFAZ, cannot lobby the government. Chiviya suggests, therefore, that

as a group squatters are not formally organized. They do not have an identifiable leadership. This creates problems for the ruling political elites. Because squatters are not formally organized and lack an identifiable leadership they do not have a direct input into the policy-making process.[3]

While it would be a mistake to argue that the communal farmers as represented by the NFAZ are a particularly powerful group in absolute terms, it is clear that in terms of traditional political analysis the squatters are, relatively, the weaker group.

Political Conflict in the Countryside

Zimbabwe has a fairly clear, if somewhat contradictory, process for selecting settlers to occupy newly acquired land. The formal process starts with the Department of Rural Development sending out qualification forms to the District Councils in each province (Zimbabwe has a total of 55 districts in eight provinces). The Councils then distribute the forms throughout their areas and collect the completed documents from peasants who want to be eligible for resettlement. When a new area opens up for resettlement, the Provincial Resettlement Officer and the District Council jointly review the returned eligibility forms and select the farmers for the resettlement scheme. The selected farmers then make their own way to the resettlement areas where they are allocated plots that have been previously demarcated.

To be eligible for resettlement a peasant must be
1) 'effectively landless, i.e. [have] no or too little land to support [him]self and dependents'; and
2) 'not employed (nor [should the] spouse [be])'; and
3) poor: 'The intention is to reach the rural poor; not, as many development programmes have, the rural rich'; and
4) 'married or widowed with dependents'; and

[3] Ibid., 218.

5)   aged 18 to 55 and able to 'make productive use of the land allocated'; and

6)   prepared to give up all rights to land in the communal areas; or

7)   a returned Zimbabwean refugee who is given special consideration; or

8)   an experienced or master farmer who is willing to give up land rights and wage employment elsewhere.[4]

The criteria are essentially the same as the ones first established in 1980, except for the provision for master farmers. This provision was added in 1982 in the hope that well-established growers would have a 'demonstration effect' among other peasants who were not as experienced in farming. This addition was a reaction by the government to the situation that had been developing in the resettlement areas.

There is a significant disjuncture between the type of resettlement programme the government was planning and the criteria it established for the selection of settlers. One of the most significant decisions that the government made on the land issue, although it is seldom discussed in Zimbabwe, was that the newly acquired plots would not simply become extensions of the Communal Lands but would be developed separately by the Ministry of Lands. The holdings in the resettlement areas are significantly larger than those in the Communal Lands, and resettlement farming means a full-time commitment by all members of the family — including the men, who are supposed to forgo other employment.[5] This differs considerably from the type of farming presently practised in the Communal Lands where most of the men are often absent because they are seeking wage employment in the urban areas. The decision not to simply append the resettlement areas to the Communal Lands was opposed by many chiefs who wanted larger Communal Lands — probably because this would result in an extension of their authority — and by some peasants.[6] The government rejected these pleas, arguing that the Communal Lands were a product of colonialism and that proper agrarian development could occur only if the resettlement areas were developed separately.

---

[4] Zimbabwe, *Intensive Resettlement Programme: Policies and Procedures* (Harare, Department of Rural Development, 1985), 23–4.

[5] B. Kinsey, 'Resettlement: The settlers' view', *Journal of Social Change and Development* [Harare] (1984), VII, 2.

[6] 'Settling debts before peasants', *Moto* (Sept. 1983), 17.

However, the government then proceeded to establish criteria for resettlement plots that favoured those who were least able to put these large areas to use, because the landless and refugees, by the very nature of their predicament, do not have significant farming experience and capital (especially in the form of draught power) to exploit the resettlement plots fully. One resettlement official estimated in an interview that perhaps only 15 per cent of the people who were actually resettled on what was sometimes prime commercial farmland were good farmers. This was more or less admitted by the government when it began to seek demonstration effects by placing master farmers in resettlement areas.[7] In the words of the provincial official, the government made a 'political decision' to favour returning refugees and the landless because, by squatting, these people had significantly helped the liberation struggle and because they were able to exert significant political pressure on the national leadership. The basic decision to settle on the newly acquired lands people who were least suited to them set the tone for the entire selection process, which has certainly not gone according to plan.

The Squatter Triumph

The resettlement process has been, and to a considerable extent still is, overrun by squatters. Officials reported in interviews that in some provinces, notably Manicaland, Mashonaland West and Matabeleland North, most of the resettlement plots have gone to squatters, and that in other parts of the country entire resettlement areas have been controlled largely by illegal settlers. A 1981 study noted: 'What actually is happening in all likelihood is that the government's programme is taking place at the same pace as that of the peasants who are occupying the land unofficially'.[8] Certainly in Manicaland almost all those resettled have been squatters, and this province accounts for approximately a third of the total number of families resettled nationwide.[9] One resettlement official, describing how squatters gain access to land planned for resettlement, said that the formal process whereby District Councils collect resettlement forms from qualified farmers and then choose the final group for the resettlement plots was so much 'wishful thinking'. He said that people in the rural

[7] *The Herald*, 7 Sept. 1982.

[8] N. R. B. Gaidzanwa, 'Promised Land: Towards a Land Policy for Zimbabwe' (The Hague, Institute of Social Studies, M.Dev.Stud. thesis, 1981), 79.

[9] *The Herald*, 8 Aug. 1984.

areas often know that land will be sold before the government does (perhaps because the farm-workers have spread the word) and that illegal settlers then move on to the farm immediately or get close enough to be able to claim occupancy once the land has been sold. In the words of one resettlement officer, 'it is just a question of getting there first'. Similarly, a Matabeleland official said in an interview: 'Anyone who knows about government land will move himself in'. It is important to note that this has not happened everywhere in the country. For instance, in Mashonaland Central, where there is not much of a squatter problem, peasants have been resettled according to established regulations. However, where there are squatters, it is almost always the case that they are the ones who have been settled on the former commercial farms.

While the government allowed the squatters to win the battle for the resettlement areas, it did not allow them to triumph throughout the country. In a number of instances the army has removed squatters in search-and-evict operations, and squatter settlements have been razed on more than one occasion.[10] The government was especially dedicated to ending the squatter menace where ongoing commercial activities were threatened. However, what has confused some is that just because the government was able to deal effectively with squatters who threatened working commercial farms, it does not mean that it was able to prevent illegal settlers from gaining control over a large percentage of the re-settlement plots.[11] Indeed, the government often moved squatters off commercial farmland on to resettlement plots. One Department of Rural Development official estimated that, of the squatters forcibly evicted by government, 50 per cent were resettled. In contrast, only a small fraction of the 800 000 families in the Communal Lands have been resettled. It is clear, therefore, who, proportionally, has benefited the most from re-settlement.

Some would claim that resettlement-by-squatting will, in the end, accomplish the goals set out by the government, because squatting is seen as a manifestation of land hunger in the Communal Lands.[12] However, studying the correlation between land pressure and squatting casts doubt on the assertion that squatting is the result solely of land hunger, and that,

[10] See, for instance, *The Herald*, 2 July 1983.

[11] See, for instance, M. Bratton, 'The comrades in the countryside: The politics of agricultural policy in Zimbabwe', *World Politics* (1987), XLIX, 192.

[12] Chiviya, 'Land Reform in Zimbabwe', 235.

therefore, all illegal settlers who have made their way on to resettlement land are deserving according to the criteria established by the government. Most of the squatting problems have occurred in the eastern province of Manicaland. In 1981 and 1982 it was estimated that 79 per cent of all squatters were in this province.[13] However, when the Whitsun Foundation surveyed the Communal Lands which were under the greatest pressure, it found that only two districts in Manicaland were among the thirty in the nation considered to have had populations furthest beyond their carrying capacity. Most of the Communal Lands under extreme pressure were in the two Matabeleland provinces and Masvingo, where dry conditions allow only very low densities of population.[14] While there is certainly land pressure almost everywhere in the Communal Lands, there is simply not a clear correlation between squatting and extreme land pressure.

Instead, squatting seems to occur where open land is available. The presence of large amounts of open land in Manicaland — as a result of farms being abandoned because of the fierce battles waged there during the liberation war — is probably what led to squatting becoming endemic in that province. It was, for instance, a Manicaland official's impression that the squatting there was 'sheer opportunism' rather than a reflection of land pressure: 'People saw some getting away with it [squatting] and decided to follow.' Another Ministry of Lands official said in an interview: 'Sometimes these people [squatters] were just trouble-makers, but government was forced to give them land. Government had to be seen as doing something.' Many of the squatters are, like the farmers in the Communal Lands, desperately in need of land; but many, clearly, are not.

Several factors contributed to the success of the supposedly weak squatters in circumventing government regulations and successfully competing against the communal farmers. Firstly, the sheer determination of the squatters must be emphasized. Owing to the poor conditions of the former tribal Reserves and the dislocations caused by the war, some people had absolutely no alternative to squatting. Many others, who might not have qualified under government regulations for land resettlement, saw squatting as a once-in-a-lifetime opportunity to improve their fortunes. Thus, squatters in one area said that 'even if they were convicted they would come back because they had not been given land and were

---

[13] *The Herald*, 16 Oct. 1981.

[14] Whitsun Foundation, *Land Reform in Zimbabwe*, 153.

hungry'.[15] Some of the squatters, up to half in certain areas, are also
Malawians or Mozambicans who previously worked on White farms and
who have no alternative to squatting. One Malawian in Karoi (Mashonaland West Province) said: 'I had to squat on this farm after my employer
had fired me because he said he could not give me the minimum wage.
Where would I have gone? Zimbabwe is my home and I cannot go back
to Malawi.'[16] One group of squatters summed up the determination of
many who tried to seize land: 'Now we have been ordered to be off by
Monday but we are not leaving. We are staying and we are prepared to
die and be buried here.'[17]

The squatters' determination was fuelled by statements from the
liberation forces and by the attitude of certain politicians immediately
after Independence. While the Lancaster House Constitution forced the
government to purchase land on a 'willing seller–willing buyer' basis, the
idea that land seizure was a part of the ongoing struggle was clearly
important to many who had spent years struggling to preserve African
land rights. For instance, Moven Mahachi, a long-time supporter of Chief
Tangwena and the Tangwena people in their struggle not to be declared
squatters on their ancestral lands by the Rhodesian authorities during
UDI, was clearly persuaded by many of the squatters' claims in post-
Independence Zimbabwe. When he was Deputy Minister of Lands,
Mahachi said of one region in Manicaland:

What I like about the Makoni people is that they do not just sit idle saying, 'We
have won the war, now we can rest'. They take action to solve the land problem
for themselves. Makoni district is more infested with squatters than any other
district in the country and this makes it easier for us: it puts pressure on the
Ministry and pressure on the owners.[18]

This attitude trickled down to the squatters. One squatter in Manicaland
said:

I had only four acres of land in Tanda. The soil was always very poor. When I
heard that I could have land here, I came. . . . A Deputy Minister, Mr Mahachi,

[15] *The Herald*, 8 May 1982.

[16] Zimbabwe Information Service, *Press Statement*, 24 Nov. 1981.

[17] *The Sunday Mail*, 8 Nov. 1981.

[18] Quoted in T. Ranger, *Peasant Consciousness and Guerrilla War in Zimbabwe* (Harare,
Zimbabwe Publishing House; Berkeley and Los Angeles, Univ. of California Press, 1985),
307.

came and told us we would get twelve acres. We are waiting to be given land. ... There is plenty of land, so why should we not have it?[19]

In the face of the determination of the squatters and support, at least initially, from part of the national leadership, the bureaucracy that was supposed to institutionalize resettlement procedures was exceptionally weak. The Ministry (Lands, Resettlement and Rural Development) which had been assigned the task of resettling people and handling the squatters was an entirely new creation. One official who was present at its creation said in an interview: 'When the Ministry was established we had no files, no phones. Everything was new. . . . We had no idea what to do in the beginning. . . . Everyone asked, "What are we supposed to do?" It took us six months just to learn the issues.' This institutional confusion was only natural for a new ministry assigned a complex task in the first chaotic months of Independence.

Typical of the weakness and institutional confusion of the resettlement bureaucracy was the government's position on the deadline after which it would refuse to settle squatters. The government's first official position seems to have been that those squatting before November 1980 would be resettled, but that no further squatting would be tolerated.[20] However, in the face of pressure from the squatters, this deadline changed several times, and there appears to have been considerable confusion within the government as to the exact cut-off date when squatting would no longer be accepted. For instance, in August 1982 the Minister of Local Government and Town Planning, Enos Chikowore, stated that people squatting after 1 June 1982 would not be resettled, while a Zimbabwe government press statement five months before had listed July 1981 as the final date.[21]

In practice, the deadlines at first did little to stop squatting. For example, in December 1983 officials in the Department of Rural Development were complaining that there was, in their words, a 'lack of political will to move back and/or halt the latest migration of squatters on the part of the government at large'. Indeed, as late as November 1986 the Governor of the province hardest hit by squatting, Senator Joshua Dhube of Manicaland, was advocating — seemingly against government regu-

[19] *The Sunday Mail*, 2 Aug. 1981.

[20] *The Herald*, 8 Nov. 1980.

[21] Compare *The Chronicle*, 23 Aug. 1982, and Zimbabwe Information Service, *Press Statement*, 4 Mar. 1982.

lations — that resettlement be first for squatters. He said that more land
had to be made available

because there has been talk of squatters — some 6 150 families which is about
37 000 people. These people are landless. They are in the wrong places —
commercial farms, Forestry Commission land and even communal areas. We are
asking government to acquire land for resettlement as a priority. We can't move
these people to nowhere.[22]

Yet, at the same time, Minister Chikowore — by then the Minister of Local
Government, Urban and Rural Development and the official who actually supervises resettlement — was stressing that land would be purchased only for those who remained in the Communal Lands, and that all
squatters had to be returned to their own areas before they would be
resettled.[23]

The institutional chaos present when the Ministry was being formed
often allowed squatters to take over resettlement areas. A Ministry of
Lands official noted in an interview, 'Our blunder was to buy land for
squatters. But everything was being done without a plan. Our hands were
being twisted by squatters.' While procedures were being established,
squatters were able to exert pressure on local officials and thereby ignore
regulations being established by the Ministry of Lands' central office.
One official recounted, 'If a group identified itself as squatters, then they
would be given a piece of land. . . . This was often done on an informal
basis, often local resettlement officers would give them a piece of land.'
The pressure that squatters applied to the weak government bureaucracy
was incessant and often ingenious. Officials in Mashonaland recall that
in one area the squatters were able to build a school and basic infrastructure and were even able to attract a foreign donor to aid them.
Another squatter group in Mashonaland came to the Department of
Rural Development and demanded, in the hope of legitimizing their
claims, that the government's extension agency, Agritex, teach them
contour ploughing so that they would not destroy the nation's resources.

Squatters also recognized that they could still call on two sets of allies
to strengthen their claims to land and thereby circumvent procedures
established by the civil servants. In the first place, many local Branch
Chairmen of the ruling party provided significant encouragement to

[22] *The Sunday Mail*, 30 Nov. 1986.
[23] *The Herald*, 26 Sept. 1986.

the squatters and these party officials often intimidated government officials. For instance, the ZANU(PF) chairman of the Vumba region in the Eastern Highlands said while helping squatters to seize land:

We were waiting hungrily for this day. I am sure that when the farmers came to destroy our properties they had the backing of their government and I don't see why our government should not back us. Now that we have come back to settle in our land they decide to call us squatters.[24]

Attempts to invoke the ruling party in order to give the squatters more leverage were common. A Manicaland resettlement officer recounted, 'I am now used to meeting different delegations [of squatters] from different areas bringing in their grievances. Some even leave with me their donations for the new ZANU(PF) headquarters.'[25] The alliance of squatters and local ZANU(PF) officials created a powerful coalition that pressed squatter demands and intimidated the bureaucracy. For instance, one resettlement official in the Mashonaland region had to get the Zimbabwe Republic Police to arrest the local ZANU(PF) leader and a spirit medium for the day so that the squatters in one area could be removed. Obviously, few government employees could be expected to confront this formidable combination of political forces.

Secondly, the squatters were also able, at first, to call upon the national leadership in their effort to circumvent the bureaucracy. In an interview, one resettlement official called the squatters 'a force to be reckoned with', and said that they were quite articulate and skilled in gaining the support of the politicians. He described the typical pattern of politics in the countryside: 'The politicians go to the squatters, hold rallies, call them the *povo* [the politically-charged Portuguese word used to describe the masses in Zimbabwe], and force government's hand to resettle them.' For instance, when Senator Chief Kayisa Ndiweni instigated a group of his followers in Matabeleland South to squat, it was decided that the illegal settlers would not be punished but, after screening, would be resettled. One newspaper noted that 'Comrade Mahachi could not punish the squatters by evicting them since it was Senator Ndiweni who instigated them into settling at the farms'.[26] Resettlement officials across the country reported similar experiences.

[24] *The Sunday Mail*, 3 Jan. 1981.
[25] *The Herald*, 20 Sept. 1982.
[26] *The Chronicle*, 10 Sept. 1982.

The alliance of squatters and national leaders was possible, in part, because the government's own regulations gave the illegal settlers unusually direct access to the most powerful politicians in the country. According to the Ministry of Lands' 1981 document, *Intensive Resettlement: Policies and Procedures*, when there is a squatter problem 'a meeting is held with the local people at which they are addressed by either the Minister or Deputy Minister of Lands, Resettlement and Rural Development'.[27] In addition having such contact with the top leadership of the Ministry of Lands, squatters often had access to other high-ranking politicians. For instance, when Chief Chikwanda and 3 000 of his followers occupied farms in the Victoria East area of Victoria (now Masvingo) Province, they were addressed by Minister Mahachi (Lands) and Minister Eddison Zvobgo (then Local Government). The next day the Deputy Prime Minister, Simon Muzenda, addressed the same group.[28]

An instructive example of the political pressure that squatters used, and the success it could bring with the help of national politicians, occurred in what is known as the Angwa River Valley between Chinhoyi and Karoi in Mashonaland West. A 1983 report noted that the squatter problem was increasing there — though it was well past all government deadlines — and that the squatters were well organized:

The leaders all appear to be self-proclaimed ZANU(PF) local leaders. Many of them are said to be charging money for distributing the privately owned farmland among their followers. They also appear to see themselves as gaining political power and prestige through their action in encouraging the squatters to occupy farms. . . . Civil authorities refuse to even serve eviction warrants on the squatters for fear of violence.[29]

By 1985 the squatters were still occupying the area. The Deputy Minister of Lands, Mark Dube, told the squatters that they had to leave.[30] However, salvation in the form of another politician was soon to rescue the squatters and confirm that they had chosen the correct tactics. Zimbabwe's major newspaper, *The Herald*, in an article entitled 'Mhangura squatters promised new home', detailed the squatters' success:

[27] Zimbabwe, *Intensive Resettlement: Policies and Procedures* (Salisbury, Ministry of Lands, Resettlement and Rural Development, 1981), 10.

[28] *The Sunday Mail*, 30 Aug. 1981.

[29] *The Financial Gazette*, 22 Dec. 1983.

[30] *The Herald*, 25 June 1985.

Squatters living along the Angwa River Valley near Mhangura are to be resettled before the onset of the rainy season. The Deputy Minister of Agriculture, Cde [Comrade] S. Mombeshora, who is also the ZANU-PF candidate for Mahonde North . . . assured the squatters, estimated to be about 500 families, that the government had plans to resettle them, but there had to be adjustments to their settlements to accommodate development. . . . The squatters vowed to vote for ZANU-PF even if it meant travelling all the way to Harare to cast their vote. . . . Cde Mombeshora said he was impressed by the squatters' political consciousness and their desire to work with the ruling party.[31]

The report concluded by quoting the squatters to the effect that their talk with Deputy Minister Mombeshora was their 'first amicable meeting with government'.[32] Given the frequency of politicians aiding squatters to circumvent the bureaucracy, Governor Dhube of Manicaland claimed that squatting occurs because people 'listen to the word of the politicians rather than the officials. The people hold to the politicians' promises, but there has been no co-ordination between this and the technical back-up of the officials'.[33]

Communal Farmer Failure

In contrast to the squatters, the communal farmers who remained in their home areas had no effective way to pressure the government on the specific issue of obtaining resettlement plots. Even Robinson Gapare, President of the NFAZ, noted that 'lack of communications between government and communal farmers is contributing to the squatter problem'. He claimed that, 'in the absence of information about resettlement plans, rural farmers were beginning to think they were being neglected'.[34] The squatters clearly saw the futility of waiting for the NFAZ to pressure government so that communal farmers might be aided, and recognized the effectiveness of squatting as an alternative strategy. One newspaper article noted: 'Squatters in the Karoi area have taken over an unoccupied farm because of growing impatience with government delays in resettling them'.[35] The squatters described their move as 'an act to draw the government's attention to our plight'.[36]

Communal farmers also lack influence because they face a much more hostile institutional arrangement when trying to lobby the government.

---

[31] Ibid.

[32] Ibid.

[33] *The Herald*, 1 Dec. 1986.

[34] *The Herald*, 22 Apr. 1981.

[35] *The Sunday Mail*, 30 Aug. 1981.

[36] Ibid.

At the national level, the problems that the NFAZ has in confronting the bureaucracy have been discussed in Chapter 3. Local action by communal farmers, too, seems not to have the potential to be effective. The branch of the government that communal farmers have most contact with is Agritex, through the latter's extension workers. However, as one Agritex official admitted in an interview, lobbying for farmers is not Agritex's job and 'extension workers have no formal training in transmitting farmers' views'. There is also still some suspicion of the extension workers on the part of some communal farmers because many of them were also agents of agricultural policy under the White minority regime of Ian Smith.

The only other government agency likely to be able to transmit the concerns of communal farmers is the Department of Rural Development.[37] However, it is clear from conversations with officials in that Department that they do not respond to communal farmers' land demands. Provincial-level Department of Rural Development officials interviewed in all eight of Zimbabwe's provinces repeatedly said that they did not recommend that a certain piece of land be bought or that more land be acquired in an area because of communal farmer complaints. Typical of official attitudes was that of one Mashonaland official who said that 'we could possibly recommend which land should be bought, but never have; I didn't want to take the initiative.' The Ministry of Lands, which actually buys the land, does not have an institutional presence at the Provincial level, and, therefore, does not come into direct contact with communal farmers. Even after ten years of Independence, Zimbabwe's institutional arrangements do not allow the communal farmers to have anywhere near the effective voice that the squatters have, because the people remaining in the Communal Lands are not provided with direct access to powerful politicians and are kept far from the civil servants who make actual decisions concerning the purchase of land.

However, within a few years of Independence the tide had probably turned against the squatters, not because of complaints by communal farmers, but because the resettlement bureaucracy had developed enough institutional resilience to resist the political pressure from the squatters. Government leaders quickly changed their views on squatting when they realized the implications for the agricultural industry, the backbone of the

---

[37] The Department of Rural Development was moved to the Ministry of Local Government when the Ministry of Lands, Resettlement and Rural Development was merged with the Ministry of Agriculture in 1985 to form the Ministry of Lands, Agriculture and Rural Resettlement.

country, of a nationwide 'land grab'. For instance, the then Deputy Minister of Lands, Mark Dube, declared an 'all-out war' against squatters in 1982, and said that they would have to vacate all land that they were on by 25 January 1983.[38] By 1985 even Mahachi, by then Minister of Lands, was telling White farmers, 'Let me assure you, the elections are over . . . the honeymoon is over. We don't want anyone twisting the arm of government and we will be acting vigorously against squatting.'[39]

In addition, Minister Chikowore's high profile and strong actions against the squatters, combined with his long tenure (for Zimbabwe) in charge of the Ministry responsible for squatters, provided the bureaucracy with a coherence and sense of mission that had previously been lacking. The Department of Rural Development's head office had also had enough time to formulate concrete positions on resettlement, institutionalize procedures, and train personnel. Significantly, the 1985 (second) edition of *Intensive Resettlement: Policies and Procedures* no longer gives squatters automatic access to ministers.[40] As a result, by 1986 the bureaucracy was able to exert enough control over local operations for established practices to be followed. In Manicaland, government appears to be less successful in stemming the squatter problem, but, in general, the squatters are not as powerful as they were.

Conclusion

There was no clash over the rules governing the political conflict between squatters and communal farmers. Indeed, the squatters were able to take the rules formulated by the government and use them effectively to pressure policy-makers into giving them more land. While the state, therefore, was structurally autonomous, it was not situationally autonomous because, until the institutions governing land reallocation were both strengthened and changed, the squatters were able to exert effective pressure in the day-to-day conflict over land. Three factors must be understood in order to explain the success of the supposedly weak squatters.

Firstly, the squatters' tactics of moving quickly against the resettlement bureaucracy and seeking allies in local ZANU(PF) officials and

---

[38] Ranger, *Peasant Consciousness and Guerrilla War in Zimbabwe*, 314.

[39] Quoted by D. Weiner, 'Land and agricultural development', in C. Stoneman (ed.), *Zimbabwe's Prospects* (London, Macmillan, 1988), 88.

[40] Zimbabwe, *Intensive Resettlement: Policies and Procedures*, 25.

some national politicians allowed them to circumvent government procedures effectively until the resettlement bureaucracy finally became strong enough to resist the claims of most squatters and limit by-passes to the national leadership. The squatters' competitors, the communal farmers, were unable to lobby the government successfully because the national organization that represented them could not successfully mobilize followers in the communal areas where its potential strength lay. Indeed, it is an interesting question whether the NFAZ actually weakened the hand of communal farmers, because the existence of a national organization may have discouraged communal farmers from taking local action which might have made their claims more salient and attracted the attention of the national leadership. The NFAZ was also ineffectual because its chief source of legitimacy, the fact that it represented rural Blacks, was not an advantage in the competition with the squatters, who were also Blacks from the rural areas.

Secondly, the fact that physical possession of the land essentially means control over it, and the fact that land can be seized and put to use by individuals with few outside resources, is exceptionally important in understanding the success of the squatters. The squatters were able to gain control of the resettlement plots because when they moved in and seized the plots they immediately had control over the land *per se* and the value that the land produced.

Because land can simply be seized and controlled, it is dramatically different from other political goods that states allocate. For instance, health clinics need government expertise and supplies to function, and these requirements effectively prevent local groups from playing a significant role in the siting of clinics. As will be noted in Chapter 8, some groups in Zimbabwe have tried to force the Ministry of Health into establishing rural health centres (clinics) in their areas, much in the way that the squatters gained land. However, they have been unsuccessful because gaining control over a resettlement plot gives a squatter automatic victory in terms of control over the crop that the land produces; gaining control over another piece of land and declaring it a clinic site means nothing unless the government agrees to provide the equipment, staff and supplies needed to make the clinic a reality. It is the nature of the political good that helps make the local groups such as squatters so politically powerful on the land issue, while other groups have had very little influence in the determination of sites for rural health centres. The fact that, for land, possession is essentially victory also meant that those who chose to stay in the Communal Lands lost out in the political conflict for very understandable reasons.

Examining the nature of the political good also helps to explain why the resettlement bureaucracy could play such an important role in the national distribution of land (discussed in Chapter 3), but be so weak initially in the conflict over who actually controlled the land that was purchased. The bureaucracy controlled the overall distribution of land because it alone made the technical decisions on which land should be bought, and it also had sole control over the funds for acquisition. However, when land was acquired, the nature of the political good caused a rapid shift in the balance of power. The fact that physical control over land meant control over its production engendered a highly decentralized battle pitting squatters (who only had to seize land) against whatever rural institutional presence the government could establish. Since the government, especially in the first years of Independence, did not have a significant presence in the rural areas, the bureaucracy was unable to duplicate its control of overall land-acquisition policy when actually determining who was to be resettled. Eventually, the bureaucracy was able to overcome the handicaps posed by the political good and institutionalize its procedures, but not before the squatters had gained control of a significant portion of the land acquired by the government.

The third factor crucial to the success of the weak squatters was the government's particular institutional structure. The squatters were more powerful than the communal farmers in this case because the institutional structure of the government was such that the type of political pressure that they were able to exert was extraordinarily effective. The weak resettlement bureaucracy, the fact that government guidelines could be circumvented by top politicians, and the access to the national leadership that the institutionalized procedures gave to the squatters, undermined the power of the civil servants who were trying to enforce the resettlement guidelines. The squatters, therefore, had the kind of direct access to the national leadership which the NFAZ dramatically lacked on the question of overall land acquisition discussed in Chapter 3. When they tried to influence the government, the NFAZ and its supporters were faced with the same problems that they had experienced in the conflict over the overall distribution of land between Blacks and Whites. They were once again faced with a government structure which did not allow them to transmit their views to the national leadership effectively, and were therefore unable to influence the central bureaucracy.

Political power cannot be judged simply by the organizational characteristics of the pressure group, but must be assessed in the light of the
institutional arrangements of that part of the government that the pressure group is trying to influence. Different groups will have varying
degrees of effectiveness in pressuring a government, depending upon
how their organizational characteristics and tactics match up against the
government's institutional framework. In the case examined here, the
characteristics of the resettlement bureaucracy, especially the poorly-
institutionalized procedures and the ability of national politicians to
circumvent civil servants, allowed the nominally-weak squatters to be
effective, while at the same time preventing the communal farmers from
exercising a significant political voice. The role that institutions play in
determining who will be politically powerful is further highlighted when
it is remembered that there are no significant class, ethnic or educational
differences between the communal farmers and the squatters.

Locus of Decision-making

The centre of decision-making in this case was at the local level of
government. The squatters were successful because they were consistently able to overwhelm the minimal state presence at the local level and
seize the land. In this case ZANU(PF) also played an important role in
helping the illegal settlers circumvent the bureaucracy. It is not surprising
that ZANU(PF) was able to play such an important role at the local level
in view of the presence it had established in the rural areas during the
liberation struggle and the stress that the nationalist armies had placed on
the land question. The ruling party was particularly prominent in Manicaland, the province with the most squatting, because this region was
ZANU(PF)'s principal theatre of operation during the war. Seizure of
land, a dramatic action that did not require any planning, could also be
justified in terms of ZANU(PF)'s vague ideology, because helping the
squatters was seen as a continuation of the liberation struggle that had
always focused on land. Also, the problem of technical expertise, which
had prevented ZANU(PF) from playing a major role in legitimate land
acquisition, was not a barrier to land seizures because physical possession of the land was the deciding factor in the political conflict. It was only
after the bureaucracy was able to strengthen its local presence — essentially extending the central government's norms and procedures to the
rural areas — that the locus of decision-making shifted to the central
bureaucracy.

The battle over resettlement plots demonstrates the fallacy of trying to judge political power in a vacuum. In Zimbabwe, the squatters, assumed to be politically weak by their very nature, actually out-performed the communal farmers, who were represented by the type of national organization normally associated with successful political influence. However, the squatters' tactics were successful only because of the nature of land as a political good and because of the particular institutional structure of Zimbabwe's resettlement bureaucracy. With a different type of political resource and a stronger bureaucracy the squatters would have done far less well.

Chapter Five

Societal Demands and Government Choices: Agricultural Producer Price Policy

---

Recent studies of Africa's continuing agrarian crisis have focused on the inadequate prices that governments pay farmers as one of the key causes of declining food production throughout the continent. However, in Zimbabwe, agricultural producer prices have, in general, provided positive incentives for crop production, and the government has avoided the disastrous trap of the 'cheap food policy' that has destroyed the agrarian base of so many other countries. To understand why Zimbabwe has differed so dramatically from the rest of Africa, it is necessary to study the price-setting process and the contrasting pressures that various lobbying groups can bring to bear upon the government. In turn, this investigation of agricultural producer price policy will also enable a further investigation of the central focus of this study: the autonomy of the state.

Power and Agricultural Producer Prices

Despite the importance of producer prices to the health of the agrarian sector, African governments have continually taxed farmers by paying them less than they would earn on the open market. The most comprehensive and challenging explanation of why this should be the case has been offered by Robert Bates. In Bates's 'rational choice' model of agrarian politics, African states tax producers through low prices in order to shift resources from the agrarian sector to industry, to increase government revenue, and to mollify urban consumers who demand a low price for their food.[1] Although these low food prices can be disastrous in the long term, they are rational from the perspective of the government because they help to meet the public sector's perceived development needs, its revenue imperative, and the government's desire to control the politically-active urban population. The only way that these low prices can be avoided is if producers can persuade the government to pay them a

[1] R. H. Bates, *Markets and States in Tropical Africa* (Berkeley and Los Angeles, Univ. of California Press, 1981), 12, 30.

higher price. Producers may succeed in influencing the government if there are historical factors which favour the producer — such as significant political support that they may have provided the victorious political party — or 'an enduring institutional bias' in marketing boards that producers helped to establish.[2] Farmers may also successfully demand higher prices because their small numbers enable them to be well organized or because other well-organized groups (such as agricultural processors) depend on adequate farm production.[3] Governments are continually able to post low producer prices because of their coercive power, the disorganization of the large number of peasant farmers in the countryside, and through the use of side-payments, including subsidized seed and fertilizer, to placate élite farmers who might lead anti-government protests.[4]

One of the key assumptions of Bates's model, and of the rational choice school in general, is that the African state is not autonomous. For pricing purposes (especially of food crops), Bates sees the state as 'an agency for aggregating private demands', and, therefore, interprets public policies as 'choices made in response to political pressures exerted by organized interests'.[5] The model, for the purposes of pricing, reduces the state to a simple response mechanism: it responds to the demands of the politically powerful and ignores those without a voice. Little attention is given to the role of institutions, to the way in which groups actually bring pressure to bear on a government, and to the nature of the issue-area itself. In Zimbabwe, all of these factors have played a significant part in the determination of producer prices.

Producer Price Politics in Rhodesia

In the colonial era, the powerful White farmers were able to convince the settler government, without great difficulty, to adopt a pricing and marketing system that was expressly in the interests of large-scale farming. Public intervention to subsidize Whites in agriculture dates back to the 1930s when the government aided maize growers in order to prevent them from leaving the land. The system reached its logical conclusion in the mid-1960s when the Agricultural Marketing Authority (AMA), a government parastatal, was formed. The law required the AMA, through its marketing organs, the Grain Marketing Board (GMB) and the Cotton

---

[2] R. H. Bates, 'The nature and origins of agricultural policies in Africa', in his *Essays on the Political Economy of Rural Africa* (Cambridge, Cambridge Univ. Press, 1983), 113.
[3] Ibid., 113–14.   [4] Ibid., 126–8.   [5] Ibid., 121.

Marketing Board (CMB), to buy the entire output of all crops regulated by the government (so-called 'controlled crops'). During White rule, the AMA was dominated by White farmers who were well represented on its board.

Prices for the controlled crops were set through a series of negotiations between the government and the farmers. The AMA would meet the Rhodesian National Farmers Union and then make a recommendation to the Minister of Agriculture who would also meet with large-scale producers. The Minister would then make his recommendations to the Cabinet. Interviews with former senior RNFU officials and personnel in the Ministry of Agriculture suggest that the pro-farmer Minister's recommendations were almost always accepted by the Cabinet. One CFU official said of the pre-1980 era, 'if the Minister of Agriculture did not get the price he wanted he would resign...and he never resigned'. Colin Leys wrote in the late 1950s: 'In this climate of opinion the farmers succeeded, in effect, in establishing a kind of guild system whereby authority of the state was largely exercised by the producers themselves in regulating production and sales'.[6]

The guerrilla war, which began after Rhodesia declared its UDI in 1965, further enhanced the power of the White farmers in the setting of producer prices. As the war progressed, it became a military imperative for the government to keep its farmers on the land. The Minister of Agriculture, for instance, noted in 1973 that 'the farmers are our first and foremost bulwark' to prevent 'the intrusion of terrorists into this country'.[7] The new leverage provided by the war allowed farmers to press for price increases and enabled them to lobby the government successfully to institute a system of pre-planting prices in the mid-1970s. Previously, prices were negotiated only after the crops were in the ground. The announcement of prices before planting meant that the farmers could make crop-mix decisions with greater certainty, because they had a much better idea of what their final returns would be. Pre-planting prices also strengthened the farmers' bargaining position *vis-à-vis* the government because they could immediately threaten not to grow crops whose prices were not satisfactory. This option was, of course, impossible if the crops were already in the ground when the prices were announced. The post-planting price negotiations were also retained so that after 1976 there

[6] Leys, *European Politics in Southern Rhodesia*, 71.

[7] Quoted in Rhodesian National Farmers Union, 'Annual Congress Report, 1973' (Salisbury, RNFU, 1973, mimeo.), 37.

were two sets of price negotiations and farmers thus had even more opportunities to obtain higher prices. In the waning days of White rule, however, the settler regime had so few resources that it could not meet the demands of even its most powerful constituency. In 1979 there was an unprecedented public protest by the farmers against the prices announced, which was led by Dennis Norman, a rich Norton farmer who was then President of the RNFU.

The Price-setting Process in Independent Zimbabwe

At Independence the new government signalled its intention to work with White farmers through repeated statements and, in a move that surprised everyone, by appointing Dennis Norman as the new Minister of Agriculture. Government co-operation with the CFU was possible because, even though it represented the most thoroughly conservative group in the country, the Union's leadership saw — before any other element of White society did — the necessity of having a constructive relationship with the new Black government. On the government's part, many officials who had lived in Mozambique during the liberation struggle had seen at first hand the damage caused by the mass exodus of the White population and were determined to avoid a repeat of that disaster. However, it is crucial to note that it was not inevitable that the government should have co-operated so openly with White agriculture and allowed it the voice in price negotiations that is described below. The government could have taken a number of measures that would have fallen far short of scaring White farmers off the land but which would have effectively curtailed their political voice in price negotiations. The government could have, for instance, ended commercial farmers' presence on the AMA, stopped formal meetings with farmers as part of the price-negotiation process, or simply restricted farmers' access to the government. It is important to note that the continued voice of the CFU is a result of a deliberate government choice, because too many people see the current situation as an inevitable result of the CFU's economic power and Norman's presence in the Cabinet. It was not, and the CFU was as surprised as anyone that the socialist government had decided to work with it.

Government Institutions in the Price-Setting Process

The new government has kept the institutional price-setting process as it inherited it from the Smith regime. The AMA still begins the price-setting process and the parastatal still has commercial farmers on its board, though they have now been joined by representatives of peasant farmers. The AMA still makes a submission to the Minister of Agriculture,[8] who then meets with the farmers. The Minister then submits his own recommendations to the Ministerial Economic Co-ordinating Committee (MECC) which is made up of all the ministries in the government which deal with economic matters. The MECC working party of Permanent Secretaries and the MECC Committee of Ministers consider the Minister of Agriculture's report and make their own submission to Cabinet. The Cabinet, in a discussion chaired by the Minister of Finance, Economic Planning and Development, then reviews the MECC report and sets the final prices. The reason that the government retained the process and structure of price-setting was because the system of massive government intervention at every stage of agricultural pricing which had been designed by the supposedly capitalist Whites appealed to the socialist sensibilities of the new Black leadership once the racially discriminatory aspects of the process had been removed.

However, while the formal process appears unchanged, the new government instituted some important reforms in the way in which the price-setting process actually works. In the first place, the meetings between farmers and government have been downgraded. One commercial farmer noted:

[During White rule] at the commodity price review the RNFU and the Minister of Agriculture would have a shouting match and at the end of the day some kind of compromise would be worked out that kept the farmers pretty happy. Now [in 1986], the commodity review is no longer negotiations but 'discussions' — our teeth have been drawn.

Secondly, and linked to the change in government–farmer discussions, the locus of decision-making has shifted. Under White rule the prices suggested by the Minister of Agriculture were expected to be adopted by Cabinet. In the new regime, so respondents in the private sector and government report, the Minister of Agriculture's recommendations are important, but no one in the governmental system expects the prices to be final until the Cabinet makes its ultimate decision. The Cabinet has, in

[8] After the 1985 elections the Ministry of Agriculture was merged with the Ministry of Lands, Resettlement and Rural Development to form the Ministry of Lands, Agriculture and Rural Resettlement. For the sake of clarity, I refer to it as the Ministry of Agriculture throughout this chapter.

fact, often made drastic changes when posting final producer prices. It is of interest to note that, apart from steel and fertilizer, agricultural products are the only commodities whose prices are determined by the full Cabinet.[9]

Finally, the pre-planting price negotiations that farmers won in the mid-1970s were dropped in 1982. Except for extreme circumstances (such as in the third year of the drought when the farmers' morale had to be boosted) the government now conducts only one set of price negotiations a year, and does not announce prices until the crops are in the ground. This reform has had the effect of passing the risk of production completely on to the farmers, because they do not know what their returns will be until well after they have decided their crop mix and done their planting. The bargaining position of farmers, therefore, has dramatically deteriorated, because they can no longer immediately threaten to change crops if they do not like the government's prices. One CFU official noted in an interview that

no pre-planting price really hurts [our] bargaining position. If you have a big crop in the ground then there's not much you are going to do. Similarly, if there is a drought year then government is going to say that no matter how much the price is increased we will still have a bad crop.

Instead, according to government, parastatal, and farmer officials, there is now an informal agreement that the price of a commodity will never go down. However, this agreement is not formal government policy, and, in 1986, prices for yellow maize, a little-used crop, were decreased. Additionally, in a country in which total variable costs for commercial farmers rose 264 per cent between 1980 and 1986, the guarantee that the nominal price will not decrease is not in itself significant.[10]

All of these changes have had the effect of giving the government greater control over the pricing process and of insulating it from farmer demands while at the same time allowing the farmers a formal role in the price-setting process and a means whereby agricultural producers can submit information to the government. This is most evident in the shift in the locus of decision-making from the Minister of Agriculture to the Cabinet, which allows the new regime to keep the AMA and, to a lesser extent, the Ministry of Agriculture farmer-dominated but which removes

[9] *The Financial Gazette,* 25 July 1986.

[10] Unpublished data provided by the Commercial Farmers Union.

much of the power that this dominance had once entailed. The appointment of Norman as Minister of Agriculture is a good example of this process. Norman provided the new government with extremely valuable expertise and information. However, because the Minister of Agriculture's powers had been curtailed and the whole Cabinet was involved in decision-making, the Black government did not have to be afraid that agricultural decisions would be controlled by White farmers, as would have been the case in the past if the President of the RNFU had been appointed Minister of Agriculture. Similarly, by no longer setting pre-planting prices, the government kept farmers involved in the price-setting process, but prevented White commercial agriculture from being able to threaten the new regime in an area as important as food supply. The sophisticated tactic of having the farmers participate in the policy process to provide information but curtailing their political power is probably a major factor in the government's development of an enlightened agricultural policy.

Actual Price Decisions

A review of the actual producer price decisions made by the government in the years since Independence naturally provides the most concrete evidence for an understanding of the nature of government decision-making in this area. In the following sections, case studies of seven controlled crops are examined to illustrate the dynamics of the price-setting process. These crops are among the most important agricultural commodities that are directly affected by government decision-making, although it should be noted that several other important export crops, notably tobacco, are sold by auction and, therefore, do not have their price determined by the government.

The government sets prices for all the controlled crops if they are grown in commercial farming areas or sold outside the communal areas (peasants can sell crops within the communal areas for the going price). Several sets of data are used to illustrate the factors relevant to pricing decisions and the implications of government's decisions. Stock-on-hand data and the surplus or deficit transferred to the trading account (the trading account is the balance between total government proceeds from crop sales and government expenditures for crop purchases) are included because these statistics are crucial to an understanding of government decision-making. An index of the return per dollar of variable cost for farmers is also included in order to provide some idea of the implications of posted prices for producers. These figures are a great improvement on the nominal-price statistics used in most studies, because they illustrate what farmers' actual profit margins are. However, the CFU cost-of-production model that generates these figures is not completely accurate, so the data must be analysed with caution. The return-to-variable-cost data applies only to large-scale farmers, but, since this is the model used by all three farmer groups and the government, it is relevant in understanding government decisions.

Maize

White maize is the nation's staple crop. At Independence, most of the country's marketed supply was provided by White farmers, but now, in good rainfall years, Black producers supply half the national crop. The most important decision in the pricing of maize was the move by the government to raise the price for the 1981/2 season from $85 to $120 per tonne. The figures for the return per dollar of variable cost show that this increase had a dramatic effect on farmers' real returns and, as a result, production increased from 1,6 million to 2,9 million tonnes.[11] All indications are that it was the Minister of Agriculture, Dennis Norman, who pushed the price through an opposed ministry and then found that the Cabinet readily agreed to the increase. Ministry of Agriculture officials report that they were 'shocked' and 'shattered' by the price increase which went well beyond their recommendations, and senior farm lobby officials also seemed genuinely surprised by the magnitude of the price rise. Respondents in the farming community agree that the impetus for the high price came from the government, and this seems likely, given that the CFU's relationship with the new government was still problematic and that the NFAZ barely existed. However, Norman and the rest of the Cabinet were aware of the failure of other African countries to feed themselves and were desperately conscious of the situation in the rural areas after the long war. The price of $120 per tonne was posted to avoid politically embarrassing food imports from South Africa by making the country self-sufficient, and to inject money into the impoverished rural areas. The maize-price announcement was the first indication of the government's determination to guarantee food self-sufficiency, even if it was at a very high price.

[11] World Bank, *Zimbabwe: Country Economic Memorandum* (Washington, World Bank, 1985), 38.

The exceptionally high producer price, which was announced before planting, and excellent rains yielded a bumper crop for Zimbabwe. Table VII shows that the government began the 1982/3 season with a stock roughly eight times the previous year's reserve. The maize surplus and the large trading-account deficits caused by the high producer price prompted the government to refuse to increase producer prices for the following two years. Beginning in the 1983 season, the farmers' returns

Table VII

MAIZE: STOCKS, PROFITS AND PRICES

Fiscal year (ending 31 March)	Opening stock ('000 tonnes)	Trading account ($)	Index of return per dollar of total variable cost	Final price ($ per tonne)
1980/1	65	–6 002 615	100,00	85
1981/2	158	–20 361 218	114,86	120
1982/3	1 201	–43 594 639	90,29	120
1983/4	1 035	–16 973 915	80,00	120
1984/5	124	–42 617 820	85,71	140
1985/6	465	–46 290 996	88,00	180
1986/7	1 426	–57 300 000	71,43	180
1987/8 *	1 806	–84 800 000	65,14	180

* Estimated.

Sources: Unless otherwise noted, sources for this and the following tables are: Agricultural Marketing Authority, *Economic Review of the Agricultural Industry of Zimbabwe* (Harare, The Authority, 1985); Agricultural Marketing Authority, *Grain Situation Outlook Report* (Harare, The Authority, various years); Grain Marketing Board, *Reports and Accounts* (Harare, The Board, various years); and unpublished CFU data.

fell dramatically as farmers were caught between stagnant prices and the worst drought that the country had ever experienced. Gary Magadzire, President of the ZNFU, said that the standstill prices created a 'crisis within a crisis'.[12] By the 1984/5 season, stocks had dropped alarmingly, so the government announced a new price of $140 per tonne as a pre-planting price in order to give farmers added confidence. However, stocks were still low at the beginning of the next season, so the government raised the price further to $180 per tonne.

[12] *The Herald*, 6 May 1983.

By 1986, the government was facing a new crisis because the good season had led to another massive maize stockpile, this time amounting to two years' supply. The government refused to increase the producer price even though, as Table VII shows, returns to farmers were again falling sharply. Additionally, in a dramatic attempt to cut maize deliveries, the government announced that it would pay only $100 per tonne, instead of $180, for any farmer's 1987 maize deliveries that exceeded 50 per cent of his previous year's deliveries. However, the government exempted any producer delivering 20 tonnes or less (i.e. most peasant farmers) from the price cut.[13] The new price announcement created major problems for some commercial farmers who had already purchased their inputs and prepared their soil on the assumption of receiving $180 per tonne. In response to the problems of some farmers, the government increased the amount of maize commercial farmers could sell at $180 and established a board to grant waivers on the quotas to some farmers.[14] However, this episode does indicate a willingness on the government's part to discriminate against large-scale farmers in order to control stock levels.

Despite strenuous lobbying by farmers to avoid this 'boom and bust' cycle which had led to (at best) erratic returns, the government continued to react according to the stockpile situation. For instance, the 1982/3 negotiating paper of the Commercial Grain Producers Association (a branch of the CFU) listed other advantages of increasing maize prices, including income generation (especially for small-scale producers), farm viability (notably in resettlement areas), and employment and wage increases on maize farms;[15] but these arguments were ignored by the government. Farmers have also tried to use Zimbabwe's export potential as an argument for why a narrow focus on stockpiles is inappropriate. This argument is potentially powerful because Zimbabwe is in charge of food security for the Southern African Development Co-ordination Conference (SADCC), and is sometimes seen as a 'bread-basket' for Southern Africa. However, Ministry of Agriculture and Ministry of Finance, Economic Planning and Development respondents indicated that they interpret the SADCC mandate narrowly to mean only that

[13] *The Herald*, 30 Sept. 1986.

[14] *The Financial Gazette*, 17 Oct. 1986. Owing to the severe drought in 1987, the Government eventually paid the full price to all farmers.

[15] Commercial Grain Producers Association, 'Maize Price Negotiating Paper, 1982–1983' (Harare, The Association, 1982, mimeo.), 5–6.

Zimbabwe should be in charge of research into problems such as foot-and-mouth disease, and, therefore, they do not attach a high priority to export potential during price-setting.

It should be noted, however, that the farmers' lobbying techniques on maize were not necessarily the most effective possible in trying to dislodge the government from its preoccupation with stock levels. The Grain Producers Association, for instance, is not one of the more visible farmer groups, and it does not make a strong effort to publicize the importance of maize and the possible welfare effects that price increases could have on smallholders. In CFU publications — such as the annual *Commercial Agriculture in Zimbabwe* — the importance of the peasant producer in maize production receives only passing mention.[16] This lack of stress on the point that could have given the CFU greater legitimacy in the eyes of the government is in sharp contrast to the lobbying techniques of other crop groups. The decision by the government to discriminate against commercial maize growers could be a reflection of this poor bargaining strategy. The failure of maize growers to take maximum advantage of the White farmer–Black farmer alliance is certainly a good example that farmers, even those as well organized as maize growers, cannot simply present their demands to the government and expect them to be granted, especially when the government is not focusing on farmers' returns as its main criterion for establishing producer prices.

Wheat

Wheat is a winter crop in Zimbabwe because of the danger of summer rust. All wheat, therefore, must be irrigated, because the rainy season in Zimbabwe occurs during the summer. Owing to the high capital costs of irrigation, and other expenses such as combine harvesters, practically the entire wheat crop in Zimbabwe is still grown by large-scale commercial farmers. In 1983, for instance, White growers produced 95 per cent of the crop.[17] Since irrigation development has not kept up with the sky-rocketing urban demand for bread, Zimbabwe is not self-sufficient in wheat and must thus ration supplies and import.

The government has long recognized the importance of a high wheat price in order to minimize the expenditure of scarce foreign exchange on

---

[16] *Commercial Agriculture in Zimbabwe* [Harare, Modern Farming Publications Trust] various years.

[17] Agricultural Marketing Authority, *Economic Review of the Agricultural Industry in Zimbabwe* (Harare, The Authority, 1985), 23.

imports. Not surprisingly, therefore, Table VIII shows that the returns of wheat producers have been consistently high. Compared with producers of other commodities, wheat growers have generally done better and had greater stability in their earnings. The trading account shows that these high prices have been granted even though the government has been running large trading-account deficits. One former official, familiar with Cabinet decisions, said that 'wheat was an easy one to argue for because

Table VIII

WHEAT: STOCKS, PROFITS AND PRICES

Fiscal year (ending 31 March)	Opening stock ('000 tonnes)	Trading account ($)	Index of return per dollar of total variable cost	Final price ($ per tonne)
1980/1	176	−153 658	100,00	135
1981/2	130	−9 333 762	113,25	165
1982/3	124	−12 143 468	104,64	190
1983/4	128	−10 184 978	100,66	220
1984/5	77	−4 439 391	105,30	250
1985/6	61	−5 832 574	99,34	285
1986/7	103	−14 300 000	88,84	300
1987/8	149	−17 100 000	82,12	330

Sources: As noted in Table VII, and Agricultural Marketing Authority, *Wheat Situation and Outlook Report* (Harare, The Authority, various years).

Cabinet related very quickly to the supply and import problems'. Similarly, a Grain Marketing Board official called the wheat lobby 'stronger than any other group' because of the fact that the government would have to import if farmers did not keep up production.

Two other factors also strengthen the wheat lobby. Firstly, because wheat is a winter cereal (the only major winter crop in Zimbabwe), there is still a pre-planting price for it. Producer prices are announced after the summer crops are in the ground but before winter crops have been planted. Wheat growers therefore have more leverage with the government because they know their profit equation before planting. Secondly, the opportunity cost of switching to another crop is relatively low for wheat growers because they can still grow a summer crop and enhance that crop with irrigation. Farmers who plant in the summer alone do not necessarily have this option because the only alternative to planting one unprofitable crop may be another unprofitable crop.

Given these realities, of which the government is well aware, wheat producers have not had to develop a powerful public lobby. Indeed, for the first five years of Independence wheat producers in the CFU did not even have their own commodity association but were instead represented by the Grain Producers Association, which is dominated by maize growers. In addition, wheat producers could not take advantage of the possibility of a CFU–ZNFU–NFAZ alliance because practically no Blacks grow wheat, and lobbyists admit that the government is 'suspicious' of the White wheat growers. However, it is not the organizational characteristics of the wheat lobby *per se* that has led to their receiving high prices but the characteristics of the crop itself — especially the fact that Zimbabwe always has a shortfall in production — that has made wheat farmers relatively successful.

Cotton

Before Independence, most of the cotton in Zimbabwe was produced by large-scale growers, but in the Independence period it is being grown by an increasing number of peasant producers as a cash crop; for instance, communal farmers produced 40 per cent of the cotton in 1985/6.[18] Cotton is ideal for peasant production because it is labour intensive, requires almost no capital investment, and flourishes in drier climates where, in Zimbabwe, peasant farmers are concentrated. Cotton seed is also quite important to Zimbabwe's oilseed industry. Finally, as an export crop, cotton earns Zimbabwe valuable foreign exchange.

In general, it can be said that cotton producers have done very well in price negotiations and cotton lobbyists compare their fortunes to those of wheat growers. In the last several years Cabinet has increased the final price of cotton markedly, often well beyond AMA recommendations. For instance, the Cotton Marketing Board, according to AMA officials, felt that no price increase should be given to cotton in 1986/7 because of the soft international market, but Cabinet approved an increase of 12 per cent. It should also be noted that the cost-of-production data (see Table IX) actually underestimate cotton's profitability, because the crop tends to do better in droughts than the model suggests. For example, although the

---

[18] Agricultural Marketing Authority, *Economic Review of the Agricultural Industry in Zimbabwe* (Harare, The Authority, 1986), 53.

model assumes a yield of 1 650 kilograms per hectare, large-scale growers had an average yield of 1 999 kilograms per hectare in 1984.[19]

Central to the explanation of cotton's excellent record is the lobbying strategy of the cotton industry. In particular, the industry's constant focus on the huge number (120 000) of peasant families who grow cotton has been a successful tactic in receiving favourable treatment for the crop. The

Table IX

COTTON: PROFITS AND PRICES

Fiscal year (ending 31 March)	Trading account ($)	Index of return per dollar of total variable cost	Final price (¢ per kg)
1980/1	4 063 340	100,00	37,5
1981/2	949 100	94,63	40,0
1982/3	–17 837 744	106,04	51,5
1983/4	4 316 667	95,97	51,5
1984/5	56 827 796	89,93	57,0
1985/6	–14 339 249	86,58	67,0
1986/7	–52 700 000	80,53	75,0
1987/8 *	–49 100 000	61,74	80,0

* Estimated.

Sources: As noted in Table VII, and Cotton Marketing Board, *Reports and Accounts* (Harare, The Board, various years), and Agricultural Marketing Authority, *Cotton Situation and Outlook Report* (Harare, The Authority, various years).

President of the Commercial Cotton Growers Association (a branch of the CFU) said, when reviewing the 1986 producer-price announcement which treated cotton significantly better than any other crop,

it cannot be disputed that cotton fared relatively well by comparison. I believe the cumulative effect of our efforts over the past few years has helped to create an awareness of the importance of cotton and the need to preserve the production base by meaningful adjustments to produce price.[20]

One cotton lobbyist argued in an interview that 'the pressure for good prices comes not so much from the White farmers but from the 120 000

[19] Cotton Marketing Board, *Report and Accounts for the Year Ended 28 February 1985* (Harare, The Board, 1985), 17.

[20] *The Financial Gazette*, 6 June 1986.

peasant families who have the same interests'. The pressure from these peasant farmers is, however, transmitted mainly through the Commercial Cotton Growers Association, which runs a professional public-relations campaign. Thus cotton, unlike maize, is taking full advantage of the alliance between the farmers groups to boost prices.

It is valuable to study the cotton producers' lobbying techniques because the commodity is a good example of the fact, so often missed in political analysis, that economic power cannot be transformed directly into political power but is dependent on, in part, a strategic evaluation of the situation by pressure groups and the adoption of proper tactics. Cotton producers succeed by using a low-profile approach to lobby government. One expert close to the industry said: 'We don't have the personal influence that American lobbyists like Michael Deaver have, and we can't twist arms. This is a socialist state that is hostile to capital. We have to go with the "soft sell" with no public threats.' One example of this type of lobbying is the Kadoma Cotton Training Centre, which is funded by White cotton growers. The Centre was established to teach peasants better techniques of growing cotton and protecting their crop against pests. Not surprisingly, several busloads of government officials are brought down to the Centre each year to see how White farmers are helping the Black masses in the rural areas. Indeed, cotton growers have managed to get the entire ZANU(PF) Politburo to visit the Centre. The Centre earns the Cotton Growers Association political kudos, and is termed 'invaluable' by lobbyists in securing the goodwill of the government. It must be stressed that this goodwill was not automatic. The cotton growers could not simply present their demands to the government, as simple models of states aggregating private interests suggest. Nor could the White farmers simply depend upon Norman to deliver a good price to them. Rather, influence was won only after years of sophisticated work by an industry that was determined to cultivate a relationship with a receptive government.

Mhunga and Rapoko

Mhunga and rapoko are millets grown exclusively in the drier regions of Zimbabwe by peasant farmers. The crops are used both for food and in the making of traditional (opaque) beer. Both crops were once controlled by the government, but were decontrolled in the 1960s. In 1984, the government, in order to aid peasants in drier areas who were particularly hard hit by the drought, recontrolled both crops, and the AMA was mandated to buy all that producers offered. As a result of this recent decision, cost-of-production data, which are available for the other crops, do not exist for the millets.

After the Cabinet decided that the crops would be controlled, AMA officials, according to informants, recommended that the price of these crops be set at a price of $10 above the then current maize price — an effective $130 per tonne. This price was seen as a subsidy by marketing officials, who wanted to help the peasants devastated by the unprecedented drought. To the surprise of everyone, the Cabinet set the final producer price of mhunga at $250 per tonne and rapoko at $300 per tonne. The Cabinet apparently decided that these high prices were justified in order to aid producers. The prices the Cabinet posted do, officials have suggested, bear some relation to scarcity prices for the millets when bought for brewing opaque beer, and Cabinet officials may have known these prices from their ties with the rural areas. Nevertheless, these prices have to be viewed as a subsidy, because scarcity prices for beer production would not normally determine producer rates. While the NFAZ certainly lobbied for high prices, respondents uniformly suggest that the impetus for this decision came from Cabinet officials who were personally concerned about the fate of the peasantry during the drought. The NFAZ could not rely on the CFU's organizational expertise to lobby government for high millet prices because no large-scale commercial farmers grew these crops.

The high prices for millets had an immediate impact on the marketing system. For instance, peasants responded to the high mhunga price by delivering to the AMA large quantities which could not be sold, because few people want to eat mhunga and supplies for traditional beer are secured in the rural areas. After two seasons of buying the crop, the AMA had a stockpile of over 40 000 tonnes of mhunga because it had managed to sell only 200 tonnes of it — mostly as birdseed. This stockpile has begun to generate huge losses for the government parastatal. For instance, the AMA lost an astonishing $10,5 million on the 1985/6 crop of 44 000 tonnes.[21] Similarly, the AMA lost over $3 million when it sold only 157 of the 13 000 tonnes of rapoko that peasants marketed in 1986.[22] In fact, when the prices were first announced, commercial farmers wanted to grow millets because they offered the best returns of any crop. Fortunately for

---

[21] Grain Marketing Board, *Report and Accounts for the Year Ended 31st March 1986* (Harare, The Board, 1987), 60.

[22] Ibid., 61.

Zimbabwe, there was a shortage of seed. In spite of the huge costs, the government shows no intention of breaking its informal agreement not to lower the producer prices. The government said in 1986 that it would pay mhunga and rapoko growers in high-rainfall regions only $100 per tonne,[23] but this means little, since most peasant growers are in the dry areas of the country.

Sorghum

Sorghum is used in Zimbabwe mainly for the brewing of opaque beer. In the past, most of the sorghum was grown by Black farmers, even though the greater part of the marketed produce has been supplied by White producers. Sorghum is a good peasant crop because it can be grown in relatively dry areas. However, since it is used mainly in the brewing of traditional beer, sorghum is not grown by many White farmers, and was mentioned only occasionally in the CFU's annual publication, *Commercial Agriculture in Zimbabwe*.[24] Sorghum is the third most important grain in peasant areas.[25]

In pricing decisions until the 1983/4 season, sorghum prices were linked to, and slightly lower than, maize prices because of sorghum's lower protein content. Prices for maize, the nation's most important crop, were set and the sorghum price was then derived from the maize price. For this reason the return-on-variable-cost figures for sorghum parallel the maize figures (see Table X).

However, in 1983/4 Cabinet made a political decision that the sorghum price should be equal to the maize price. The Cabinet made this decision, AMA officials recalled, against all recommendations that sorghum should continue at a price slightly lower than maize, because the political leadership wanted to help peasant farmers during the drought. There was a feeling, one official reported, that the Cabinet linked sorghum directly to maize so that peasants who could not grow maize could still receive some drought relief from the government via its pricing policy. No official attributes the lobbying power of any farmer group as being instrumental in the higher sorghum price, although the NFAZ undoubtedly did help to highlight the plight of

---

[23] *The Herald*, 30 Sept. 1986.

[24] See, for instance, *Commercial Agriculture in Zimbabwe* (1984/85), 59.

[25] Zimbabwe, *Report of the Commission of Inquiry into the Agricultural Industry* [Chairman: G. M. Chavunduka] (Harare, Govt. Printer, 1982), 42.

the peasant farmer. The CFU, however, does not seem particularly concerned about sorghum.

The result of the government's effective subsidization of sorghum has been, as Table X shows, a build-up of sorghum stocks in Zimbabwe. The demand for opaque beer does not seem to change greatly, and there is nothing else that Zimbabwe can do with the crop. One Ministry of Agriculture official described Zimbabwe as 'swimming' in sorghum.[26]

Table X

SORGHUM: STOCKS, PROFITS AND PRICES

Fiscal year (ending 31 March)	Opening stock (tonnes)	Trading account ($)	Index of return per dollar of total variable cost	Final price ($ per tonne)
1980/1	5 500	127 053	100,00	105
1981/2	4 037	−146 112	94,38	115
1982/3	15 852	−523 692	81,25	115
1983/4	8 463	−666 683	71,88	120
1984/5	3 865	−1 930 065	84,38	140
1985/6	10 688	29 926	90,00	180
1986/7	56 600	−5 400 000	73,13	180
1987/8 *	100 947	−1 800 000	35,00	180

* Estimated.

Sources: As noted in Table VII.

Groundnuts

In Zimbabwe, groundnut production is dominated by the peasant farmer, although most of the nuts that are actually sold to the AMA are grown by commercial farmers. Groundnuts are an excellent peasant crop because they are labour intensive, provide a good source of protein, and, being legumes, are appropriate for the sandy areas of the country where they can be grown in rotation with other crops. Groundnuts are also of great use to the nation as a whole since they can be used to manufacture cooking oil and have substantial potential as an export crop.

Unfortunately, despite their innate advantages, production of groundnuts in Zimbabwe has not shown the same dramatic increase as that of

[26] *The Sunday Mail*, 7 Sept. 1986.

other crops. By 1975 the peasant sector was growing between 30 000 and
40 000 tonnes of groundnuts a year, while in 1985 it probably produced
less than 10 000 tonnes. AMA purchases from African producers in 1975
totalled 25 000 tonnes (84 per cent of total government purchases), while
in 1984 peasant farmers sold only 584 tonnes (9 per cent of total purchases).[27] There are a variety of factors responsible for this decline,
including the poor availability of seeds and a lack of knowledge on the
part of the growers in handling the delicate seeds. However, the consistently low producer price is the primary reason why there has been a
decline in groundnut production. Melanie Ross, former chief economist
of the AMA, has written: 'The evidence indicates that the target group of
producers (peasant farmers) are responsive to price, and that the overwhelming problem in the groundnut industry is low prices — in both
relative and absolute terms'.[28] An examination of the return per dollar of
variable costs in Table XI shows that returns on groundnuts have consistently declined, except when the producer price was increased in 1985 and
1987. Another indication of groundnuts' low price was the black market
for the commodity: in 1986/7 farmers could get between $1 000 and
$1 500 per tonne for groundnuts, while the government price was only
$750 per tonne.[29] A similar black market does not exist for any other crop
in Zimbabwe.

It would seem that farmers are well placed to lobby for high groundnut prices. There is a similar mix of White large-scale and Black peasant
farmers that works so well in cotton, and Robinson Gapare, the leader of
the NFAZ, also heads the AMA's Oilseeds Committee. Groundnuts'
appropriateness for the peasant farmer and their potential to raise health
and incomes, as well as the possibilities for export, should have appealed
to the government during price negotiations. Yet everyone agrees that
groundnuts have fared the worst among all controlled crops in Zimbabwe.

One reason for this poor performance seems to be the NFAZ's lack of
assertiveness. AMA officials recounted that Gapare personally did not
lobby hard for groundnuts, and often left AMA officials to press for price
increases by themselves. Similarly, the Commercial Oilseeds Producers

[27] *The Herald*, 16 Aug. 1985, and M. A. Ross, 'The Role of Producer Price in the
Groundnut Industry of Zimbabwe' (Harare, 1985, mimeo.), Table 3.

[28] Ross, 'The Role of Producer Price in the Groundnut Industry of Zimbabwe', i.

[29] Ibid., 30.

Association (a branch of the CFU) is not primarily concerned with groundnuts since it is not a very significant crop for large-scale growers. The Oilseeds Producers Association also does not seem to have the same dynamism as the Cotton Growers Association and lacks a flair for public relations: unlike the cotton producers, groundnut farmers do not employ a professional public-relations consultant. However, even without an

Table XI

GROUNDNUTS: PROFITS AND PRICES

Fiscal year (ending 31 March)	Trading account ($)	Index of return per dollar of total variable cost	Final price (per tonne)
1980/1	327 109	100,00	390
1981/2	–458 126	87,94	420
1982/3	–631 597	78,89	450
1983/4	170 756	71,36	450
1984/5	–232 833	68,34	500
1985/6	–365 684	83,42	750
1986/7	–600 000	70,35	750
1987/8 *	–930 000	71,35	900

* Estimated.

Sources: As noted in Table VII, and Agricultural Marketing Authority, Oilseeds Situation and Outlook Report (Harare, The Authority, various years).

assertive lobbying campaign, there was for a considerable time during the middle and late 1980s an awareness in the agricultural establishment, and throughout the civil service and marketing parastatals, that the groundnut price was simply too low.

Respondents throughout the agricultural system were unanimous in saying that the main reason for poor groundnut prices was the attitude of Cabinet officials who believed that groundnuts were primarily a 'woman's crop' — studies show that women do grow most of the groundnuts in Zimbabwe[30] — and, therefore, that price increases would not lead to gains in production because women were not responsive to increased prices. One former AMA official said: 'The system wasn't just letting groundnuts die, it was killing them. I must have heard it a million times that

[30] K. Truscott, 'The Wedza Project, Evaluation 10' (Harare, Department of Agricultural, Technical and Extension Services, 1985, mimeo.), 1985.

groundnuts were not price responsive.' Another official who was privy to Cabinet discussions said,

Officials in Cabinet rejected it [a proposed groundnut price increase]. They felt that it was a traditional crop grown by women, who if they were to get a surplus, would just give the money to their husbands. . . . they said that women didn't need any more money.

Minister Norman, in fact, recommended a price of $1 000 per tonne, above even AMA suggestions, for three successive years in the early 1980s, but the Cabinet rejected these suggestions each time. The one significant increase in the groundnut price (from $500 to $750 per tonne in 1985) also strengthens this explanation. While there was certainly some awareness that the groundnut price needed to be increased, the main reason for this jump, officials explain, was that the ZANU(PF) Cabinet wanted to pump more money into rural areas before the 1985 election against its arch-rival PF-ZAPU. This suggestion seems to be confirmed by the fact that in the following year, 1986, there was not even a symbolic increase in the groundnut price, even though there was widespread agreement through-out the agricultural community that further price increases were in order.

     Since 1986, as Zimbabwe tries to move away from the production of cereals and into oilseeds — because of the massive surpluses — there has been a new urgency to promote groundnuts, so government attitudes may be changing. The price of $900 per tonne for groundnuts in 1987/8 (up from $750) was the first indication that policy-makers understood the important role of groundnuts. Government officials at least say that they have realized the importance of an attractive price for groundnut growers if the nation is to produce enough, and that they are prepared to shed their previous beliefs. This evolution of beliefs is due to pressure from the agricultural industry and civil servants, as well as to the self-evident failure of previous groundnut policies.

Pressures for Inexpensive Food

Describing the Zimbabwe government as being vitally concerned with food self-sufficiency, and therefore responsive, at times, to the lobbying of agricultural producers, does not explain entirely why Zimbabwe has avoided being pressured into the kind of cheap food policies that have hurt other African nations so badly. It must also be explained why the urban minority, so vocal in other countries, has not acted as a force to keep producer prices low.

For several reasons institutional practices in Zimbabwe tend to deflect demand for cheap food away from the producer price-setting process. Firstly, the price at which the commodity will be sold to consumers is not determined at the same time that the producer price of the crop is set. For instance, when Minister Norman was asked how the announced produce cer prices would affect 'the man in the street', he said:

What I have announced today is an agricultural blueprint with an indication of likely producer prices. I do not set the consumer prices. When we come to discuss consumer prices, then obviously it is a Cabinet decision and I would not be in a position to stand up and make an announcement . . .[31]

In the second place, while officials are concerned that the trading account between government sales and government purchases balances, there is no institutional imperative when setting producer prices even to consider what the final consumer price will be. Nor are groups who represent consumer interests involved in the relatively secret price-setting process. The separate timing of the process of setting producer prices from that of setting consumer prices, and the lack of an institutionalized concern or an outside agent to represent consumer interests, has meant that whatever pressure there is to keep food prices low is not transferred directly to the price-setting process. As a result, officials throughout the AMA and the Ministry of Agriculture seldom, if ever, point to consumer pressures as the reason for a specific price.

While the pressure for a cheap food policy has not significantly affected producer prices, it has influenced the final selling price of basic commodities. The government has not kept producer prices low because of concerns about consumer prices, but, equally, it has generally not raised consumer prices to the open market level and has thus incurred huge subsidy costs. In 1984/5, for instance, subsidies paid for all agricultural goods through the Ministry of Agriculture totalled $128 million, while another $22 million in subsidies was paid through the Ministry of Trade and Commerce. Agricultural subsidies accounted for 47 per cent of total government subsidies, and food subsidies amounted to 20 per cent of the total government deficit.[32] These subsidies have obviously played a role in forestalling strong pressure from consumers for low prices, but,

[31] Zimbabwe *Parliamentary Debates, House of Assembly. Second Session, First Parliament comprising Periods from 8th September, 1981 to 2nd October, 1981, 19 January, 1982 to 10th February, 1982*, IV, 10 Sept. 1981, 164.

[32] World Bank, *Zimbabwe: Country Economic Memorandum*, 15 and 111.

even if consumer pressures were brought to bear on the government, it is not certain that they would affect the process of setting producer prices.

Determinants of Agricultural Producer Price Policy

The overwhelming consideration in Zimbabwe's pricing policy for agricultural produce over the last ten years has been food self-sufficiency. When threatened with shortages of its staple, maize, the government has provided a price high enough for adequate production. Wheat, the other crop studied that has been in chronic short supply, has also generally received a high price. Farmers' lobbying has promoted high prices for products in short supply, but in this instance the producers are clearly pushing the government where it already wants to go. The farmers' organizational ability is less important in the setting of these higher prices than the government's general fear of running short of food and its very specific worry of becoming dependent on South Africa. The case of the $120-per-tonne price of maize and the generally high prices of wheat are the best examples that indicate that government concern, rather than producer pressure, led to higher prices. Even during the financially troubled late 1980s, when the returns on most products have decreased, the government has increased prices in order to retain self-sufficiency and to increase the production of valuable commodities such as oilseeds.

A second, and almost as pervasive, goal of government pricing policy has been to increase the welfare of the peasant farmer. The Cabinet has, mainly on its own volition, increased the prices of mhunga and rapoko far beyond what was justified in terms of national needs, has made the sorghum price equal to that paid for maize, and was receptive to arguments for increases in the cotton price. The national leadership has demonstrated this sensitivity to the peasant farmer — which is so lacking in most African countries — because the ruling party has strong links to the rural areas dating from the long guerrilla war and because many in the government are genuinely committed to the betterment of the lives of the majority of the population that is still on the land. It would be a mistake to believe, however, that the conduct of the guerrilla war alone prompted close links between the peasantry and the government. In Mozambique, for example, pricing policy has been unfavourable to peasant farmers,[33] despite the fact that Frelimo undoubtedly had a stronger peasant base than either of the Zimbabwe nationalist armies did. Only in the case of

[33] F. Ellis *et al.*, *Agricultural Pricing Policy in Mozambique, Tanzania, Zambia and Zimbabwe* (The Hague, Institute of Development Studies, 1985), 253.

cotton can it be said that farmers' lobbying pressure was instrumental in the setting of higher prices. Indeed, a strong case can be made that the least well-organized producers in Zimbabwe—the peasants who grow mhunga and rapoko and who cannot tap the CFU's expertise—have done the best from government pricing policy.

The case of Zimbabwe demonstrates that a shift of political power to the peasantry is not necessarily a condition for relatively high producer prices. In the rational choice model it appears that peasants will achieve better prices only if they become better organized and are therefore able to exert more pressure on their government.[34] However, the evidence presented here demonstrates that a government committed to a viable agricultural sector can post producer prices favourable to farmers, without significant overt political pressure from peasants. This is especially true if, as in Zimbabwe, the government's own institutional structure invites input from farmers and deflects some of the pressure for inexpensive food away from decision-makers. Continual agrarian decline and poor urban–rural terms of trade are not inevitable, even given the continuation of existing political systems in Africa. For instance, the remarkable increase in producer prices in several African countries in recent years can in no way be attributed to a sudden empowerment of the peasantry.[35] Rather, these increases are due, in part, to the growing realization (strongly promoted by the International Monetary Fund and the World Bank) by national élites across Africa of the importance of agrarian development and the deleterious effects of low producer prices. Bates recognizes the possibility of leaders' attitudes changing,[36] but only at the cost of going outside the rational choice model, since his analytic framework does not seem to allow for this type of evolution in the thinking of élites, given the political pressures for inexpensive food.

Conclusion

As in the other case studies, state autonomy in the area of agricultural producer prices must be examined on two levels. In the design of the

---

[34] Bates proposes a coalition of food producers and urban industry to unite for higher prices. However, it seems unlikely that African food producers will become organized enough in the foreseeable future to form any type of coalition, Bates, *Markets and States in Tropical Africa*, 130–1.

[35] For instance, ten African countries have de-controlled producer prices since 1982, *The Financial Gazette*, 20 Mar. 1987.

[36] Bates, *Markets and States in Tropical Africa*, 132.

structures governing the setting of producer prices the state was autonomous. In Zimbabwe, it was not inevitable that the new government would allow farmers, and the CFU in particular, an institutionalized voice in the price-setting process. The decision that farmers should have a voice in the price-setting process was an autonomous one taken by the new government in order that farmers' information, demands and lobbying could enter the system. At the same time, the government set constraints on how influential the farmers could be. Farmers could not and did not lobby on the issue of granting themselves access to the government, because this issue was recognized by everyone as one in which the new regime, and specifically Robert Mugabe, would have to take the lead. Similarly, it was the government itself which firmly established peasant welfare as a consideration in the price-setting process. Finally, the government's surprise decision in 1986 to develop a two-tier price for maize that discriminated against the commercial farmers showed once again that it set the rules by which the political game would be played.

However, at a second level, the level of everyday government decisions that are made within the overall institutional framework, the government was not autonomous. The cotton case study showed that a sophisticated campaign which stressed peasant welfare (even though large-scale farmers also benefited directly from high cotton prices) could have a strong impact on the decision-making process. Similarly, the CFU lobbied successfully in 1986 to get waivers for as many commercial farmers as possible so that they could receive the full maize price. The government was receptive to the CFU's claims, but it must be stressed that the farmers were lobbying within the process established by the government: they were not lobbying against the structure of a two-tier price for maize that included the potential for waivers. Lobbying techniques do matter at the level of everyday decisions, because the government has deemed that lobbying is legitimate.

Part of the reason for the state being willing to yield some of its autonomy lies in the design of the new price-setting process. The new leaders paid careful attention to the design of the government institutions which would mitigate the pressures from producers. By allowing the farmers — both in the person of Norman and also more generally through organizations — an institutionalized voice in the price-setting process, valuable information that the farmers possessed could be transmitted to the government. In view of the amount of expertise resident in private agriculture in Zimbabwe, such a compromise greatly enhanced the possibility that the 'right' prices would be chosen. At the same time, by shifting the responsibility for setting producer prices to the Cabinet, the government ensured that the farmers, and Norman in particular, would not exercise undue influence in such an important issue. Zimbabwe's institutions also shielded policy-makers from pressure from consumers for low producer prices, although the urban populations have success-fully influenced the retail prices. Thus, Zimbabwe has continued to have a favourable pricing policy toward farmers, even after Norman was forced to leave the Cabinet when Prime Minister Mugabe decided to punish the White population for supporting Ian Smith in the 1985 elections.

Unfortunately, the rational choice model cannot account for the kind of sophisticated tactics that the government used to shape institutions in Zimbabwe. The premise that the state serves simply to aggregate public pressures causes the government's basic decisions on the overall struc-ture of public institutions to be ignored. Similarly, the model allows for little consideration of the effects of different institutional arrangements on everyday government decisions. As a result, a rich process of institu-tional formation, change and influence is lost.

Another important aspect of the agricultural producer price issue-area is that it requires an iterated decision-making process. In order to take account of stockpiles, climate and world economic trends, new prices must be set every year. The iterated nature of the decision-making process has important implications for the politics of the issue because the repetition allows the actors involved to learn from their experience. While the CFU recognized very early on that it needed to co-operate with the new government, it was much slower in forging ties with the Black farmers' unions. However, over time the sophisticated and well-organ-ized CFU learned that its most effective strategy was to combine with the Black farmers so that the three unions could benefit jointly from their individual strengths. An iterated process, almost by necessity, would seem to benefit supplicant groups who seek to influence a government, because, unless the state is completely resistant to outside pressure, those who seek to pressure a government will learn better tactics as time goes by. This is especially true in a country like Zimbabwe where groups such as the CFU were initially unsure as to their standing with the new government, and did not know what kind of pressures the new regime would be susceptible to.

An investigation of the politics of agricultural producer prices in

Zimbabwe also reveals the striking importance of the tactics chosen by interest groups in determining their ultimate effectiveness in influencing the government. The White farmers, despite their economic power and organizational capability, could not simply demand higher prices from the government, except in the unusual case of wheat where the nation was unable to meet demand because of the crop's production structure. Similarly, the Black farmers could not simply pressure the government in the name of peasant welfare to get higher prices. It was only when they joined forces — combining White organizational capability and Black legitimacy — that the farmers were a truly effective interest group. Those farmer groups which did not use the most effective combination of tactics, notably the White maize farmers, seem to have suffered the consequences.

Locus of Decision-making

There was a distinct change in the point at which decisions were made on agricultural producer prices when the new regime transferred power from the Ministry of Agriculture to Cabinet as a whole. The change in the locus of decision-making to Cabinet level was made specifically to allow the parastatal marketing authorities and the Ministry of Agriculture to remain White-dominated in order to benefit from the agricultural expertise of commercial farmers. At the same time, the change allowed Cabinet to retain final control over producer pricing. In the maize, mhunga, rapoko and sorghum cases, the Cabinet used its final control over the decision-making process not only to increase prices but to introduce a new norm — the welfare of the peasant producer — into the policy-making process.

The characteristics of agricultural producer prices, unlike those of land reform, allow an easy upward shift in the locus of decision-making. While producer price debates do rest on some technical points, in an agricultural country such as Zimbabwe all government leaders feel comfortable discussing the issue, because most of them grew up either in peasant areas or on commercial farms. The fact that producer prices require only one set of decisions each year also allows the busy Cabinet more influence in the price-setting process than in the process of land acquisition, where hundreds of technical decisions slowly shape the nature of the programme. The move to eliminate pre-planting prices (effectively reducing the number of price decisions by half) can therefore be seen not only as a way of limiting the leverage of the White farmers but also of increasing the influence of Cabinet *vis-à-vis* the bureaucracy in the overall decision-making process.

While the Cabinet has been intimately involved in the producer price process, ZANU(PF) has not, except to the extent that the top government leaders also head the party. One lobbyist noted in an interview that 'in technical areas such as agricultural pricing the party really doesn't get involved. It doesn't have the staff that would look at an issue like production. The structure of the party is weak below the provincial level.' Similarly, a long-time Ministry of Agriculture official said:

The party is not involved in agricultural pricing. They don't play a technical role. . . . [There] was much greater intervention by the RF [during UDI]. Many more people came to me saying they were founding members of the RF than have come to me saying they were founding members of ZANU(PF).

Finally, the poorly-developed ideology of ZANU(PF) also prevented it from playing a significant role in the setting of producer prices. Apart from a general policy to help the peasant, which was immediately adopted by the government, the party really had no guidelines on how to participate in the setting of prices. Therefore, not only did it lack the ability to participate, but it would also have had very little to contribute had it been allowed to.

One of the great dangers of political analysis is the fallacy of inevitability. It may seem, according to the rational choice model, that it was inevitable that Zimbabwe would have high producer prices because of its well-organized and rich White commercial agricultural sector. Similarly, it would be easy to say that Zimbabwe's agricultural policies were determined mainly by Dennis Norman. However, while the CFU and Norman were no doubt important, because they provided information and lobbied government leaders, it was the independent decisions and beliefs of the Black government that played the crucial part in determining the pattern of producer prices. Perhaps because Zimbabwe is a new country, where people still remember the basic debates over government policy, it is easy to see that the process of government is much more complex, interesting and confusing than those who would reduce a rich political process to a simple model can imagine.

Chapter Six

Zimbabwe's Policies towards Foreign Investment

Foreign investment has been an integral part of Zimbabwe's economy since the country was founded by a multinational corporation, the British South Africa Company, in the 1890s. The years of Company rule laid the foundation for foreign investment to play a pivotal role in the economy, and in independent Zimbabwe several hundred foreign companies are deeply involved in almost every aspect of Zimbabwe's economy. The new government has pledged to capture the 'commanding heights' of the economy from the multinationals by putting key sectors of the economy under state control. At the same time, the government has continually stressed the need for new foreign investment in order to transform the war economy into one that can produce jobs for Zimbabwe's burgeoning population. Because the state's relationship with foreign capital is a crucial part of the country's evolving political economy, it is important to study how Zimbabwe is reintegrating itself into the world economy after fifteen years of sanctions. Zimbabwe's policy on foreign investment also provides the opportunity to assess the degree of influence that foreign capital and certain Western countries can bring to bear on an apparently weak state. Finally, foreign-investment policy provides a particularly good perspective from which to view factional politics in Zimbabwe.

Industrial Power in Rhodesia

The manufacturing industry was the last of the 'three legs' of the Rhodesian economy to develop a formal lobbying mechanism. Before the Second World War, industry did not formally seek to influence the government. David Murray writes that,

since commerce and industry, at least till the Second World War, had little positive use for the powers belonging to the government, there was not a significant political system focusing on governmental power operating in the sector. The change came during the Second World War. From that time commerce and industry took on a recognizable shape as a governmental sector, though then the peculiar characteristics of commercial and industrial enterprise gave the sector its own distinctive features.[1]

The first 'distinctive feature' of industry that had an impact on its relationship with the government was in the separation of the organizations representing the manufacturing sector from those representing commerce. Industry's main representative body, the Federation of Rhodesian Industries, was formed in 1949. However, commercial enterprises were represented by another organization, the Rhodesian Federated Chamber of Commerce, which was established during the 1950s.[2]

The second feature of the industrial sector was its lack of unity. Almost inevitably, the diversity of industrial concerns caused severe splits within the sector. Leys notes that even in the 1950s, when the manufacturing sector was still in its infancy, several sub-sectors, including the clothing and textile manufacturers and the steel users, had gone outside the manufacturing industry's major representative body in order to lobby the government.[3] In addition to splits according to function, the manufacturing industry was divided between foreigners and local Rhodesians, but this distinction would not become important until after UDI.

The third characteristic that influenced industry's relationship with the government was its status as 'poor sister'. Agriculture was the settler base of the country, while mining was the oldest part of the economy and traditionally provided most of the colony's exports. Manufacturing, as a relatively new sector of the economy, had neither farming's impressive lobbying mechanism nor the sheer economic dominance of the mining industry, and therefore tended to lose out in a conflict with the two other industries. However, this conflict did not occur between 1945 and the end of Federation, because the boom economy engendered by the world-wide economic expansion and the substantial benefits the colony derived from Federation allowed all sectors of the economy to thrive.

UDI and Industrial Development

Because it needed a co-ordinated approach to sanctions, and because of the demands of supporting the war economy, the Rhodesian government imposed heavy regulations over the industrial sector during the UDI

---

[1] Murray, *The Governmental System in Southern Rhodesia*, 162.

[2] Leys, *European Politics in Southern Rhodesia*, 105, 108.

[3] Ibid., 108.

period. One banker with long experience in the commercial sector explained in an interview that

since Whites had such a stake in the country they didn't allow multinational corporations to milk the country. Whites developed firm exchange-control mechanisms and vested more and more power with the ministries and committees that were shrouded in secrecy. Whites also gained managerial control over many of the firms during UDI and this effectively prevents exploitation . . . many Whites actually detest MNCs but see them as an agent of development.

The most important of these controls on business were the exchange-control regulations introduced in 1965.[4] Exchange control was vital to the rebel regime, because sanctions limited the amount of hard currency available, and shortages of foreign exchange had a significant impact on Rhodesia's industrial sector which was heavily dependent on imported inputs. The regulations allowed the government to impose almost any kind of restriction on imports, exports or currency transactions that it deemed necessary.[5] It was estimated that during UDI the foreign-exchange controls restricted official outflows of capital to a remarkably low five per cent of gross operating profits.[6] The stringent exchange-control regulations and other emergency provisions also had the effect of forcing companies to maintain business activity and reinvest profits, even though the political situation and business climate were extremely unfavourable.[7]

Although the overall business situation was poor, especially immediately after UDI, Rhodesian industrialists were able to make significant strides between 1965 and 1980. During UDI, when foreign subsidiaries were effectively cut off from their parent companies, the presence of a local capitalist class allowed for substantial indigenization:

The local executives of foreign companies (who were nearly all White Rhodesians) found themselves cut off from their parent company to a large extent, and therefore free to make their own decisions and to reinvest locally-made profits

[4] Rhodesia, Exchange Control Act (Nos. 62 of 1964, 8 of 1967, and 15 of 1970).

[5] C. Sylvester, 'Continuity and discontinuity in Zimbabwe's development history', *African Studies Review* (1985), XXVIII, 24.

[6] A. Seidman, 'A development strategy for Zimbabwe', *Zambezia* (1982), X, 22.

[7] W. Schneider-Barthold, 'Determinants and forms of external and internal dependence in Rhodesia and Namibia: Possible solutions to the problem of twofold dependence', in German Development Institute, *Perspectives of Independent Development in Southern Africa: The Cases of Zimbabwe and Namibia* (Berlin, The Institute, Occasional Paper 62, 1980), 12.

that would have been repatriated otherwise; in such ways the distinction between foreign and domestic capital became blurred.[8]

UDI, therefore, continued the process of state-promoted indigenization that had begun with the achievement of self-rule status in 1923.

Local industry also benefited from the continuation and enhancement of industrialization through import substitution. In 1965 tobacco accounted for 32 per cent of all exports, and 35 per cent of all imports were manufactured goods. Fifteen years later exports had increased by 280 per cent, tobacco amounted to only 15 per cent of total exports, and manufactured goods accounted for only 28 per cent of total imports.[9] By 1980 the colony's industrial sector was relatively well developed in comparison with the rest of Africa (except for South Africa) and extremely sophisticated. For instance, the manufacturing sector accounts for 24 per cent of Zimbabwe's GDP, three times as much as in the average Black African country.[10]

However, indigenization of management and increasing sophistication did not free the colony from overall foreign control. While almost all industries are run by Zimbabweans, many are still owned by foreign companies (Table XII demonstrates that foreign ownership is pervasive). Sylvester concludes: 'It would be hard to find a case comparable to Zimbabwe in which the role of foreign investment is so long established, deeply integrated into the sectors producing the bulk of output, and so strongly interconnected with local capital.'[11]

Government Attitudes towards Foreign Investment

The new government that came to power in 1980 pledged to reduce overall foreign control of the economy. Since the founding of the country by the BSA Company, foreign companies, especially those based in South Africa, were viewed as supporting White settler power, and there were lingering suspicions, increased by the Whites' bravado over their performance during UDI, on the part of many nationalists that these companies had been instrumental in allowing Rhodesia to survive the

[8] Stoneman, 'Foreign capital and the prospects for Zimbabwe', 50.

[9] Economist Intelligence Unit, *Zimbabwe's First Five Years* (London, The Unit, EIU Special Report 111, 1981), 62.

[10] United Nations Industrial Development Organization, *Study of the Manufacturing Sector in Zimbabwe* (Vienna, Unido, DP/ID/SER.A/631, 3 vols., 1985), I, 3.

[11] Sylvester, 'Continuity and discontinuity in Zimbabwe's development history', 28.

Table XII

ESTIMATES OF FOREIGN CONTROL BY SECTOR, 1986

	Agriculture	*Manufacturing*	*Mining*	*Distribution*	*Transport*	*Finance*	*Overall*
Domestic	55	48	25	75	65	25	50
Total foreign	45	52	75	25	35	75	50
of which: South African	35	25	35	15	15	0	24

Since the government purchased a substantial portion of Delta Corporation, I assigned Delta's share of the economy to the 'domestic' sphere. However, it should be noted that the government may not actually gain control of all of Delta's operations, and therefore this company could still be seen as South African. Delta controlled 3 per cent of the manufacturing sector and 10 per cent of the distribution sector.

Unlike the author of the original Table, I treat Wankie Colliery as a Zimbabwean-controlled company because the government has majority ownership. Anglo American owns 40 per cent of the colliery and managed it until 1989. Wankie Colliery accounts for 10 per cent of the mining sector.

Sources: C. Stoneman, 'Foreign ownership/control of the economy', in J. Hanlon, *Beggar Your Neighbours: Apartheid Power in Southern Africa* (London, Catholic Institute for International Relations, 1987), 305.

imposition of mandatory sanctions. Companies owned outside Zimbabwe were also criticized for draining the country of scarce foreign exchange through dividend remittances. The *Transitional National Development Plan* noted:

A considerable stock of capital and the technical know-how that goes with it come from, and are under, foreign control. This pattern and structure of property relations is obviously opposed to the socialist and nationalist principle of vesting the ownership of our country's resources in the people of Zimbabwe through their socialist or state organs. Our independence and political power should now transform into an instrument for establishing an equitable socio-economic order.[12]

[12] Zimbabwe, *Transitional National Development Plan*, I, 18.

At the same time, and somewhat paradoxically, the Zimbabwean government is relying on new foreign investment to provide a significant portion of capital for new economic growth and to create more jobs. The government's economic blueprint for 1983–5 assumed that foreign inflows would total $1 222 million over the three-year period and would therefore account for 20 per cent of total Gross Capital Formation during the life of the plan.[13] The ambitious goals of the *Transitional National Development Plan*, Prime Minister Mugabe wrote, recognized

the existing phenomenon of capitalism as an historical reality, which, because it cannot be avoided, has to be purposefully harnessed, regulated and transformed as a partner in the overall national endeavour to achieve set national plan goals.[14]

The *First Five-Year National Development Plan*, covering the years 1986–90, lowered expectations of private investment inflows in the light of Zimbabwe's poor record of attracting foreign investment, but still assumed that foreign inflows would amount to $200 million, or 3 per cent of Gross Capital Formation, during the period of the Plan.[15]

The resolution of the tension between the desire to wrest control of the commanding heights of the economy from foreigners and the dependence upon foreign investment for new economic growth is a fundamental problem for the government. Some analysts claim that attempting to reform the capitalist structure to the advantage of the African majority is impossible, as foreign companies will, if they are not eliminated from the economy, be able to dictate state policy. For instance, John Bradbury and Eric Worby argue that

in essence the role of the state has become subordinate to the forces of capital and the government's policies have become articulated with the needs of capital reshaping the socialist programme and modifying any attempts to promote worker control and ownership of the means of production. Today, nearly five years after Independence, the state reflects the needs of big business and transnational capital, to a large degree adopting a social democratic economic, social and labour model to work within the interstices of capital.[16]

These charges are vigorously denied by Zimbabwe government officials who argue that they are taking the only realistic path available to them,

---

[13] Ibid., 39.   [14] Ibid., i.

[15] Zimbabwe, *First Five-Year National Development Plan*, I, 45.

[16] J. Bradbury and E. Worby, 'The mining industry in Zimbabwe: Labour, capital and the state', *Africa Development* (1985), X, 143.

given the structure of the economy. Nevertheless, even those sympathetic
to the new regime have warned that 'the very advancement and attractiveness of the economy, as well as the need to guarantee future consumption will continue to invite a *rapprochement* with settler and international
capital . . .'[17]

The best way to examine how the ambivalence over foreign investment is being resolved is to look first at the government's policy towards
existing foreign investment and then to study its policy towards investors
who have tried to enter the country since 1980. It is important that each of
these policies is studied independently, because the government has
considered existing and prospective investment to be distinctly different
when formulating its policies.

Policy towards Existing Foreign Investment

The government's highest priority, particularly in its rhetoric, was to
curtail the scope of existing foreign investment and implement measures
to increase the level of state involvement in the economy. However, the
government faced severe constraints in pursuing this goal. Firstly, the
government was constrained by the Lancaster House Constitution, which
committed the Zimbabweans to compensating property-owners for any
assets taken over by the government. It is estimated that buying out
foreign investors would have cost upwards of $2 500 million.[18] Given that
the new regime faced many other demands on limited funds, only a small
portion of the foreign-investment stock could have been purchased in the
short to medium term.

However, even without the constitutional provision, it is unlikely that
Zimbabwe would have seized foreign capital assets because such an
action would have meant alienation from the West and, therefore, the loss
of a good part of the aid that the country has received since Independence:
approximately $2 700 million had been committed by aid donors, almost
all of them Western countries, up to 1986.[19] This aid, especially the
commodity import programmes which provide vitally-needed foreign
exchange for imported inputs, is an important element of the government's economic plans. Indeed, Zimbabwe has used its scrupulous

[17] Bratton, 'Development in Zimbabwe: Strategy and tactics', 474.

[18] C. Stoneman and R. Davies, 'The economy: An overview', in Stoneman (ed.),
Zimbabwe's Inheritance, 123.

[19] Zimbabwe, *Socio-Economic Review of Zimbabwe 1980–1985*, 32.

adherence to the Lancaster House Constitution as a tactic to gain more aid.[20] The importance of good relations with the West was also undoubtedly stressed by many Zimbabweans who had received advanced technical training abroad. Indeed, Bernard Chidzero, who had been a senior official in the United Nations and was noted for his cautious approach to economic policy, was named Minister for Economic Policy and Development at Independence, and he soon became the most important official in the area of economic policy. In contrast, politicians such as Enos Nkala, the first Minister of Finance, who had fought in the war and who might have attached less importance to good relations with the West, were soon moved out of their economic portfolios.

Dramatic moves against foreign capital would probably also have meant the flight of more of the White population who possessed invaluable economic skills and who were essential to the operation of the economy.[21] Many of Zimbabwe's leaders had been in Mozambique when Frelimo gained power, and had witnessed at first hand the chaos caused by the rapid departure of the White population. The new regime was committed to avoiding this disaster, especially as Zimbabwe's industry was much more developed than the manufacturing sector of the former Portuguese colony.

It was also a special concern of the government to maintain a productive private sector that generated significant tax revenue, because after 1980 Zimbabwe embarked on a massive programme to increase social services, particularly health and education. For instance, in the first seven years after Independence the recurrent Education budget increased from $118,6 million to $771 million, while the Health budget rose from $52,8 million to $260 million.[22] In the light of this huge expansion in social expenditure, the government needed all the tax revenue it could get. Thus, Robert Mugabe noted in an interview,

I, myself, am determined that as we move, we do not disrupt our economic system . . . a socialist does not have to start by destroying the infrastructure which he finds. . . . I think it is calamitous for you to do so. . . . How can we bring about change, for example, in respect of the schemes we have for the resettlement of our

[20] Davidow, *A Peace in Southern Africa*, 94.

[21] Bratton, 'Development in Zimbabwe', 457–8.

[22] Zimbabwe, *Statistical Yearbook, 1987,* 98, and Zimbabwe, *Budget Statement 1987* (Harare, Ministry of Finance, Economic Planning and Development, 1987), 24–5.

people if we do not have the necessary finances. True, we have the ideas, but we may not have the necessary funds, and this will be a restricting factor.[23]

The special situation that Zimbabwe faces in Southern Africa also plays a significant part in the general risk-averse approach of Zimbabwe's leaders towards dramatic changes in the economy. These leaders have seen, sometimes at first hand, South African destabilization in Mozambique and Angola. They were aware that South Africa was able to create such destruction partly because of the poor economic position of the former Portuguese colonies. To threaten foreign companies and thereby create economic instability within the country at a time when Zimbabwe was facing a grave external threat would obviously have been an extremely hazardous policy with little guarantee of significant gains. Instead, Zimbabwe's leaders have used the revenue generated by foreign companies to, among other things, fund its forces in Mozambique that are helping the Frelimo government fight South African-backed rebels. The irony of using tax revenue from South African-owned companies to confront South African-backed rebels is an indication of both the strengths and weaknesses of Zimbabwe's position and strategy.

The Zimbabwe government also showed restraint because it did not have at Independence, as it still does not, a real strategy for seizing the commanding heights of the economy. Dan Ndlela notes: 'The government in fact does not seem to have a clue on what its priorities are if industry should be the lynch pin of a transformation towards socialism'.[24] This lacuna is not surprising, as it is part of the overall problem of the government coming to power without a clear policy agenda indicating which sectors of the economy should be under state control.

Table XIII shows the government's major acquisitions between 1980 and 1987. The Table shows the relative insignificance of government investment in an economy whose capital stock in the manufacturing sector alone amounts to $2 400 million. The government's purchases have also been on an *ad hoc* basis, with many vital sectors untouched. For instance, there have been no government purchases of foreign firms in the strategic agricultural, ranching and forestry sectors, even though, as Table XII shows, foreign investment is very significant in these areas.

---

[23] BBC Television, Newsnight, 9.50 p.m., 16 Apr. 1980, cited in *Foreign Broadcast Information Service: Daily Report: Near East and Africa*, 17 Apr. 1980, U5–U6.

[24] D. B. Ndlela, 'Manufacturing industry: A critical review', *Journal of Social Change and Development* [Harare] (1983), V, 5.

Table XIII

MAJOR GOVERNMENT PURCHASES OF COMPANIES SINCE 1980

Purchase	Amount ($ millions)
43% of Zimbabwe Newspapers from Argus Group *	2,4
61% equity in Zimbank from Nederlands Bank *	26,6
42,6% of Caps Holdings (pharmaceutical)	4
49% joint venture in Olivine Industries (edible oils)	29
40% joint venture in Wankie Colliery with Anglo American *	14,1
Control of MTD Mangula group (copper) from Messina Transvaal *	5
Control of Kingstons (retail) from CNA Investments *	1,2
85% share in Astra Corporation * (engineering) from Bomende Houstermaatschappi	25,5
35% share of Delta Corporation *	n.a.
91,3% of Kamativi Tin Mines from Canadian nationals	n.a.

* Indicates government purchase from a South African company.

Sources: The Herald, 27 Oct. 1982; 19 Jan. 1984; 10 Apr. 1986; 12 Apr. 1987; 7 May 1987; *The Sunday Mail,* 4 Jan. 1981; *The Financial Gazette,* 28 Nov. 1986.

Some of the government's investments were designed to give Zimbabwe more general control over its economy, and specifically to reduce South African involvement in important companies. For instance, it was obviously unacceptable to the new leaders that a South African company (Argus Group) owned the daily newspapers (Zimbabwe Newspapers) or that another South African-owned company (CNA Investments) controlled the major retail agent for those newspapers (Kingstons). As one foreign-aid official noted, 'the expansion of the the state is driven by the facts of foreign ownership; it has nothing to do with socialism'. However, the government takeover of MTD was primarily done to preserve employment at a mine that was about to shut down. Similarly, the purchase of 49 per cent of Olivine Industries, a company that had been wholly owned by a Zimbabwe family, actually caused a *reduction* in the level of domestic ownership, because the other 51 per cent was bought by the American multinational, H. J. Heinz Company.

The Regulatory Alternative

Finally, because it had inherited the regulatory apparatus and a local capitalist class from the Rhodesians, the government knew that the alternative to buying or seizing foreign capital was not, as many simplistically assume, unfettered exploitation by the multinationals. The administrative aspects of the Socialism-for-the-Whites system developed by successive settler regimes, and the intrusive regulations required to combat sanctions between 1965 and 1980, have been retained by the new government. These regulations allow the state a strong governing hand over company operations and, to a certain extent, over the entire domestic allocation of resources. For instance, Zimbabwe's system of total administrative control over all foreign currency in the country gives the state tremendous power to influence patterns of production, and allows it to regulate which new economic activities firms can enter. Thus, the government, through its foreign-exchange allocation system, is trying to create a new class of Black businessmen by giving them preferential access to import licences.

In addition to keeping almost all the regulations affecting business that had been enacted by the settler state, the new government has actually enhanced its regulatory power in several areas. For instance, the government has extended retrenchment regulations to cover all workers with the result that employers cannot fire workers without permission from the Ministry of Labour. In addition, the government has instituted minimum wages for every sector of the economy,[25] and placed a ceiling on the wage increases allowed to high-income earners in order to force a compression of the wage structure. The new regime has also established

[25] See Chapter 9.

a parastatal to market all of the nation's mineral exports in order to gain more control over a strategic sector of the economy that is dominated by foreign companies.[26] While the retention and enhancement of the previous regulations preserves bottle-necks in the economy and places severe constraints on entrepreneurial dynamism, the state structures do allow the government a large degree of control over the economy.

The existence of a comprehensive regulatory environment means that the government's relationship not only with foreign investors but with the entire private sector has to be seen in a new light. It is simply incorrect to assume that, unless the government actually intervenes in the economy by seizing or purchasing private-sector assets, it has no control over the economy. Indeed, in view of the constraints, discussed above, on decreasing the level of foreign involvement in the economy, the preservation of the comprehensive regulatory environment developed by the Rhodesians was seen by the new regime as its best alternative for achieving at least some control over the economy.

The effective 'Rhodesianization' of foreign enterprises during UDI also meant that foreign control of the economy is less of a concern to government than the figures on total capital stock might indicate. While the business class is overwhelmingly White at present, these Whites are Zimbabweans, and the government can see that significant numbers of Blacks will soon move into the operational ranks of foreign businesses. Indeed, one striking phenomenon in Zimbabwe is the number of Blacks who serve in senior positions in the government and then move into high-paying jobs in foreign-owned companies. Once the government began to deal with foreign operations as they actually are in Zimbabwe, it found them much less threatening and much less 'foreign' than they had appeared when the guerrillas were writing their propaganda.

Not surprisingly, the government's decision not to try immediately to gain control of large numbers of enterprises met essentially no opposition from local or foreign-based businesses. Business interests were so delighted by the government's determination to avoid disruptive policy measures that few objected to continuing to work under the highly restrictive business environment that had evolved under settler rule. Most business were, in fact, extremely comfortable working in an economy where the state intervenes extensively. This is not to say that businesses do not object to specific decisions and practices taken within

---

[26] Chapter 7 is a detailed study of the creation and implementation of the Minerals Marketing Corporation.

the regulatory environment: industrialists constantly complain about their foreign-exchange allocation or that the government did not allow them a high enough price increase. There are also an increasing number of complaints concerning 'the lack of agreed formulas and procedures for the determination of prices and wages which inhibit long-term planning'.[27]

However, there are many fewer objections to the fact that the government allocates foreign exchange or has a comprehensive system of price controls. Indeed, some of Zimbabwe's industrialists have been noticeably reluctant to endorse World Bank suggestions that the country should abolish much of the present regulatory structure governing business. Even if business interests within the country did not like the regulatory environment, there was little they could do about it. They could not divest from Zimbabwe without getting government permission to remove their money from the country, and divestment would hurt the company's reputation in other areas where it might be interested in investing.[28] Those companies that have divested have had to sell their assets at discounts as high as 70 per cent — which is not an attractive option for many.

The Zimbabwe government's actions towards existing foreign investment, as opposed to its rhetoric, have been fairly clear. The government has intervened only occasionally to purchase companies owned by foreign interests. It is constrained from seizing foreign assets because of constitutional and political considerations, and it cannot purchase assets because of financial constraints. In addition, faced with the complicated role that foreign investment played in Zimbabwe's relatively developed economy, the government lacked a detailed approach towards foreign investment and its energies for developing radical new policies lay elsewhere. Finally, the leaders found that it was actually much easier than they had thought to live with foreign investment, owing to the extraordinary controls that the settlers had placed on businesses and the blurring of the demarcation between domestic and foreign capital that had occurred during the UDI years. Given the political and financial constraints, and the lack of a comprehensive plan to counter foreign involvement in the economy, living with the inherited regulatory environment became an attractive alternative for the new government.

---

[27] R. C. Riddell, 'Zimbabwe's experience of foreign investment policy', in *Papers and Proceedings of the Seminar on Foreign Investment: Policies and Prospects* (London, Commonwealth Secretariat, 1985), 40.

[28] Ibid, 133.

Policy towards New Investment

Zimbabwe's policy towards foreigners who want to invest for the first time is, in many ways, much more interesting and significant than its policy towards existing foreign investors. While the government was constrained by many factors from tampering with existing foreign investment, new foreign investment could be considered on its own terms. The new government had a more-or-less consistent policy towards new investment until 1989. In 1989, new approaches to foreign investment were announced which involved radical changes in the government's policies.

Procedure and Institutions

There was a procedure before 1980 for the approval of new capital inflows before a foreigner was allowed to invest. One former Reserve Bank official explained in an interview that

before Independence the exchange-control branch of the Reserve Bank took care of all foreign-investment decisions. . . . The Reserve Bank acted autonomously from Treasury, even though there was liaison. All the real decisions [on foreign investment] were made by the Reserve Bank as Treasury ceded authority.

Not surprisingly, given that the exchange-control branch of the Reserve Bank was charged with reviewing new investment proposals, this former official reported that 'the net foreign-exchange position of the new investment was the main concern' in a decision to approve new investment. In the last few years of UDI, when the economy was buffeted by sanctions and the war, the Reserve Bank insisted that a new investment become a net foreign-exchange earner within a year of the investment, either through increased exports or by import-substitution. If this criterion were met, the new investment was approved within a week or two. The guiding attitude of the time, as one merchant banker said in an interview, was that 'we didn't see the need to interfere with people who wanted to risk their money in this country'.

The new government adopted a very different institutional structure for considering new foreign-investment proposals before 1989. While the Reserve Bank still vetted proposals, the centre of the decision-making process shifted to the newly-created Foreign Investment Committee (FIC) housed in the Ministry of Finance, Economic Planning and Development. The FIC was composed of all the ministries dealing with economic affairs, the Ministry of Justice, Legal and Parliamentary Affairs, and the Minister in the President's Office with special responsibility for State Security. Each foreign-investment proposal went through a three-stage process at the FIC. It was first reviewed by the secretariat of the committee to see whether the proposal met basic information requirements. The proposal then went to a working party of the FIC composed of senior officials from each of the ministries represented on the Committee. Finally, the Ministers themselves reviewed the proposal. The prospective investment might also have been discussed by other government committees. For instance, any project involving manufacturing also had to be considered by the Industrial Projects Committee. The Cabinet might also have discussed a new foreign-investment proposal.

It was not clear to anyone exactly what the Foreign Investment Committee took into account when reviewing proposals, but it appears that government more or less kept the requirement that the investment should become a net foreign-exchange earner within one year. In addition, the FIC and the government generally considered the proposal's potential to increase jobs, transfer technology, open new markets for exports, and promote industrial development in the rural areas.[29] Owing to the government's information demands, the number of committees and people involved, and sheer inefficiency, it often took six months to a year, and occasionally as long as two years, for a definite decision to be made on an investment proposal.

The national leadership decided to move the centre of decision-making on new foreign investment both horizontally (from the Reserve Bank to the Ministry of Finance) and vertically (from middle-level officials to the ministerial level) in order to increase its actual control over the approval process. A former Ministry of Finance official said in an interview: 'At Independence it was decided that the Reserve Bank did not take into account the aspirations of government. The Reserve Bank was White dominated.' Although the government moved very quickly to Africanize the Reserve Bank (something not difficult to do given the flight of Whites from government to the private sector), it was still felt that real control over foreign-investment policy could be achieved only if a new institution was created that allowed the ministers to be directly involved in approving specific proposals.

---

[29] Zimbabwe, *Foreign Investment: Policy, Guidelines and Procedures* (Harare, Govt. Printer, 1982), 5.

Regulations Affecting New Investment

Government policy towards new investment must be divided into two parts: specific policies towards new investment, and measures affecting the general business climate. When a foreign investor is deciding whether to invest in a country, that decision is predicated not only on the host country's policies towards new investment but also on an evaluation of how well business functions generally in the country. The business climate, which is only partly determined by the government, must also be considered, because it will affect decisions by foreign investors and will, to some degree, strengthen or weaken the attractiveness of the government's investment policy.

The first element of the government's foreign-investment policy was the definition of 'foreign'. Between 1980 and 1989, the government adopted a highly restrictive definition that equated 15 per cent foreign involvement with foreign ownership.[30] Thus, if even 20 per cent of a Zimbabwean company was controlled by a White person with a British passport who had lived in the country for thirty years (a very common occurrence), the company was considered to be 'foreign'. While restrictive, this definition enhanced the government's regulatory framework because it effectively gave the government control over all new capital inflows. The constraining definition also set the tone for the government's whole approach to new investment.

The Foreign Investment Committee's approach towards new investment was cautious, in the eyes of the government, but was perceived as highly negative by those in the private sector. The Committee's vague procedures, its exceedingly long period of consideration (investors generally had no idea when they would actually receive word that their investment had been approved), and its seemingly negative attitude towards potential new investment caused the FIC to deter potential new foreign investors from coming to Zimbabwe. John Robertson, a Zimbabwean economist, summarized the effect of the FIC as perceived by potential investors: 'The handicaps faced by established companies are nothing like as severe as those by any that might be coming, especially as the Foreign Investment Committee appears to function as a barrier to investors and not as a magnet.'[31] One former government official noted that, repeatedly, foreign investors' initial enthusiasm for Zimbabwe

---

[30] Ibid., 4.   [31] *The Financial Gazette*, 25 Nov. 1983.

diminished as they encountered delays in receiving FIC approval: 'Lots of interested parties fall aside because of delays; it simply takes too long.' Government officials replied by saying that they were simply being cautious about approving new foreign investment in an economy that was already dominated by foreign capital, although they did admit that the FIC had been slow to approve proposals.

Part of the adverse effect that the FIC had on new investment was inadvertent, particularly at the time when the Committee was first established by an inexperienced government after Independence. One former government official familiar with the FIC noted in an interview that

the fundamental problem [of the FIC] was that it did not know what its development priorities were, what sectors foreigners could go into, what sectors they could not, what the relationship of the committee was to other committees. They couldn't co-ordinate priorities.

However, the government, even after several years of experience with the FIC, refused to change the Committee's basic operating procedures. Merchant bankers reported that they and the successor to the Association of Rhodesian Industries, the Confederation of Zimbabwe Industries (CZI), had tried 'over and over again' to change the FIC procedures without success. One banker went so far as to claim that the government was 'looking for excuses to set up barriers to foreign investment'.

The government had been unwilling and unable to reduce the barriers to new foreign investment because of the important symbolic part that foreign investment plays in the new country's political project. Multinational corporations are a particularly vivid emblem of the continuing capitalist nature of the White-dominated economy because they have the potential to develop an alternative political power base, which is very threatening to a regime unsure of its own power. One businessman familiar with government thinking said in an interview:

Cabinet . . . is just concerned with the overall situation. They don't want enough economic power to accumulate in one place that it becomes political power. . . . They just don't want a powerful Tiny Rowland [the Chairman of Lonrho Corporation] to develop who can dictate policy to government. They don't want to be told what to do.

Or, as one former official in the Ministry of Finance said, 'they [the government] like foreign investment but they do not like foreigners'.

Thus, foreign investors were accorded far less legitimacy when they lobbied government than the commercial farmers were, even though the farmers had been the mainstay of Ian Smith's Rhodesian Front. Government considers the CFU to have more legitimacy than new investors because the farmers are now Zimbabweans and have shown their dedication to the country by staying on the land; therefore, the government allows the commercial farmers an important role in policy issues such as the setting of producer prices. On the other hand, even though prospective investors were not involved in UDI, they were initially unable to influence the policy process because of government's fears about their foreign origin. The difference between the two groups is demonstrated to the government by the fact — constantly mentioned in Zimbabwe's development plans and in conversations with officials — that foreign investors remit their profits and thereby use scarce foreign currency, while the farmers invest their money in the land or, at the very least, keep the funds in the country.

The symbolism of foreign investment became especially important because of factional politics in Zimbabwe. The more radical faction of the government has lost out in many policy battles: the Constitution makes many concessions to Whites, land has not been seized, and existing companies have not been nationalized. Hindering new foreign investment, therefore, was a way of placating the radical segment of the Cabinet with an important symbolic issue, because the left-wing ministers were particularly concerned with Zimbabwe's relations with multinational capital. Indeed, several officials — including the Minister of Foreign Affairs, Nathan Shamuyarira, the Minister of Information Posts and Telecommunications, Witness Mangwende, and, to some extent, Robert Mugabe himself — have lashed out against those who wanted more foreign investment, saying that greater multinational participation would further decrease Zimbabwe's control over its own resources. For instance, the Prime Minister taunted backbenchers in Parliament by stating:

I do not know whether our honourable members and other party stalwarts in ZAPU who constantly cry for investment, foreign investment, have ever stopped to think about the state of ownership at present. Who owns what in this country? More investment capital means more ownership of our resources.[32]

[32] Zimbabwe, *Parliamentary Debates, House of Assembly. Third Session, Second Parliament comprising Periods from 23rd June, 1987 to 19th August, 1987, 20th August, 1987 to 3rd November, 1987*, XIV, 8 July 1987, 198.

Officials who favoured foreign investment were unable for many years to make effective counter-arguments, because of the symbolic importance of foreign investment in Zimbabwe and because of their own weak political position. For instance, Bernard Chidzero, who by 1987 had become the Senior Minister with responsibility for all the ministries dealing with economic affairs, was ineffective, especially in the early years of Independence, in arguing for more foreign investment, because he did not fight in the war and, therefore, had little standing on ideological issues. As one respondent who frequently lobbies Cabinet officials noted,

Chidzero is inclined to economics. He is not a good politician. He has very good ideas — he is the best we have — but he cannot get the ideas through Cabinet. The others who are more political gain the ear of Mugabe.

Indeed, Chidzero is the only major figure in the government who was not a member of the Politburo, despite his obvious importance in all spheres of economic decision-making.[33]

The Business Environment

As mentioned earlier, it is also necessary to look beyond specific government investment policies to the general business climate in order to understand the growth, or lack thereof, of foreign investment since Independence. The business environment in Zimbabwe has been poor for reasons both within and beyond government's control. In the first place, the regulatory environment that the government inherited from the settlers would obviously have been a deterrent to those seeking to enter the Zimbabwe economy for the first time. Robertson describes how the business environment created by government policies appears to the investor who does not already have his money locked in the economy:

High wages against low prices, high productivity against protection for disruptive or lazy workers, high investment against low profits, and hopes of savings to invest almost destroyed by high taxation. Put bluntly, our investment policies and the investment climate to which they give rise were not compatible with the needs of investors. We are offering him a near certainty that he won't make money.

---

[33] With the creation of the United ZANU(PF) party at the end of December 1989, Chidzero was appointed to the new Politburo (*The Herald*, 23 Dec. 1989). However, his position is simply that of an ordinary member, with no specific responsibilities — the responsibility for finance is given to Emmerson Mnangagwa, and that for economic affairs to Naison Ndlovu. This would seem to indicate that Chidzero's influence on the Zimbabwe economy will continue to lie at the government, rather than at the party, level.

We've told him that we don't want to see him getting rich and our legislation tells him that we have every intention of interfering with everything he does.[34]

However, these intrusive controls cannot simply be dismantled because it was the very existence of a comprehensive regulatory environment that was partly responsible for the government's decision not to significantly disrupt ownership patterns in the economy. New government regulations which have adversely affected the business environment, including the establishment of a national minimum wage and severe limitations on the ability of companies to lay off workers, were also part of the government's effort to gain greater control of the economy. The strategy of preserving and extending the regulatory environment that the government followed in order to be able to live with the existing high level of foreign investment disallowed the possibility of making Zimbabwe particularly attractive to new investors.

The business environment in Zimbabwe has also been depressed because of factors outside the government's control. The dramatic decrease in world commodity prices, the global recession, and an unprecedented three-year drought between 1982 and 1984 seriously affected the economy. The country was forced to suspend remittance payments temporarily in 1984 because of severe balance-of-payments stress largely caused by the drought,[35] and in 1987 the government temporarily reduced by 50 per cent the amount of dividends that could be remitted out of the country.[36] Foreign currency is still in extremely short supply: Zimbabwe was exporting about the same in real terms in 1987 as it was in 1980.[37] A potential investor looking at Zimbabwe would be guaranteed that his new enterprise would not have a constant supply of imported inputs, and it is doubtful that the country can avoid further interruptions in remittances of profits if commodity prices remain low.

Zimbabwe's business climate is also severely damaged by a problem not faced by most Third World countries: dependence on South Africa. As noted in Chapter 2, a large portion of Zimbabwe's total external trade passes through its southern neighbour's transportation network. Zimbabwe's transport dependence on South Africa makes the country

---

[34] *The Financial Gazette*, 25 Nov. 1983.

[35] Zimbabwe, *Socio-Economic Review of Zimbabwe 1980–1985*, 60.

[36] *The Herald*, 29 May 1987.

[37] A. M. Hawkins, 'Introduction', in *Commercial Agriculture in Zimbabwe* (1987/88), 3.

dangerously vulnerable to South African destabilization such as slow-downs in the movement of goods or an outright refusal to accept Zimbabwean exports or imports. While it is hoped that Zimbabwe's efforts to disengage from South Africa will reduce its dependence, it is clear that for the short to medium term Zimbabwe will be vulnerable to South African destabilization. The generally turbulent climate in Southern Africa, and the possibility that violence may spill over from South Africa even without conscious destabilization, also serves to deter investors.

All these factors have created to an unprofitable business environment that is unattractive to new investors. Local economists estimate that the return on investment since Independence has been only 8,5 per cent, while inflation has averaged approximately 14 per cent and the Zimbabwe dollar has depreciated significantly against major currencies.[38] The low returns have been aggravated by high taxes on the earnings of foreign companies. While Zimbabwe once had a low level of taxation, it now has a higher effective tax rate than any other country in Southern Africa except Zambia.[39] The combination of low returns on investment and high taxes have clearly made Zimbabwe an unattractive place in which to invest; indeed, a recent study of the business environment in SADCC states actually rated Zimbabwe as having the worst overall position towards investment when government attitudes, bureaucracy, foreign exchange, markets and incentives are all taken into account.[40]

Official Agreements concerning Foreign Investment

While Zimbabwe cannot do anything about many of the factors which have led to the creation of the poor economic environment, it could have taken measures to alleviate some of the problems that existed between 1980 and 1989. For instance, the United States Overseas Private Investment Corporation (OPIC) agreements are designed to improve the business environments of Third World countries by allowing companies to take out insurance against political risks and disruptions of the flow of remittances. Other Western nations, such as Great Britain and West Germany, have similar agreements. While it is highly unlikely that there

[38] Return-on-investment figures are from an interview. Inflation estimate from Zimbabwe, *Annual Economic Review of Zimbabwe 1986*, 29.

[39] Whitsun Foundation, *Trade and Investment in Zimbabwe: Volume II: Investment* (Harare, The Foundation, 1983), 252.

[40] A. W. Whiteside, *Investment Opportunities in Southern Africa: The Business Climate in SADCC States* (Braamfontein, South African Institute of International Affairs, 1987), 15.

will be any political disruption of foreign-enterprise operations in Zimbabwe, the country's foreign-exchange problems and its history of suspending remittances make OPIC's remittances coverage extremely relevant for new investors. Many potential Western investors insist on such an agreement being in place before they will consider investing: West German trade officials in Harare, for instance, said that there would be no German investment until Zimbabwe signed Bonn's equivalent of OPIC. These sentiments were echoed by representatives and businessmen from several major Western countries. Even the Chinese were 'not really happy about the investment climate in Zimbabwe because of lack of guarantees on their investments'.[41]

However, Zimbabwe consistently refused to sign such agreements, despite lobbying by foreign companies and the United States and other countries. It was argued that OPIC was not necessary because Zimbabwe's Constitution protected private investment, and Zimbabwe's leaders have labelled OPIC-type agreements an infringement on their sovereignty.[42] Officials in the government suggested that avowedly-socialist Zimbabwe did not want to appear to be signing an apparently-capitalist document — although over thirty-five other African countries, including such self-consciously radical states as Mozambique, Ethiopia and Tanzania, have signed such an agreement.[43] In view of the lack of foreign investment, many in Zimbabwe, especially officials in the Ministry of Finance, Economic Planning and Development, would have liked Zimbabwe to have reconsidered before 1989 its refusal to sign OPIC-type agreements, but the issue became so politicized that advice from technocrats was not heeded by the Cabinet. The government's highly publicized refusal to sign OPIC-type treaties, frequently reiterated by more radical members of the Cabinet,[44] has made these agreements a benchmark of Zimbabwe's refusal to collaborate with international capital. The new government, therefore, was sending a strong message to potential investors that Zimbabwe would not make efforts to improve its investment climate if this effort impinged at all on its political aspirations.

[41] *The Financial Gazette*, 16 May 1986.

[42] See, for instance, Mugabe's speech reported in *The Herald*, 15 May 1986.

[43] Overseas Private Investment Corporation, *1985 Development Report* (Washington, OPIC, 1986), inside back cover.

[44] Libby, 'Developmental strategies and political divisions within the Zimbabwean state', 153.

New Foreign Investment in Zimbabwe

As a result of government's pre-1989 policies on new investment, the poor business climate, and the government's refusal for almost a decade to sign OPIC-type agreements, Zimbabwe has attracted little new foreign investment since Independence. According to the Ministry of Finance, Economic Planning and Development, Zimbabwe received only about $110 million between 1981 and 1986, $80 million of which was in cash and $30 million in kind.[45] This is obviously a trivial amount, given the country's assumptions about direct capital inflows. Indeed, in the first four years of Independence Zimbabwe received about as much foreign investment as the Ivory Coast gains in six months.[46] In a striking appraisal of the country's economic future, no company that has divested from South Africa has relocated in Zimbabwe.

The major new investments in Zimbabwe have been the purchase by H. J. Heinz of 51 per cent of Olivine Industries, the establishment of a chewing-gum factory by Dandy, the investment by Aberfoyle Investments in a palm-oil plantation, and an expansion of gold-mining operations by Cluff Minerals. The Heinz investment, which accounts for a substantial portion of total new investment, was not significant in itself because the American company purchased an already profitable company — an investment that did not represent a substantial risk. The Heinz purchase was viewed by the government as a precedent-setting investment which would convince other companies to come to Zimbabwe; indeed, the government broke its own rule of not allowing domestic ownership to be diluted when it approved the Heinz purchase. However, no American company has followed the Heinz lead. Dandy established a new industry in Zimbabwe with a factory in a rural area, thereby meeting two of Zimbabwe's investment goals. However, the investment was for only $3 million and it, too, does not appear to be serving as a precedent for other companies.

It is extremely difficult to determine to what extent the lack of new investment is due to factors beyond Zimbabwe's control or to government policy. Certainly, at Independence dozens of foreign business delegations visited Zimbabwe because they were impressed with the

[45] Personal communication from Foreign Investment Committee Secretariat.

[46] C. B. Thompson, 'Statement of Carol B. Thompson', in *Zimbabwe: Four Years of Independence; An Assessment: Hearing before the Subcommittee on Africa of the Committee on Foreign Affairs, House of Representatives, Ninety-eighth Congress, Second Session*, 24 May 1984, 31.

relatively well-developed economy, the sophisticated infrastructure, and the business acumen developed while evading sanctions.[47] One newspaper reported that 'something approaching investment fever is already stirring among US businessmen seeking overseas operations or export markets' in Zimbabwe.[48] These delegations seemed willing to invest despite the hazards of doing business in Southern Africa; however, government policies deterred many of them when they began to formulate concrete investment plans. Merchant bankers indicated that at Independence they expected between ten and twenty times the volume of investment that Zimbabwe has actually received. While these estimates were probably overly optimistic, Zimbabwe would have received more investment if it had adopted policies aimed at improving the business climate. Stoneman estimates that, after UDI, Rhodesia received over £100 million ($330 million at 1989 exchange rates) in foreign investment for mining alone.[49] If investors had placed their money in the highly risky UDI environment, they would certainly have invested in stable Zimbabwe if government policies had been more favourable. It was one banker's view that 'government policies that discourage investment have been more important in the lack of investment than have unfavourable domestic or foreign economic factors'. Even the Minister of Finance, Economic Planning and Development, Bernard Chidzero, agreed that 'economic management issues and administrative matters may lie at the heart of the lack of investment inflows'.[50]

Reforming the Foreign Investment Regime

In May 1989 the government radically changed the procedures that had guided new foreign investment in Zimbabwe. In the first place, the definition of a 'foreign' company was amended to describe one that has at least 25 per cent of its shares owned by a non-Zimbabwean. Secondly, and more importantly, it eliminated the FIC and created a 'one-stop' facility known as the Investment Centre, which is designed to give investors a response to their application within ninety days. The Invest-

[47] See, for instance, the *Herald* reports for 12 June 1980 and 28 June 1980.

[48] Quoted in A. Astrow, *Zimbabwe: A Revolution That Lost Its Way?* (London, Zed, 1983), 164.

[49] Stoneman, 'Foreign capital and the prospects for Zimbabwe', 53.

[50] Quoted by A. Rusinga, 'Why do foreign investors hesitate', *African Business* (May 1986), 49.

ment Centre will initially be part of the Ministry of Finance, Economic Planning and Development but will eventually become an autonomous body. The remittability regulations were also modified to allow foreign investors, especially those involved in high-priority projects, to take more money out of the country. Finally, Zimbabwe acceded to the World Bank's Multilateral Investment Guarantee Agency and pledged itself to negotiate bilateral investment accords such as OPIC.[51] The announcement of the new regulations was coupled with a change in rhetoric towards new foreign investors: President Mugabe noted in his 1989 Independence-day speech that foreign investors can play 'an important role' in the investment process.[52]

Several factors seem to have led to the leadership's decision to change the regulations regarding new foreign investment after almost a decade of policies which were all but hostile to it. Firstly, it has become abundantly clear to everyone that Zimbabwe faces a very significant unemployment problem and that the previous regulations were simply not addressing the problem of the hundreds of thousands of school-leavers who will, by 1990, be entering the job market with little prospect of employment.[53] President Mugabe mentioned the unemployment issue when he announced the new foreign-investment regulations, and he admitted that previous government policy had been a failure in this respect.[54]

Equally importantly, by 1989 officials who advocated a technocratic approach to policy had won a new prominence at the apex of government. Chidzero in particular, seems to have 'the firm backing of Mugabe and ZANU to thoroughly re-make Zimbabwe's economy'.[55] In part, this new stature has come about because the evidence for the failure of the previous policy has become increasingly obvious on the streets of Harare. Also, as Zimbabwe matures as an independent state, it is only natural that the legitimacy of individuals depends less and less on what they did during the liberation struggle and more and more on their performance in the post-Independence years. The prominence of technocrats was acceler-

---

[51] Zimbabwe, *The Promotion of Investment: Policy and Regulations* (Harare, Govt. Printer, 1989).

[52] *The Herald*, 19 Apr. 1989.

[53] See A. M. Hawkins *et al.*, *Formal Sector Employment Demand Conditions in Zimbabwe* (Harare, Univ. of Zimbabwe Publications, 1988), 5–7.

[54] *The Herald*, 19 Apr. 1989.

[55] A. Meldrum, 'Mugabe's maneuvers', *Africa Report* (May–June 1989), 40.

ated because many officials long known for their doctrinaire approach to policy — including heroes of the Independence struggle, Enos Nkala and Maurice Nyagumbo — were forced to resign in 1989 because of a scandal involving the resale of cars from the Willowvale car-assembly plant.[56] The *Financial Gazette* noted the importance of élite conflicts in the design of the new foreign-investment policy:

it does not take three years to draft a code, however much consultation takes place and however many other codes are examined for guidelines applicable to Zimbabwe's situation. The delays have occurred because of deep differences within the government and ruling party over the principle of encouraging foreign investment at all.[57]

Finally, after nine years in power, Zimbabwe's leaders may have achieved enough self-confidence not to view international commercial treaties as infringements on their sovereignty. They have, in other words, come to the conclusion that the war they started against the Rhodesians and (in the guerrillas' view) their international collaborators is finally over.

The new guidelines do go a substantial way towards addressing many of the complaints of foreign investors. The new regulations defining a foreign investor are less restrictive, and the new Investment Centre should dramatically reduce the time that foreign investors have to wait for a response to their applications. In addition, the signing of the OPIC-type agreements should reassure investors about the stability of Zimbabwe and the flow of dividends. However, the new regulations do not guarantee a significant inflow of foreign funds into Zimbabwe. At the most general level, there are simply not that many investors seeking to place their money in any part of Africa at present. Also, the factors which make Zimbabwe's business climate unattractive — government policies and the external conditions over which the government has no control — will continue to deter many investors.

Conclusion

The Zimbabwean state was not autonomous when trying to formulate policy towards existing foreign investment. The political, regional and

---

[56] The scandal became known as 'Willowgate'; see Zimbabwe, *Report of the Commission of Inquiry into the Distribution of Motor Vehicles* [Chairman: W. R. Sandura] (Harare, Govt. Printer, 1989).

[57] *The Financial Gazette*, 5 May 1989.

economic constraints faced by the new regime allowed almost no room for manœuvre in either the rules governing existing foreign investment (structural autonomy) or in everyday policy (situational autonomy). That the existing regulatory environment gave Zimbabwe substantial influence over the multinational corporations was fortunate, but the government was extremely limited in the kind of action it could take. In contrast, when designing policies for new investment, the government enjoyed substantial autonomy. At the structural level, the government at first created new institutions, designed an elaborate and hostile approval process, and refused to sign international investment-protection agreements, even though (or perhaps because) these agreements were prerequisites for new investment. Even when the state changed the foreign-investment guidelines, it was because of factors inside the state — the changing influence of technocrats and new realizations on the part of the leadership of the effects of their policy — rather than because of a change in the bargaining power of multinational companies. Between 1980 and 1989 the state was also situationally autonomous because, in the day-to-day decisions on foreign investment, multinationals did not have the ability to influence government policy. However, the changes made in 1989 suggest that at the day-to-day (situational) level the government is willing to allow foreign investors much greater influence in the investment-approval process.

Existing Investment: The Coincidence of Power and Interests

A more or less stable position has evolved between the government and existing foreign capital in Zimbabwe. Foreign companies presently in Zimbabwe are most interested in preserving their existing investment and in trying to obtain more favourable government policies towards their companies within the existing regulatory framework — for example, being able to get more foreign exchange allocated to them. While foreign-owned companies would have welcomed new investment, primarily because it would have been a reflection of an increased desire on the government's part to co-operate with the private sector, these enterprises have other, more pressing, concerns. Clearly, the most important issues in government–business relations in the late 1980s, and for the foreseeable future, are foreign-currency allocations, trade liberalization and the reform of the economy.[58]

[58] *Business Opinion Survey* [Harare, Univ. of Zimbabwe, Dept. of Business Studies, MBA Programme] (1987–9), XIII–XVII.

At the same time, the government is constrained by the Lancaster House Constitution and a host of economic, political and strategic factors from tampering with existing investment. The regulatory state and the existence of a domestic capitalist class which Blacks will eventually penetrate also make living with the current level of foreign investment in the economy an acceptable, though hardly desirable, alternative to the total control of the economy that the guerrillas' heady rhetoric called for. The new government's leaders, therefore, have made the best of a bad situation and used their country's inability to act against existing foreign investment to their advantage by ostentatiously adhering to the Lancaster House agreement.

A policy of not tampering with existing foreign investment could have caused significant problems for the regime since its own ideology seems to demand radical action against multinational companies. However, the government has used its harsh policies against new investment — most notably the tough approval procedures for new proposals and its refusal to sign OPIC-type agreements — to prove its socialist credentials and to demonstrate that some of the rhetoric from the liberation struggle has carried over into actual policy. By venting so much of its hostility and its political project on potential new investors, the socialist government has been able to live with the current level of foreign penetration and placate the more radical members of the Cabinet.

New Investment: Factors Promote State Autonomy

Several factors allowed Zimbabwe to be hostile to foreign capital. Firstly, the bargaining position of new foreign investors is exceedingly poor. While analysts often speak of 'international capital' as if it were a conspiratorial monolith, it is actually quite a fractured group in Zimbabwe. The Confederation of Zimbabwe Industries does try to influence the government on various issues, but it is concerned with the entire gamut of government–private sector relations rather than simply with foreign investment. In addition, the CZI does not appear to have an effective lobbying presence. As with the Chamber of Mines,[59] and in direct contrast with the CFU, the Confederation's president is an executive who cannot lobby government on a full-time basis. The CZI does not have a high public profile, partially because it is not a devoted lobbying organization and partially because the companies it represents are so diverse

[59] See Chapter 7.

that it simply cannot represent every single concern of each industrialist. Most importantly, the CZI reflects the general orientation of its members, who are certainly not concentrating on easing the way for new investors, especially when new investors face regulations that pose less problems than the regulations that affect existing companies. It is doubtful that, even after nine years, the bargaining power of multinational corporations had changed significantly in Zimbabwe, and it is probably not the case that an increase in the power of foreign investors was the direct impetus for the changes in the foreign-investment guidelines that were introduced in 1989.

Before 1989, therefore, foreign companies had to individually confront policy-makers when they tried to convince the government to approve an investment proposal. There was really nothing that a company which wanted to invest in Zimbabwe could threaten the government with in order to get a favourable ruling or policy, since Zimbabwe had made it repeatedly clear that it wanted investment on its own terms and was willing to forgo economic gains from new investment if companies made unacceptable demands. One businessman familiar with approaches to the government by foreign companies said in an interview: 'You cannot give them [the government] a take it or leave it proposition because they'll leave it'.

The existence of Zimbabwe's relatively sophisticated industrial sector further reduced the leverage of new foreign investors, because there is often the possibility that many of the large number of well-established companies already in the country can expand their productive capacity. For instance, the Permanent Secretary in the Ministry of Finance, Economic Planning and Development, Dr Elisha Mushayakarara, said when addressing Zimbabwean industrialists:

We Zimbabweans are very imaginative and those fields which are not already being attended to by our industrialists and manufacturers, really we would feel more comfortable by having those of you in this hall moving into those areas. . . . I can only imagine possibly that if we decided to manufacture atomic bombs, maybe that's where we might fail.[60]

Zimbabwe has, in fact, attempted to encourage existing foreign companies to reinvest by reducing the interest rate paid on surplus funds held

[60] *The Financial Gazette*, 17 July 1987.

by multinationals from 9 per cent to 5 per cent, and by loosening the regulations on how companies can use blocked funds.[61]

The difficulties that foreign firms had in trying to pressure Zimbabwe were amply demonstrated by negotiations surrounding the Heinz investment. Both an informant inside the company and several bankers close to the negotiations attributed Heinz's success in getting its applications approved despite the dilution of domestic control to smart negotiating tactics on the company's part and to the government's desire to have a prestigious foreign firm come into the country. One businessman said: 'The Heinz negotiations were done with skill and that is the key point. Heinz woos Zimbabwe and is quite persistent. Their reputation proves they are genuine and they do have something to offer.' No one attributed Heinz's success to pressure from foreign capital; everyone suggested that it was the company's own tactics and the government's own desires that led to successful completion of the negotiations. Indeed, it is hard to see why existing firms, foreign or domestic, would care whether it was Heinz or a Zimbabwean company that produced cooking oil and baked beans.

Even if there were formidable political pressure for foreign investment in Zimbabwe, the government's institutional structure for regulating foreign investment between 1980 and 1989 was so dense that it was unlikely that foreign capital could have significantly influenced government actions. For instance, the FIC's proceedings were secret, and it seemed to operate behind an institutional veil which prevented outsiders from understanding, and therefore successfully influencing, its actions. Informants who would have known these facts if they could were unable to describe how the FIC operated, what exactly it considered, and who on the Committee was particularly important. All of this information was vital if a proper lobbying strategy was to be developed.

The new structure that the government adopted in 1989 was designed, at least in theory, to significantly reduce the insulation of state officials from investors and to make the entire investment process more transparent. At the very least, the requirement that it should take only ninety days for a decision to be made on a foreign-investment proposal removed a crucial buffer between state officials and potential investors: applicants were previously told simply that their proposal was still being considered and that they should come back later.

---

[61] See, Chidzero, 'State of the economy, foreign exchange and investment', in Zimbabwe, *Annual Economic Review of Zimbabwe, 1986*, 74–5.

The nature of the issue-area may possibly have helped foreign companies influence the government, because Zimbabwe will always have to make decisions regarding foreign investment. Individual firms may not initially have had the leverage against the government, but it is possible that, as time went by, a large number of unrelated decisions by different firms gradually forced the Zimbabweans into a position more favourable to foreign capital.[62] To a limited extent, this appears to have been the case, because foreign investors added their voice to the continual torrent of written and verbal advice to government that its investment policy was not addressing the unemployment problem. However, what is probably more important is that the people who had always argued that the previous investment policy was not working finally gained enough prominence to enact their preferences.

Locus of Decision-making

Changing the locus of decision-making was central to the national leadership's approach to new foreign investment. Fearing that they could not control the state apparatus, the leadership deliberately created a new institution soon after Independence, the FIC, to give ministers or their immediate aides direct control over new foreign investment. This control was possible because foreign-investment decisions are discrete: there are relatively few decisions that have to be made at one time, so ministers could personally consider the issues and have a direct impact on the policy process. The structural distinctness of the FIC also prevented the kind of downward shift in policy-making that occurred in land acquisition. If the ministers were overwhelmed with technical decisions they did not allow bureaucrats to make decisions; rather, they simply held the proposal in the FIC until they had time to consider the proposal. The institutional structures created by the new regime before 1989, and the fact that few decisions had to be made at any one time, therefore prevented the kind of bureaucratic takeover that occurred on the land issue.

The importance of the locus of decision-making becomes even clearer when examining the changes in the investment regulations enacted in 1989. The new regulations effectively move the locus of decision-making away from Cabinet, with the result that the government has less control over the day-to-day decisions regarding foreign investment, thereby making Zimbabwe more attractive to foreign investors. Indeed, the new

---

[62] I am indebted to James Scott for suggesting this point.

structures encourage technically-minded bureaucrats to become more involved in the decision-making process and exclude Cabinet members, who might be more inclined to make political statements in response to foreign-investment applications.

There is no evidence of ZANU(PF) being involved in the policy-making process on foreign investment. Once again, the party seems to lack the technical expertise and organizational structure required to play a significant role in this issue. The party's ideological stance was also taken up by certain members of the Cabinet who were dedicated to being hostile to foreign investment, so there was little that the party had to contribute. By 1989, when the new regulations were formulated, the party seems to have been acknowledged as being largely irrelevant to the making of economic policy. In addition, when the foreign-investment regulations were being finalized, the party was still reeling from the loss of many of its most prominent leaders as a result of the 'Willowgate' car scandal, which probably contributed to its marginalization to some extent.

Zimbabwe's leaders are in many ways in the same situation as the settlers were after 1923: they have achieved a political victory but are still uneasily dependent on foreign capital for economic advancement. While the present government is much more antagonistic towards international capital than its White predecessors, the basic problem of how to carry the political victory into the economic sphere is the same. The Black government tried to follow the policies of previous governments in attempting to consolidate its political victory through the enhancement of state mechanisms to enable the public sector to better regulate large portions of the economy. However, the fact that the new government has to try to provide economic benefits for eight million people, rather than for 250 000, has meant that it has been much less successful in trying to control foreign investment and promote growth. Whether the new regulations will attract significant new investment and still preserve what the government feels is its political prerogatives remains to be seen, but this is clearly a delicate balance which the government will have to monitor closely in the future.

Chapter Seven

State Power versus the Multinationals: Minerals Marketing Policy

The conflict between the multinational corporations, which played an integral role in the development of Rhodesia, and the new socialist government of Zimbabwe is a major political drama. Nowhere is this conflict more evident than in the mining industry, where a few large foreign companies control a strategic sector of the economy that accounts for 8,3 per cent of the country's Gross Domestic Product and approximately 38 per cent of its exports.[1] In the most important new legislation affecting existing foreign investment, the government has sought to gain control over Zimbabwe's mining sector, in the face of strong opposition from the mining companies, by creating a parastatal organization, the Minerals Marketing Corporation of Zimbabwe (MMCZ), to market Zimbabwe's mineral exports. The development of the MMCZ is a significant example of the way in which Zimbabwe's government has met the challenge posed by the continuing White dominance of the economy, and of how the process of reconciliation between Whites and Blacks has been carried out.

The Mining Sector and Government in Rhodesia

The early history of Zimbabwe, as Arrighi has noted, turns on the overestimation of the country's mineral resources.[2] When the settlers began to re-evaluate the significance of the colony's mineral resources, they moved into other activities and the economy become much less dependent on mining. One of the effects of this change was that the mining sector quickly lost its electoral base. In 1936, for example, there were 3 000 smallworkers exploring claims, and these miners had the potential to provide the same kind of electoral support for mining that the farmers

---

[1] Zimbabwe, *Statistical Yearbook, 1987*, 77, and Zimbabwe, *Annual Economic Review of Zimbabwe, 1986*, 11.

[2] Arrighi, *The Political Economy of Rhodesia*, 19.

gave to commercial agriculture. However, by 1946, technical, economic and legal changes had reduced Rhodesia's smallworkers to 756, and the large mining companies would soon completely dominate mineral production.[3] Without electoral pressure to force it to intervene constantly, as it did in agriculture, the government sought a different relationship with the mining industry. Murray notes that

rather than an administrative system constructed on the basis of direct government action, or on a close partnership between government and individuals, the government sought to create the conditions in which private individuals, and, even more, companies, could operate with the incentive of securing a profit from exploiting the colony's mineral resources and selling them in the world market.[4]

The result was a different pattern of politics from the one experienced in agriculture where the Rhodesian National Farmers Union was to play a consistently strong and public role in lobbying the government on agrarian issues. Again, Murray points out:

In the public service and agricultural sectors much depended on the representative associations.... A comparable governmental system was nearly created for the mining sector but [this] attempt had failed, and the sector had been reorganized after the Second World War on the basis of a system of competitive free enterprise. The situation in the sector, however, had a significance for the general governmental system of the society. The established administrative system did not provide for itself a support in the electoral political system: it relied on other forces to produce an acceptance in the electoral political system for a free enterprise administrative system in the mining sector.[5]

The absence of an electoral base meant that the mining companies exercised political influence in a way radically different from the way in which the farmers did: without a mining lobby in the electorate, mining interests could not use the farmers' public lobbying techniques. Therefore, the mining companies sought to exercise influence through less public means, utilizing their long-time contacts in government, especially in the Ministry of Mines. Leys noted in the late 1950s that '[mining] influence through official and informal channels is more important than participation in politics'.[6]

At the same time that the industry was losing its electoral base, the

[3] Murray, *The Governmental System in Southern Rhodesia*, 149.
[4] Ibid., 158.   [5] Ibid., 161.
[6] Leys, *European Politics in Southern Rhodesia*, 105.

government was taking action to protect the industry from the hostile international environment. For instance, during the Second World War, Prime Minister Godfrey Huggins was afraid that the South African Iron and Steel Corporation (ISCOR), which owned the colony's only steel plant, would concentrate production in South Africa when the war ended, and leave the colony without a steel works. Realizing the importance of the steel industry to the country's future economic growth, Huggins purchased the Bulawayo company from ISCOR.[7] This purchase set the stage for the important steel operations at Redcliff which are major consumers of mineral production in independent Zimbabwe. During this period, the government also established a roasting plant to process ores at Que Que (now Kwekwe).[8] Both actions provided valuable processing plants for Rhodesia's minerals and set the stage for other facilities which would allow Rhodesia to develop its mining and manufacturing industry further and export more valuable commodities.

Between the end of the Second World War and UDI there was little conflict between government and the mining houses because of the booming economy and because the colonial regime did not interfere while the companies were consolidating their hold on the extractive industry.[9] The expansion in the mining sector led, as Table XIV demonstrates, to an ever-broader array of mineral exploitation. This diversification is particularly impressive because the mining industry shifted from the production of mostly low value-added ores to the higher value-added production of refined metals.[10] However, as the boom years of the Federation came to an end, the mining industry and the rest of the Rhodesian economy stumbled into an era of grave and unprecedented problems.

The 1965 Unilateral Declaration of Independence and the resulting sanctions must be seen as a major set-back for the mining industry. The mining sector was among the most export-oriented in the Rhodesian economy and, therefore, had a great deal to lose from the economic sanctions that followed UDI. The fact that, at the same time, mining companies in newly independent Zambia were working out a *modus vivendi* with the Black government must also have emphasized the

---

[7] Gann and Gelfand, *Huggins of Rhodesia*, 160.

[8] Arrighi, *The Political Economy of Rhodesia*, 31.

[9] Phimister, 'Zimbabwe: The path of capitalist development', 282–3.

[10] I am grateful to Paul R. Thomas for suggesting this point to me.

Table XIV

RANGE OF SIGNIFICANT MINERALS PRODUCED, 1945–1984 *

1945	1956	1965	1984
Asbestos	Asbestos	Asbestos	Asbestos
Chrome	Chrome	Chrome	Chrome
Coal	Coal	Coal	Coal
Gold	Copper	Copper	Copper
Mica	Gold	Gold	Gold
Tungsten	Lepidolite	Iron Ore	Iron Ore
	Limestone	Limestone	Limestone
	Tin	Lithium	Lithium
	Titanium	Nickel	Nickel
		Tin	Phosphate
			Silver
			Tin

* A mineral was considered significant if it amounted to at least 0,5 per cent of total mineral production by value.

Source: Ministry of Mines, *Report of the Secretary of Mines*, various years.

potential cost of continued White minority rule. Clearly, mining companies would have preferred the moderate Black option to the unknown, and highly dangerous, business environment induced by sanctions. Table XV demonstrates that mining exports were initially hit hard by sanctions, although they soon recovered and began to grow. However, it should be remembered that the sanctions premium — the cost of sanctions-busting operations and the necessity of sometimes selling goods below the world price in order to attract buyers — continued to reduce the mining companies' profits throughout the UDI period. One key actor in the sanctions-busting operations estimated that the sanctions discount was equivalent to a 15 per cent decrease in total trade.[11]

Nevertheless, the UDI period was a time of rapid development for the mining industry. Unfortunately, it is difficult to trace the exact growth of the industry because many statistics from that era have apparently been destroyed in an effort to protect those who helped Rhodesia evade sanctions. However, it is clear that mining became more diversified

[11] E. Cross, 'Economic Sanctions as a Tool of Policy against Rhodesia' (Salisbury, Univ. of Zimbabwe , Centre for Applied Social Sciences, Seminar Paper 22, 1980, mimeo.), 4.

Table XV

DISRUPTION AND RECOVERY OF MINERAL EXPORTS, 1965–1978

Commodity	1965	1966	1975	1978
		($ *millions*)		
Crude materials, inedible, except fuels (SITC sect. 2) *	38 782	33 418	89 987	125 368
Crude asbestos	21 552	14 772	48 827	57 344
Ferrochrome	3 380	2 774	38 900	31 600

* Standard International Trade Classification (SITC) 2 includes all raw mineral exports. It therefore includes crude asbestos but not ferrochrome, which is considered a manufactured product.

Sources: Rhodesia, *Annual Statement of External Trade, 1965* (Salisbury, Central Statistical Office, 1966), and Rhodesia, *Statement of External Trade by Commodities 1966, 1975, 1976, 1977, 1978* (Salisbury, Central Statistical Office, 1980).

during this period as production of nickel, cobalt and silver, all of which were insignificant before 1965, grew to $58 million in 1979.[12] Overall, in spite of the difficulties of doing business during UDI, the value of mining output increased in nominal terms from $54 million to $315 million between 1964 and 1979.[13]

During the UDI years, the mining companies were affected both by the stringent regulations that the Rhodesians applied uniformly to multinational companies and by special regulations applying only to the extractive industry. For instance, when Lonrho attempted to lay off half of the workers of a non-mining subsidiary, the Rhodesian government enacted the Emergency Regulations (Control of Manpower) provisions which prevented the dismissal of White workers without the permission of the Ministry of Labour.[14] Even more importantly, when the US State Department requested Union Carbide to stop ferrochrome shipments to Mozambique, the Smith government used emergency regulations to force the company's Rhodesian subsidiary to sell all its production to the

[12] Zimbabwe, *Transitional National Development Plan*, I, 12.

[13] The 1979 figure represents a real increase of 85 per cent, ibid., 12.

[14] S. Cronje *et al.*, *Lonrho: Portrait of a Multinational* (London, J. Friedmann, 1976), 166.

state-controlled trading corporation, Universal Exports (UNIVEX), that played a significant part in the sanctions-busting exercise.[15]

In contrast to most African states, the renegade colony was not only able to enact these regulations, but was also able to enforce them. One of the reasons for the Rhodesians' success in affecting company behaviour was the competence of the civil service that was drawn from the settler population. One former Ministry of Mines official observed in an interview that 'most Rhodesian civil servants were career people, they were a highly efficient group who knew each other in a very small service and were able to get things done'. The mining sector, because of its strategic importance, came under special scrutiny by this highly trained cadre of officials. The former official noted: 'We were very nationalistic. Rhodesia was basically independent since 1923 and very independent during UDI. . . . We didn't let the [mining] companies get away with anything. The companies were always closely monitored.' He said, for instance, that the Ministry of Mines, in addition to enforcing the regulations mentioned above, was very concerned that companies might try to transfer profits illegally from unstable Rhodesia by under-invoicing (selling products to their parent companies for artificially low prices so that profits can be realized outside the country). The official noted that the exchange controls prohibited transfer pricing, and that the companies were constantly monitored to see that they were selling minerals at the right price.

The nature of the relationship between Rhodesia and the multinational mining houses discussed here is fundamentally different from the pattern seen in the rest of Africa. Even in the early years of the colony, the settlers were able to exhibit a certain degree of independence from the multinational company that had founded it. As the settlers' government grew stronger and mining receded in importance in the national economy, Rhodesia was able to lessen its dependence on the mining companies by processing some of its minerals. Eventually, during UDI, the government was able to significantly affect almost every aspect of the multinational mining companies' conduct of business in order to promote its war effort.

The Government and the Mining Companies in Zimbabwe

In 1980, when the new government came to power, it immediately made clear that business could not continue as usual in the mining sector. In the

[15] G. Lanning, *Africa Undermined: Mining Companies and the Underdevelopment of Africa* (Harmondsworth, Penguin, 1979), 189.

Transitional National Development Plan the government singled out the mining sector as an area where it desired 'increasing the degree of domestic, particularly state participation, ownership, planning and control'.[16] Inevitably, these goals would bring the new government into conflict with the large mining houses which dominated this strategic sector of the economy. To further emphasize its intentions the new government named Maurice Nyagumbo, an important nationalist leader who had spent many years in gaol, as the new Minister of Mines.

In fact, the conflict in the mining sector was particularly severe, because at Independence the mining companies were almost entirely foreign-owned: as much as 90 per cent of the capital stock in this sector was controlled by multinational corporations.[17] Of the fourteen mines that accounted for 73 per cent of total output in 1974 (later data are not available), all but one or two were foreign-owned.[18] There was certainly no sector of the Zimbabwean economy in which foreign dominance was greater or more well established than in the mining sector.

The companies involved in mining in Zimbabwe represent a veritable 'Who's Who' of powerful transnational enterprises. As the indirect successor of the British South Africa Company, Anglo American Corporation has pride of place among foreign-owned mining houses in Zimbabwe. The Corporation, which is undoubtedly the pre-eminent economic institution in Southern Africa,[19] has significant investments in several minerals.[20] Rio Tinto Zinc, listed by some sources as the world's largest mining company,[21] also has a significant involvement in the mining sector.[22] Significant interests in Zimbabwean gold and copper are also held by Lonrho, a British multinational that had its origins in Rhodesia several decades ago.[23] Lonrho itself claims to be 'the largest and most

[16] Zimbabwe, *Transitional National Development Plan*, I, 70.

[17] Economist Intelligence Unit, *Zimbabwe's First Five Years*, 87.

[18] Clarke, *Foreign Companies and International Investment in Zimbabwe*, 61.

[19] Green and Thompson quote one Southern African official as saying, 'SADCC does not have to worry about regional co-ordination of mining; Anglo American Corporation already does it!', R. H. Green and C. B. Thompson, 'Political economies in conflict: SADCC, South Africa and sanctions', in P. Johnson and D. Martin (eds.), *Destructive Engagement: Southern Africa at War* (Harare, Zimbabwe Publishing House, 1986), 265.

[20] Clarke, *Foreign Companies and International Investment in Zimbabwe*, 66.

[21] R. West, *River of Tears* (London, Earth Island, 1972), 11.

[22] Clarke, *Foreign Companies and International Investment in Zimbabwe*, 76–8.

[23] Ibid., 72.

widely-established company on the African continent'.[24] Certainly, there is no other company that has been so singularly successful in developing a multinational enterprise by concentrating on investment in Africa. Finally, a number of other large multinationals, including Union Carbide (chrome), Falcon Mines (gold), and the British-based Turner and Newall (asbestos), also have significant mining operations in Zimbabwe. After his comprehensive survey of the mining sector, Clarke summarized the economic position of the mining multinationals in Zimbabwe:

> TNCs [Transnational Corporations] have a major controlling interest in the mining sector. They command large-scale units and are major producers for the export market. Their organizational structures are complex and well integrated with national and international business and finance. . . . The TNCs also own large tracts of land and control vast areas held by them under Exclusive Prospecting Orders.[25]

The current pattern of ownership in the mining industry is basically the same as it was before Independence, except that the government bought the financially troubled Messina Transvaal Development Company (copper) and the Kamativi Tin Company (tin). These interests are now operated by the government-owned Zimbabwe Mining Development Corporation.

The multinationals and other mineral producers are represented by the Chamber of Mines. Voting power in the Chamber is determined by a complex formula that 'gives large-scale foreign companies an in-built advantage in the management and control of the Chamber and the industry'.[26] The Presidency of the Chamber rotates between the chief executive officers of the major mining companies. Unlike the President of the Commercial Farmers Union, the President of the Chamber of Mines has to undertake his duties while continuing to work full-time for his company.

In the face of this extraordinarily rich group of companies, the new government was up against the problem of wanting to increase its control and participation in the mining industry without having the expertise and skilled manpower needed even to contemplate replacing the mining houses. As in all other sectors of the economy, Whites had dominated the

---

[24] *Lonrho Annual Report 1985* (London, Lonrho, 1986), 5.

[25] Clarke, *Foreign Companies and International Investment in Zimbabwe*, 80.

[26] Ibid, 145.

administrative positions in the mining industry. For instance, the government's 1981 manpower survey found that Whites occupied 74 per cent of the administrative and managerial positions in the mining and quarrying industry.[27] The government also could not draw upon the skills built up during the years of self-rule because so many White civil servants had left the government for the private sector. In a telling example, Michael Harris, a Deputy Secretary in the Ministry of Mines, left the civil service to become President of a mining company and, eventually, President of the Chamber of Mines. The skills problem was aggravated by the fact that Zimbabwe produces a broad range of minerals and has significant downstream processing capability: if Zimbabwe had been a producer of just one or two minerals and had exported them in their raw state, then the skills problem might not have been so serious.

The political conflict in the mining sector was centred around two related issues. Firstly, it was unacceptable to the new socialist government that a sector that made a significant contribution to the national economy and provided a significant portion of total foreign exchange was almost completely under private, foreign control. Although the sector had been heavily regulated by the Rhodesians, the only area in which the government actually participated on a regular basis was in the marketing of gold and silver, which had traditionally been done by the Reserve Bank. Minister Nyagumbo expressed the government's unhappiness with the situation in the mining sector:

These [mining] companies determine the rate of growth of the mining sector. They determine how much to produce, when to produce, how to sell and when to sell, the degree of local beneficiation [i.e. processing] and so on. The government has little or no say in any of these decisions.[28]

Private enterprise, according to Minister Nyagumbo, could not continue to dominate this sector: 'In the main, therefore, the production and disposal of minerals is not within government's control. This situation is totally unacceptable in our new social order.'[29] In an interview, one mining official made government's point even more vividly: 'Government did not like the idea of a large part of exports being controlled by six or seven firms. One person in the mining industry [an Anglo American official] alone controls 10 per cent of the country's exports.'

[27] Zimbabwe, *National Manpower Survey* (Harare, Ministry of Manpower Planning and Development, 3 vols., 1983), III, 166.

[28] *The Herald*, 22 Jan. 1982.   [29] *The Herald*, 25 July 1981.

In addition to the government's general complaint that it was not sufficiently involved in the mining industry, there was the specific issue of transfer pricing, which the new government claimed to be rampant in the mining industry. Minister Nyagumbo argued that, 'under the present system of marketing our minerals, producers can sell to their sister companies abroad, at low prices, or could similarly sell commodities with a low level of processing like metal concentrates'.[30] Professor Ann Seidman, in her inaugural lecture at the University of Zimbabwe, went so far as to claim that Zimbabwe was losing in the order of $150 million a year through under- and over-invoicing, because studies done elsewhere suggested that 'the typical Third World country' lost that much through illegal transactions by corporations.[31]

The government also argued that the exchange controls that the Rhodesians had enforced were unlikely to stop transfer pricing in independent Zimbabwe because the government lacked the expertise to supervise the companies and because the multinational companies could deceive the government by changing their books. Indeed, the Minister of Mines argued in Parliament that *no* form of regulation in the existing free-enterprise system could effectively regulate the mining industry:

Despite the offer by the Chamber of Mines to examine books of its members, I can assure honourable members that no company is prepared to disclose to government in what manner it is abusing this system. The present system of control depends on the good faith of too many private producers and metal brokers, and offers numerous loopholes for under-invoicing and transfer pricing.[32]

There was also the feeling, according to some, that, because many branches of government, such as the Reserve Bank, were still White-dominated after Independence, they could not be trusted to regulate the foreign companies. The Deputy Minister of Trade and Commerce, M. J. Mvenge, quoted a newspaper article during the Parliamentary debate on the MMCZ:

[30] Zimbabwe, *Parliamentary Debates, House of Assembly. Second Session, First Parliament comprising Periods from 8th September, 1981 to 2nd October, 1981, 19th January, 1982 to 10th February, 1982*, IV, 26 Jan. 1982, 1380.

[31] Seidman, 'A development strategy for Zimbabwe', 31.

[32] Zimbabwe, *Parliamentary Debates, House of Assembly. Second Session, First Parliament comprising Periods from 8th September, 1981 to 2nd October, 1981, 19th January, 1982 to 10th February, 1982*, IV, 26 Jan. 1982, 1382.

It appears that white civil servants in Zimbabwe and foreign companies that traded with Rhodesia during the sanctions years have kept a hold on government contracts. . . . Companies which broke sanctions during the UDI are still monopolizing the economy, while those businesses which observed sanctions are in an unfavourable position following Independence.[33]

Rejection of Nationalization

Even though it had strong concerns about continued foreign involvement in the mining sector, the government realized after some consideration that it would be impossible to nationalize the mining industry. Zimbabwe's mining sector was recognized as a dynamic and diversified industry which could greatly aid the nation by expanding exports and employment. There was also, in the light of general African experience, some scepticism as to how well the government could run the mining sector, and this wariness was compounded by the fact that Zimbabwe's diversified and sophisticated industry would be much harder to administer than mining industries in most African countries. Minister Nyagumbo explained the government's thoughts on nationalization: 'We believe that free enterprise should be left undisturbed because this gives incentives for higher production which enables more profits and therefore more employment and better money and conditions of service for workers.'[34] The government did purchase two companies, as mentioned above, but all indications are that those actions were mainly *ad hoc* interventions designed primarily to prevent closures which would have caused large increases in unemployment.

The Imposed Solution: The MMCZ

Instead of nationalization, the new regime seized on the marketing of minerals as something that could be administered by the government and which would give it substantial control over the entire industry. A Ministry of Mines official explained in an interview,

The nature and structure of mining is such that it is a diversified industry. Government is extremely weak in terms of personnel and know-how to enter into production with any reasonable chance of success. MMCZ allows government to group together people who have knowledge . . . and initiate participation through marketing rather than production. Unless you know how to sell it you are not controlling it. We see that other African countries are unable to market.

---

[33] Ibid., 21 Jan. 1982, 1294.   [34] *The Herald*, 29 Apr. 1980.

The attraction of a marketing parastatal was enhanced by the generally successful experience other African countries have had with state-operated minerals marketing organizations. The World Bank, for instance, identified minerals marketing agencies and some export crop trading boards as the only successful types of parastatals in Africa.[35] Control over marketing would also curtail the dangers of transfer pricing because it would be the government, rather than the companies, that would set the prices for exports and collect the revenues from sales.

Therefore, the government created the Minerals Marketing Corporation of Zimbabwe in 1982.[36] The MMCZ is a parastatal under the control of the Minister of Mines. The Chairman of the Board and four Board members are chosen by the Minister. The Minister also selects four other directors, two are chosen by the Chamber of Mines, one represents the mine-workers, and the general manager of the Corporation also sits on the board. The MMCZ has broad powers to 'act as the sole marketing and selling agent for all minerals' in Zimbabwe (Section 20 of the MMCZ Act), but in practice it leaves the marketing of gold and silver to the Reserve Bank. In order to carry out its role as the sole marketing agent, the Corporation is given the power to require all mineral producers to sell their products to the Corporation. The MMCZ also has the power to negotiate the sale of minerals on behalf of other producers, or to authorize, once given all the details of the sale, the direct sale of minerals from the producer to a foreign buyer (Section 37). The Corporation receives all monies paid by buyers from contracts authorized or negotiated by the Corporation and, after taking a commission, must within thirty days pay the remaining monies to the producer (Section 42).

In addition to its powers and obligations in the marketing area, the Corporation is given broad powers to control actual rates of production by any mining company in Zimbabwe. The Corporation can, for instance, under Section 44 of the Act, set the maximum mineral stockpile that a person or company may own or control. It can also order the stockpile to be reduced by any amount it considers necessary and within any time period it considers appropriate. The Corporation may, at its own prerogative, demand information relating to the quantity, type, grade and location of any mineral owned, processed, controlled, smelted, refined,

[35] World Bank, *Accelerated Development in Sub-Saharan Africa: An Agenda for Action* (Washington The World Bank, 1981), 38.

[36] Created by the Minerals Marketing Corporation of Zimbabwe Act (No. 2 of 1982). All clauses listed are found in the Act.

produced or sold before or after the announcement of the Act (Section 45).
Finally, the Corporation can order that any existing contract be modified,
varied or terminated, according to its mandate (Section 52).

These provisions give the MMCZ control not only over what the
mining houses decide to market but over Zimbabwe's entire potential
production. The MMCZ is, therefore, more than a simple marketing
agency because it has the power to exert substantial control over the
whole industry. However, by letting the mining companies proceed
without government interference unless the MMCZ is unhappy with
company performance, the Act saves the government from the burden-
some, and possibly grossly inefficient, task of taking up large-scale
production itself.

Political Conflict

The MMCZ goes directly against the interests of the multinational
corporations. First of all, by removing the mining houses from direct
contact with the market, the MMCZ separates the companies from their
customers, and, therefore, makes their business decisions potentially
much more difficult. For instance, Zimbabwe can produce four different
types of ferroalloys (high carbon, low carbon, ferro-manganese and ferro-
silicon) in varying quantities, depending on what the market demands.
However, companies must obviously feel the pulse of the market if they
are to produce the right mix to meet demand. The companies feared that
if they lost control of marketing they would be unable to make the correct
production-mix decisions. The mining houses were also concerned that
the slowness of paperwork in a government bureaucracy would lead
them to lose sales in a market where competence and speed are demanded
by customers. Finally, the corporations feared, and were bewildered by,
the stockpile provisions of the Act which had the potential to affect their
production rates and thus leave every aspect of their business in the
control of a socialist government's parastatal. In an interview, one
mining executive called the stockpile provisions the 'fire and brimstone'
of the Act.

The idea of establishing a parastatal corporation to control marketing
was developed soon after Independence, and the corporation was a legal
reality by 1982 and in operation by 1983. The period during which the Bill
was formulated and drafted was short; correspondingly, the mining
companies had very little time to lobby against it. According to mining
company officials, there was considerable dismay in the industry because

they had almost no indication of what was being planned before they saw the draft, and were shocked to see that the government planned to take over all minerals marketing and to regulate production.

Initially, the companies tried to act independently to convince government either that the Bill should be scuttled or that the provisions of the Bill should be changed to make it more amenable to the mining industry. One of the mining houses, according to an industry official, even convinced Lord Soames, the colonial Governor who presided over the transition to Independence in late 1979 and early 1980, to lobby the Zimbabwe government because of the close ties that he had with the leadership. This strategy was a disaster, because the new Black government saw it as proof of the collusion between international capital and the British government to prevent it from enacting its socialist project. Although the fact that it was Lord Soames who was lobbying was never made public, Chris Ushewokunze, the Permanent Secretary in the Ministry of Mines, complained about countries whose companies mine in Zimbabwe: 'They didn't just want us to modify the plans — they wanted us to drop them altogether. . . . That wouldn't be right.'[37] After the Soames fiasco, Ian Smith volunteered to try to lobby the government on the marketing issue, but this offer was wisely turned down by the mining companies.

The companies then tried to act jointly to lobby the government through the Chamber of Mines. This was a somewhat unusual position for the Chamber because the companies usually acted on their own when they wished to pressure the government. The Chamber adopted a low-profile approach, saying very little publicly while trying to impress its view on government through meetings and reports. Foreign companies that were potential new investors also weighed in with more public complaints. One news article in late 1981 reported as follows:

Millions of dollars in new mining investment in Zimbabwe are likely to be lost if the draft Bill to establish a Minerals Marketing Corporation goes through Parliament in its present 'draconian' form. . . . Already two major Swedish mining organisations are preparing to withdraw from proposed mining development here if the clauses of the Bill recently published in a local newspaper remain unchanged. It is also believed that two other foreign mining groups, one from West Germany and the other from America, will similarly lose interest in mining in Zimbabwe if the Bill is approved as it stands.[38]

[37] *The Sunday Mail*, 8 Nov. 1981.   [38] *The Financial Gazette*, 18 Dec. 1981.

Despite these pressures, the companies' campaign was a failure; the government refused to listen to any of the suggestions that the mining houses put forward. The Chamber of Mines, for instance, argued that the mining industry should be allowed to appoint at least four members to the MMCZ board and that the whole provision regulating stockpiles should be dropped.[39] Both of these suggestions were rejected. Chamber of Mines' officials report that the President of the Chamber met with Permanent Secretary Ushewokunze and went through each clause of the Bill giving mining industry suggestions that, at the very least, would have made the Bill more favourable to the industry. These sources report that *every* suggestion made by the mining industry was rejected and that the very few changes in the draft Bill made before it became law had the effect of tightening it up and rendering it even more unfavourable to the industry. Mining company officials express doubt that the government was even interested in the mining industry's suggestions. Roy Lander, the former President of the Chamber of Mines, said: 'But we were not (with hindsight) being asked to suggest changes; that was the government's prerogative. The purpose of the consultation was to brief us and advise us.'[40]

Corporate Weakness and State Strength

Several factors contributed to the dramatic victory of the apparently weak Zimbabwean government over such a powerful set of multinationals. Firstly, while the mining interests are economically powerful, they suffer from real political disadvantages that stem directly from the industry's economic structure. Unlike the commercial farmers, the mining industry never developed a sophisticated lobbying organization. It was only after the mining companies failed individually in lobbying government that they tried to work collectively through the Chamber of Mines. One Chamber of Mines official said, 'Each of the Chamber's dozen members has its own method of lobbying and public-relations strategy; the approaches are totally different'. Correspondingly, the Chamber is not really a dedicated lobbying organization, particularly in comparison with the CFU. One former President of the Chamber of Mines said, 'The President of the CFU sits in his office and says: "Who should I lobby next?" We can't do that; we have jobs to do.' The industry's failure to develop an effective lobbying organization was aggravated after Inde-

---

[39] *The Herald*, 10 Dec. 1981.   [40] *The Herald*, 11 Feb. 1982.

pendence because the contacts it had cultivated in the Ministry of Mines and other relevant ministries disappeared when White civil servants left for the private sector or emigrated. In many cases these contacts were replaced by people who were hostile to foreign capital. Minister Nyagumbo and Permanent Secretary Ushewokunze were said to be particularly unsympathetic to corporate concerns.

Secondly, the mining houses are politically weak because they are foreign-owned, and, therefore, have little legitimacy in Zimbabwe. They are particularly vivid examples of the political symbolism discussed in Chapter 6 because they are so large and wealthy and because so many of them are either based in South Africa (as is Anglo American) or have strong connections with South African businesses. Mining houses understand that they are seen as illegitimate by the government, and this recognition has a direct impact on their lobbying and public-relations strategies. Unlike the Commercial Farmers Union, the Chamber of Mines never says how big its industry is or how many people it employs, because big foreign enterprises are seen as threatening in Zimbabwe. The mining companies, therefore, have to keep a very low profile. For instance, one mining company official noted that his approach to lobbying government often begins by his asking himself, 'How do I convince people that I am a human being and also head of a multinational company?' The mining industry's great strength — the presence of a few, foreign-owned companies in a strategic sector of the economy — is also its greatest political weakness.

The mining industry also could not, as the commercial farmers successfully did in the agricultural producer price-setting process, align with Black peasants in order to lessen the government's mistrust of their motives. While the government is committed to developing mining cooperatives (primarily in chrome), there is simply no way that these fledgling Black miners can become significant enough to aid the mining companies in the way that 800 000 peasant families help the CFU in its search for higher prices. That the multinational companies turned first to a British Lord while the White farmers were forming alliances with the Black farmers demonstrated the domestic weakness of the mining companies when trying to lobby government.

The government's consideration and implementation of the MMCZ also came at a time when mining companies were facing grim economic prospects, and their condition may have also weakened their position with the government. The low base-metal prices of the early 1980s, and the large wage increases imposed by the government in 1980 and 1981,[41] dramatically squeezed mining company finances. Mining profits dropped from $86 million in 1980 to $40 million in 1981, when the return on capital investment was a poor 4 per cent.[42] Many said that the mining industry was suffering from the worst crisis in its history. Several companies, including Zimbabwe Alloys (Anglo American's ferrochrome producer) and Rio Tinto Zinc, had to apply for government aid to keep their mines operating. The government, in order to forestall mine closures which would drastically increase unemployment, responded by making $50 million dollars available for the economic support of the mining companies.[43] Obviously, there was only so much the companies could do in opposing the new marketing agency at the same time that they were in the process of asking the government to aid their ailing industry.

However, the complete explanation as to why the government managed to create the MMCZ does not reside only in the mining companies' political weakness. Although weak in manpower and expertise, the government did have the juridical power that came with its victory in the liberation struggle; the Blacks inherited a state that had a long history of regulating the mining industry. Although many key Ministry of Mines personnel left, the new government inherited the procedures, controls and, perhaps most importantly, the accepted idea that it was quite normal for the state to regulate the mining industry. Although the MMCZ is definitely a state intervention of distinctly greater magnitude than previous state interventions, it was not altogether unlike them, particularly that during UDI which required to minerals be sold to UNIVEX. Minister Nyagumbo noted: 'For the second time therefore, mineral producers in partnership with the state will be able to fight international marketing problems together, in order to gain maximum advantage for Zimbabwe.'[44]

The government was also able to compensate for its weakness by borrowing from the experience of other countries. Ministry of Mines officials admitted that they 'drew quite a lot from the lessons of other countries'. Zambia, for instance, had established a parastatal in the mid-1970s to market all its minerals, the Metal Marketing Corporation of

---

[41] See Chapter 9.   [42] *The Herald*, 22 May 1982.

[43] *The Herald*, 1 June and 2 Aug. 1982.

[44] Zimbabwe, *Parliamentary Debates, House of Assembly. Second Session, First Parliament comprising Periods from 8th September, 1981 to 2nd October, 1981, 19th January, 1982 to 10th February, 1982*, IV, 21 Jan. 1982, 1282.

Zambia (MEMACO), and Zimbabwe had extensive knowledge of this parastatal because the Permanent Secretary in the Ministry of Mines, Chris Ushewokunze, had been a lecturer in the Department of Law at the University of Zambia and had studied the mining industry there. Ushewokunze, in fact, thanked MEMACO in the first annual report of the MMCZ for the assistance it had provided him when Zimbabwe's marketing corporation was being set up.[45]

Partly as a result of this outside help, even mining industry officials were able to note that 'mining policy has been singularly straightforward'. For instance, the MMCZ Bill was much better prepared than most government legislation. A mining company official commented upon 'the sheer legal quality of the Bill. It was comprehensive legal drafting at a time when government drafting was pretty poor. It was done in a way that was watertight.' Demonstrating a high level of competence and confidence, Ministry of Mines officials were actually able to write the whole Bill in house. One official said in an interview that

when we [the Ministry of Mines] went to the legal draftsmen we had the entire framework of the Bill. Everything was done in the Ministry. Some Ministries just send vague ideas to Justice [the Ministry of Justice, Legal and Parliamentary Affairs] but the Ministry of Mines knew what it wanted.

The government's competence in this area can also be gauged from the fact that it moved quickly on minerals marketing when delay has characterized so many other government initiatives in the post-Independence era. For instance, while it took less than three years to establish the state marketing agency, the new regime allowed almost seven years to pass before it institutionalized the wage-setting process.[46]

The government's preference for control of the industry, even if it meant sacrificing new investment, also made irrelevant many forms of leverage that the companies usually possessed. For instance, the MMCZ probably did deter some mining houses from coming to Zimbabwe with potentially large investments; however, this loss was not seen to be important by the new socialist government, which was already suspicious of foreign investment and was unsure whether it wanted further economic development of the mining sector if it meant even greater

[45] Minerals Marketing Corporation of Zimbabwe, *Annual Report 1983* (Harare, The Corporation, 1984), 3.

[46] See Chapter 9.

dependence on international capital. In response to White critics who complained that the MMCZ would stop new investment, for instance, Minister Nyagumbo said in Parliament:

> If it is true . . . that there is a big company contemplating withdrawal from Zimbabwe because of the establishment of the Minerals Marketing Corporation then, Mr Speaker, Government is on the correct course. The rip-off must end. The company concerned must be aware that Government is at last catching up with their unfair profiteering in mineral sales at the expense of this country.[47]

Just as the mining companies' overall economic position could not be translated into political power, the threats of new companies not to invest were politically irrelevant to a new socialist government with priorities other than simply fostering economic growth.

Implementation of the MMCZ and Reconciliation

The creation of the MMCZ by Act of Parliament did not automatically guarantee the state's effective participation in the mining industry: once the MMCZ started operations, an efficient marketing organization still had to be established. Many officials acknowledge that the most important problem the government faced when implementing the MMCZ was to regain the co-operation of the mining industry. This co-operation was essential, because the Ministry of Mines realized that it would have to borrow heavily from mining company expertise and personnel in order to market the commodities effectively. The government also knew that the effort to establish an effective marketing corporation would be much more difficult if the mining companies actively engaged in obstructing the parastatal.

In order to defuse tensions between the government and the embittered mining industry, Minister of Mines Nyagumbo appointed Mark Rule as the first General Manager of the MMCZ. Rule, a White, was an expert in minerals marketing and was well known to the mining industry because he was managing director of UNIVEX during the UDI years and was the Smith regime's chief ferrochrome 'sanctions buster'. His appointment was welcomed in the mining industry because it was expected that, given his expertise and experience, he would be able to run a competent marketing organization.

---

[47] Zimbabwe, *Parliamentary Debates, House of Assembly. Second Session, First Parliament comprising Periods from 8th September, 1981 to 2nd October, 1981, 19th January, 1982 to 10th February, 1982,* IV, 26 Jan. 1982, 1382.

Rule succeeded in gaining the trust and co-operation of the mining industry. Mining company officials report that he acted 'incredibly responsibly' in getting the mining industry to work with the MMCZ. To gain this co-operation while preserving the its basic mission, the MMCZ developed a sophisticated policy of trying to foster co-operation, exerting its authority only when it knew that it could enforce it. One MMCZ official explained in an interview that

> the Corporation tried to institute the business of co-operation by consent not authority. . . . We didn't want to give an order when our organization was young only to have it resented and sabotaged. We realize that we have to live with these people [the mining companies]. Rather than confrontation we have to start bent but not be allowed to bend. We cannot be seen to lose authority. MMCZ has never gone back on authority. Until the Corporation got up to speed it would not use authority that could not be enforced.

For instance, Rule and the Ministry of Mines knew that they would not have the capability to market all of Zimbabwe's mineral production competently at once. Therefore, they started out by marketing only a few products through the MMCZ itself, and used the provisions of the MMCZ Act (Sect. 37(1)(a)(iii)) which allowed private companies to sell minerals as long as those sales were authorized by the MMCZ. This practice enabled the MMCZ to take over the marketing as it gained confidence, rather than having to be responsible for marketing a large share of Zimbabwe's exports immediately. Rule also staffed the MMCZ with marketing personnel from many of the major mining houses, and this also boosted co-operation with the industry. For instance, the first Deputy General Manager of the MMCZ, Tobias Chizengeni, was formerly employed by Anglo American, and most of the staff of the major asbestos marketing company were moved *en masse* to the MMCZ. As the marketing corporation consolidated its staff's expertise and gained more experience, it took over the direct selling of more and more commodities. Four years after the MMCZ began operations, Ministry of Mines officials reported that almost no sales were handled by the companies themselves because the MMCZ acted as the agent for almost all of Zimbabwe's mineral production.

Since the MMCZ has acted responsibly, and because they lacked alternatives, the mining companies have co-operated with the MMCZ. Marketing experts from the parastatal report, for instance, that they have had to use the Act's legal enforcement provisions only twice — just one of them in an important case — because mining companies have voluntarily decided to act in accordance with MMCZ promulgations. The heads of mining companies still do not like the MMCZ — indeed, they can become quite agitated when discussing it — but they have found that they can live with it and view it only as, in the words of one company president, 'another tax, another obstacle to business'.

The MMCZ's operations have gone relatively smoothly, but export revenue has not noticeably increased: government and MMCZ officials now admit that they overestimated the amount of transfer pricing. The lack of transfer pricing was undoubtedly due to the strong exchange-control regime imposed by the Rhodesian government during UDI that was continued by the new government, and perhaps also to the fact that local residents, as opposed to expatriates, were managing the mining companies. The lack of windfall profits points to the danger of assertions, such as those made by Seidman, that transfer-pricing experiences can be extrapolated from one country to another without regard to a nation's history or differences in its administrative structure.

Conclusion

The Zimbabwe government was structurally autonomous in the conflict over the marketing of minerals. It designed the political rules governing future mineral policy, and it did not allow the mining houses to have any significant influence over the decision-making process that created the MMCZ. The government was also situationally autonomous, because the sophisticated tactics that it followed, and the nature of mining itself, prevented the multinationals from having any significant influence on the day-to-day decisions of the MMCZ.

The institutional weaknesses and strengths of the Zimbabwean state must be understood in order to explain why it prevailed in the minerals marketing area. The state was too weak, especially in terms of funds and personnel, to consider nationalization seriously. There were, however, several strengths which the new government capitalized on. Firstly, the state had the juridical power to create a legal monopoly to buy all of Zimbabwe's minerals and sell them on the world market. This organization could be created by legal fiat, and its mission was simple to enforce because mineral exports cannot leave the country except in bulky shipments on only a few rail lines that are already examined by Customs officials enforcing Zimbabwe's exchange-control regulations. The relative ease with which the government was able to enforce the new parastatal's mission is significant, because, as Thomas J. Biersteker has noted, 'a state's capacity to implement policy is at least as important as (and possibly more important than) its capacity to formulate policy'.[48]

The level at which policy decisions were made within the government was also an important factor in the successful creation of the MMCZ. Almost all the planning for the MMCZ was done in the Ministry of Mines, much of it by Permanent Secretary Ushewokunze himself. There was, therefore, no advance warning to the mining companies as to what the government was planning, because information did not (as it so often does in Zimbabwe) leak from the lower ranks of the civil service. Correspondingly, when the mining companies were trying to pressure the government, their efforts could have made a difference only if they had been able to convince two people: Permanent Secretary Ushewokunze and, perhaps to a lesser extent, Minister Nyagumbo. There were no other parts of the institutional structure that the mining companies could have turned to for a more favourable ruling in the way that the squatters were so successfully able to do. Since the Permanent Secretary and the Minister were both committed to the concept of the MMCZ — even to the point that the prospect of new investments being curtailed did not matter — efforts by mining companies to change the government's plans were futile.

The state was situationally autonomous because it had other institutional strengths that were realized as a result of the sophisticated tactics adopted by top government officials. In the first place, the government rejected simple racial politics and named a White man as the parastatal's first General Manager. Mark Rule brought with him a vast knowledge of minerals marketing and of the practices of multinational corporations, which freed the government from relying on companies in the formulation of the MMCZ's policies (although it did attract personnel from the mining companies). The government also adopted a strategy in the implementation of the MMCZ which maximized its strengths even though the Corporation itself was quite weak. The choice of these tactics, and the resulting strength of the state, was not inevitable, as poor policy-making in other African states clearly demonstrates. State strength is, therefore, not solely a given, depending on static advantages in personnel and organizational structures, but is plainly reliant on the wisdom of government officials in using the resources that are available to them.

The nature of the issue-area, involving basically a one-time decision, also worked to the government's advantage. The government was able to

---

[48] Biersteker, *Multinationals, the State and Control of the Nigerian Economy*, 296.

use shock tactics on the unsuspecting corporations, and enacted the MMCZ legislation while the corporations, with no history of working together, were still trying to regroup and lobby through the Chamber of Mines.[49] If the decision-making process had been repetitive, then there might have been the possibility that the mining companies, who are among the most politically sophisticated corporations in the world, would have developed better strategies to influence the government. The commercial farmers have certainly benefited from the iterated nature of agricultural producer price-setting decisions, as they have gradually learned to work with peasant farmer groups in order to increase their legitimacy in the eyes of government; this opportunity was not available to the mining corporations.

Finally, the nature of the mining houses as an interest group must be examined if government decisions in the minerals marketing area are to be understood. The industry was unable to convert its economic power into corresponding political power. Indeed, the very factors which caused the mining industry to be economically powerful — the dominance of a few, large foreign firms in a strategic sector of the economy — prevented it from developing an effective lobbying organization during White rule and, once the Black government took over every aspect of the mining industry's economic structure, worked against it. The mining industry's political weakness was particularly important, because it would have taken a very powerful lobbying organization to dissuade government from adopting a policy that derived from its juridical power.

Locus of Decision-making

The creation of the Minerals Marketing Corporation can be seen as an effort by the government to shift the responsibility for decision-making from the White-dominated mining sector to a parastatal.

Within the government itself, the locus of decision-making was clearly at the level of the Permanent Secretary. Actors throughout government and private industry assigned primary credit (or blame) for the MMCZ to Ushewokunze. The rest of the civil service did not seem involved, and part of it, especially the Reserve Bank, was distrusted by the new leadership because of the number of Whites who still held important positions. The ministers did not have a primary role in the formation of the MMCZ

---

[49] On the uses of 'blitzkrieg' tactics, see S. P. Huntington, *Political Order in Changing Societies* (New Haven, Yale Univ. Press, 1968), 346.

because of the technical knowledge required. For the same reason, no one even indicated that ZANU(PF) was significantly involved in the decision-making leading up to the creation of the MMCZ. In this area the government was also proceeding in a manner favoured by the party, so there was little need for the party to become involved in the actual decision-making process.

Relations between the government and the mining companies have come almost full circle in Zimbabwe. Ninety years ago the country was administered by a multinational mining company, the BSA Company, which set the pattern for the oppression of Blacks. Today, a Black government administers marketing policy for the multinational mining companies. The case of the Minerals Marketing Corporation clearly demonstrates that a careful examination of political conflicts is necessary in order to trace the reasons for eventual outcomes, rather than a simple assumption that the economically strong will automatically become the politically powerful.

Chapter Eight

Ethnic and Class Claims on Health Services

The increased provision of health care by the new government of Zimbabwe has been one of the most visible fruits of the liberation struggle, and the new regime's health programme has entailed a massive increase in funds devoted to medical care. In this chapter, I will examine demands for health services by two groups and the government's response to those requests. I first investigate government provision of rural health centres (clinics) to see whether there is a discernible bias in the distribution of these political goods along regional or ethnic lines, and then I examine the effort to provide health care for Zimbabwe's least organized and most exploited group: commercial farm-workers and their families.

Inequalities in Health Care

The field of health care dramatically illustrates the inequalities that emerged during Rhodesia's period of economic development. By the 1970s the Whites had developed a modern health-care system for themselves with large, capital-intensive hospitals that had a curative focus. John Gilmurray, Roger Riddell and David Sanders estimated that the doctor–patient ratio for the 230 000 White Rhodesians was 1 : 830 in the late 1970s, which put level of medical care for the settler population at the general level of that available in developed Western countries.[1] There was one hospital bed for every 219 Whites, and these hospitals, especially in the urban areas, had much of the same sophisticated equipment commonly found in Western hospitals.[2] Approximately $144 per year was spent on health care for each White.[3]

The contrasts between the sophisticated medical-care system for

---

[1] J. Gilmurray et al., The Struggle for Health (Gwelo, Mambo Press, 1979), 38.

[2] Ibid., 36.

[3] Zimbabwe, Planning for Equity in Health: A Sectoral Review and Policy Statement (Harare, Ministry of Health, 1984), 30.

Whites and the services available to the Black population, especially the vast majority who lived in the rural areas, were enormous. For instance, it was estimated that there was only one doctor for 50 000 to 100 000 people in the rural areas; there was only one hospital bed for 525 Blacks and the facilities were of poor quality and overcrowded.[4] One provincial health official noted in an interview that, in contrast to the well-organized medical system for Whites,

before Independence, there was no administrative framework for delivering services. The PMOH [Provincial Medical Officer of Health] was responsible for only provincial [i.e. province-wide] programmes. There was no organizational structure. The PMOH was really only responsible for preventative programmes, nothing else.

Only $31 was spent on health care for each urban Black and only $4 was spent on the care of each person in the rural areas.[5]

The disparity in health services, compounded by the general inequalities of Rhodesia's socio-economic system, had a direct impact on the kind of diseases the two population groups suffered from and on their life expectancy. Before Independence, the crude White death rate was 8,2 per 1 000 (it was 11,2 per 1 000 in Britain) and the infant-mortality rate was 17 per 1 000 live births (compared to 16 per 1 000 for Britain).[6] According to one observer, 'the disease pattern of the [White] population [was] almost identical to that seen in industrialized societies with degenerative and stress diseases and cancer accounting for the bulk'.[7]

In contrast, Blacks in Rhodesia had the health profile typical of citizens in a Third World country. It was estimated in the late 1970s, for instance, that the infant-mortality rate for rural Blacks was between 120 and 220 per 1 000 live births.[8] Africans suffered mainly from malnutrition, air-borne diseases such as measles and tuberculosis, water-borne ailments such as trachoma, and vector-borne diseases including malaria and bilharzia.[9]

[4] Gilmurray et al., The Struggle for Health, 36–7.

[5] Zimbabwe, Planning for Equity in Health, 30.

[6] Gilmurray et al., The Struggle for Health, 15.

[7] D. Sanders, 'A study of health services in Zimbabwe', in United Nations Conference on Trade and Development, Zimbabwe: Towards a New Order: An Economic and Social Survey: Working Papers (n.p., United Nations, UNDP/UNCTAD Project PAF/78/010, 2 vols., 1980), II, 408.

[8] Gilmurray et al., The Struggle for Health, 22.

[9] Ibid., 24–9.

Demand and Distribution of Rural Health Centres

At Independence the government was committed to establishing a new health system whose top priority was increasing the availability of medical care, with a large preventive element, to Blacks in the rural areas. An integral element of this programme is the rural health centre, or clinic, because it is 'the first point of contact between the people and the formal health sector'.[10] According to the Ministry of Health,

the Rural Health Centres provide basic but comprehensive promotive, preventative, curative and rehabilitative care . . . delivery of uncomplicated births, child spacing, child health and nutrition, routine immunizations for children and anti-tetanus immunizations for women of child-bearing age, environmental sanitation, especially in relation to small-scale water supplies and excreta disposal systems, control of communicable diseases, other special problems, including mental illness, eye diseases and physical and mental handicap, general curative care, including basic dentistry. Health and nutrition education form a routine part of all the above activities.[11]

Ideally, the rural health centres will be staffed by two medical assistants (one of whom is a maternity assistant) and a health assistant who specializes in promoting community awareness about safe water and sanitation practices. The centres are designed to serve a catchment population of approximately ten thousand people who should be within eight kilometres' walking-distance of the centre.[12]

Government studies indicate that the catchment and distance requirements of the rural health centre programme necessitates the building of 316 new centres and the upgrading or reconstruction of approximately 160 others in order to reach the full complement of 766. By the end of fiscal year 1985, approximately 210 new centres had been constructed at a cost of $17,6 million.[13] The rural health centre programme is, therefore, an ideal policy to investigate for ethnic bias because the new government will have had to make a large number of allocation decisions since Independence.

Ethnicity in Zimbabwe

Much speculation, but little thorough work, has been given to ethnicity in Zimbabwe and to how ethnic claims affect government operations. Part of the reason for the absence of a systematic understanding of ethnic

---

[10] Zimbabwe, *Zimbabwe 'Health for All' Action Plan* (Harare, Ministry of Health, 1985), 8.
[11] Ibid., 164–5.   [12] Ibid., 9 and 166.   [13] Ibid., 186.

dynamics in Zimbabwe is due to the remarkably superficial coverage of the country by Western journalists.[14] However, part also derives from a reluctance by many who are sympathetic to the new government even to admit to the existence of, much less analyse, ethnic divisions in an avowedly socialist country.[15] Zimbabwe is divided into several different communities that vary tremendously in the strength of their ethnic identification. The Shona–Ndebele conflict has always been the most public in Zimbabwe because of the dramatic split in the nationalist lines during the liberation struggle; this split was carried into independent Zimbabwe. Table XVI shows that in the 1980 elections ZANU(PF) was by the far the most popular party in the Shona areas but received very few votes in the predominantly Ndebele provinces of Matabeleland North and Matabeleland South. Although there was initially a unified government of ZANU(PF) and PF-ZAPU, the PF-ZAPU office-holders were soon forced to relinquish power when Prime Minister Mugabe charged that PF-ZAPU was supporting dissidents who were wreaking havoc in Matabeleland. Communal tensions increased in 1982 when the government sent the Army's 5th Brigade into Matabeleland in order to apply a military solution to the dissident problem. The 5th Brigade was responsible for grievous human-rights violations, including imprisonment without trial, torture and rape. The Army was also responsible for numerous civilian deaths, and whole areas of Matabeleland were reported to be deserted because so many people had fled from government troops.[16] The parties formally united in 1987, but the ethnic split is still a potentially important question in distributional issues.

The 5th Brigade's intervention left the Ndebele population wounded but no more likely to support the Shona-dominated ZANU(PF). In the

[14] For instance, Nick Davies claims that the Shona–Ndebele conflicts 'go back through thousands of years of tribal rivalry in which the Ndebele in the south oppressed the weaker Shona . . .', *The Guardian*, 11 Mar. 1983. Actually, the Ndebele did not even arrive in what is now Zimbabwe until the nineteenth century, and the concept of the Shona is even more recent; see T. Ranger, *The Invention of Tribalism in Zimbabwe* (Gweru, Mambo Press, 1985).

[15] Note, for instance, the almost complete absence of the ethnic issue from Stoneman (ed.), *Zimbabwe's Prospects*.

[16] Information on human-rights violations in Matabeleland is provided in Lawyers Committee for Human Rights, *Zimbabwe: Wages of War* (New York, The Committee, 1986), and R. Hodder-Williams, *Conflict in Zimbabwe: The Matabeleland Problem* (London, Institute for the Study of Conflict, Conflict Studies 151, 1984). An optimistic portrayal of Matabeleland after the unity accord was signed in 1988 can be found in T. Ranger, 'Matabeleland now', *African Affairs* (1989), LXXXVIII, 161–74.

1985 elections, as Table XVI also shows, although ZANU(PF) won even more convincingly in every other area of the country, it was unable to make significant inroads in Matabeleland where PF-ZAPU won every parliamentary seat (the only seats it won at all in the election). Careful examination of the Table shows that ZANU(PF) increased its meagre support in Matabeleland in 1985 by attracting votes from minor parties

Table XVI

1980 AND 1985 ELECTION RESULTS BY PROVINCE

| | *Percentage of votes* | | | |
| | 1980 | | 1985 | |
Province	ZANU(PF)	PF-ZAPU	ZANU(PF)	PF-ZAPU
Manicaland	84,1	1,6	88,6	1,4
Mashonaland Central	83,8	2,3	98,3	0,8
Mashonaland East	80,5	4,6	91,8	2,9
Mashonaland West *	72,0	13,4	94,4	3,4
Masvingo	87,3	1,9	97,9	1,7
Midlands	59,7	27,1	82,9	14,8
Matabeleland North	10,0	79,1	15,1	82,6
Matabeleland South	6,9	86,4	12,9	86,6

* Does not include results for Kariba.

The percentages do not add up to 100 because of votes for minor parties.

Source: The Herald, 9 July 1985.

rather than from PF-ZAPU. In fact, the PF-ZAPU vote *increased* in both Matabeleland provinces. After the vote, in a reflection of the fundamental communal split that was both symbolized and aggravated by the election, many Ndebele people in urban areas throughout the country were attacked by members of the ZANU(PF) Women's League and had their property destroyed.[17]

The ethnic split between the Shona and the Ndebele is aggravated by the fact that the division coincides with regional and administrative boundaries. Most of the Ndebele population is contained in two provinces, Matabeleland North and Matabeleland South, and there are very few significant Ndebele communities outside these two provinces. The

[17] *The Herald,* 9 July 1985.

coincidence between administrative and ethnic boundaries means that allocation decisions made on a regional basis automatically have an ethnic component, because all actors are likely to perceive provincial distributions in ethnic terms. Ethnicity in Zimbabwe is, therefore, not simply an anachronistic phenomenon surviving from historical conflicts but a potentially very real element of the political game, because leaders who gather ethnic support may be able to influence national allocation decisions.

However, the Shona–Ndebele split is not the only salient communal division in Zimbabwe. There are also significant intra-Shona conflicts that have appeared occasionally in the nationalist movement and in independent Zimbabwe. The intra-Shona splits are present because the Shona never were one community. Indeed, the idea of 'Shonaness' is a new one dating only from the last century.[18] The Shona are composed of a number of distinct communities spread across Zimbabwe who speak a more or less mutually intelligible language. The most important of the Shona communities are the Manyika in the Eastern region of the country, the Zezuru in the area around Harare, and the Karanga in the south of the country centered around Masvingo.

There have been repeated, though seldom discussed, incidents of intra-Shona conflict in the operation and staffing of the government. Exercises in ethnic arithmetic abound; it was, for instance, fairly clear that the portfolios in the first ZANU(PF) Cabinet were carefully balanced among the major Shona groups.[19] Occasionally, intra-Shona conflicts come out into the open. For instance, during the Parliamentary debate on corruption in the National Railways of Zimbabwe, the then Minister of Transport, Herbert Ushewokunze, said:

What you saw unfolding here was the thin edge of the wedge of a grand strategy by a given region of Zimbabwe which prides itself in being the chosen tribal grouping of this country . . . these people can kill. They have killed before, both inside the country as part of the former regime and outside the country, acting as agents of imperialism. One does not want to sound unrealistic, but if this were not so, Herbert Chitepo and others would be with us today.[20]

[18] Beach, War and Politics in Zimbabwe 1840–1900, 14–15.

[19] X. Smiley, 'Zimbabwe, Southern Africa and the rise of Robert Mugabe', Foreign Affairs (1980), LVIII, 1075.

[20] Zimbabwe. Parliamentary Debates, House of Assembly. First Session, Second Parliament comprising Periods from 30th September, 1985 to 11th December, 1985, 21st January, 1986 to 25th April, 1986, XXII, 9 Apr. 1986, 1994–6. He was referring to the Karanga.

Zimbabwe's regional and administrative boundaries also aggravate intra-Shona conflicts because some of the provinces are associated with one sub-group or another. Thus, Manicaland Province is the home of the Manyika, Masvingo Province is the home of the Karanga and, to a much lesser extent, Mashonaland West, Mashonaland Central and Mashonaland East are identified with the Zezuru. (The identification of the Zezuru with one particular province is not as strong because they are distributed throughout three provinces and because minor groups, such as the Korekore, also live in these provinces.)[21] Once again, because of the coincidence between ethnic and administrative boundaries, there is a clear incentive for leaders and communities to stress ethnic allegiances in the hope that by mobilizing support around communal identities they will be able to have more leverage when bargaining with the government.

Siting Procedures for Rural Health Centres

Within the context of an ethnically charged environment, the stated procedure for locating rural health centres has been clearly established. In each province, district health officials submit their priorities for rural health centre sites to the Provincial Medical Director (PMD). The district officials have in turn received these site selections from sub-district officials who constitute the Village Development Committees (VIDCOs) that are supposed to cover each village (about 100 families) and from the Ward Development Committees (WADCOs) that consist of several VIDCOs.[22] The PMD compares the needs of each of the districts and then sets province-wide priorities.[23] The PMD's decisions are supposed to be based on catchment area, walking-distance, and technical criteria. The most important of these technical specifications are the availability of water (the Ministry will not build a centre unless it has a guaranteed potable water supply) and easy access to a road so that the health centre can be restocked with medical supplies. The Ministry of Health's head office in Harare receives the PMD's requests and allocates health centres to each province according to funds made available by the Treasury.

---

[21] M. F. C. Bourdillon, *The Shona Peoples* (Gweru, Mambo Press, 2nd edn., 1982), 16–18 and 346–7.

[22] The local-government schemes are described in Zimbabwe, *Delineation of Village and Ward Development Committees in District Council Areas of Zimbabwe* (Harare, Ministry of Local Government and Town Planning, 1985), 1.

[23] Zimbabwe, 'Rural Health Centres (Clinics) — Procedure for the Selection of New Sites' (Harare, Ministry of Health, 1986, mimeo.), 1–2.

Health officials report substantial pressure from communities for these centres. This is hardly surprising, given the impact that health centres can make in an area. Indeed, only after visiting a centre and seeing sick people who have walked miles for treatment can one appreciate the importance of the provision of basic health care. Symbolically, the centres are also exceptionally important because they are one of the most significant benefits of the achievement of Independence and one of the clearest indications in the rural areas that there has been a change in regimes. A Provincial Health Service Administrator (an official in the PMD's office) in Mashonaland echoed the comments of many officials by noting that 'the siting of rural health centres is very controversial in the communities. Everyone wants a centre in their village.' Similarly, a Masvingo official said: 'Everyone would like a centre; people want a centre in every village. The strong councillors try to get their centres near their homes.'

Pressure for new centres is often brought to bear in the name of the ruling party, ZANU(PF). Indeed, officials report that at the local level of government — the VIDCO and WADCO levels — it is impossible to differentiate between the party and the government. One Mashonaland West health official said: 'the WADCOs and VIDCOs tend to be party structures'. In Matabeleland, before the unification of ZANU(PF) and PF-ZAPU in 1987, these Committees were similarly identified, and health officials there report considerable distrust of local-government structures because the Ndebele populations feared that the VIDCO and WADCO structures were simply another way for ZANU(PF) to extend its authority.

Biases in the Distribution of Rural Health Centres

The key question when examining the importance of ethnic influence in health care is: Has there has been a bias in the distribution of new centres? Table XVII displays the number of health centres per 100 000 people in each province for 1980 and for mid-1985. However, the data also include figures for centres under construction in each province, so the display is actually a realistic portrayal of health-service delivery projected into the future.

The data show that the new Zimbabwe government inherited a highly unequal health-care system in 1980. Before 1980, there had been exceptionally little planning and co-ordination on a national scale for health services aimed primarily at rural Blacks. Many centres from the pre-1980 era owe their existence solely to the initiative and personal interest of local officials such as District Commissioners and missionaries. If government and mission personnel were interested in health care, then some facilities might be provided. However, if an area did not have such committed White officials, then even the most basic facilities might be lacking. It should be noted that, owing to the limited resources available for health care for Blacks, it would have been extremely unlikely that even those

Table XVII

RURAL HEALTH CENTRES IN 1980 AND 1985 *

Province	Centres per 100 000 people		Percentage increase
	1980	1985	1980–1985
Manicaland	12,29	16,87	37,3
Mashonaland Central	7,64	13,38	75,1
Mashonaland East	12,59	19,28	53,1
Mashonaland West	9,54	14,77	54,8
Masvingo	7,71	12,17	57,8
Midlands	10,52	15,09	43,4
Matabeleland North	5,98	11,87	98,5
Matabeleland South	9,68	13,83	42,9
Zimbabwe	9,49	14,66	57,9

* The Table covers a total of 51 districts. Harare and Bulawayo districts were excluded because they are urban and, therefore, have unusual concentrations of centres. One district in Mashonaland West could not be included owing to border changes between 1980 and 1985. Bubi District in Matabeleland North was also excluded as an outlier; in 1985, Bubi had 120 centres per 100 000 people, while the rest of the province averaged only 12.

Sources: Ministry of Health, 'The Health Institutions of Zimbabwe' (Harare, The Ministry, 1985, mimeo.), and Zimbabwe, *Main Demographic Features of the Population of Zimbabwe* (Harare, Central Statistical Office, 1985), 62–77.

areas where local authorities were concerned with health-service delivery would have received adequate facilities.

The 1985 column in Table XVII presents a radically changed situation. An analysis of the statistics shows that the government, while increasing the total level of services by 58 per cent on a national basis, managed to improve the balance in the provision of centres by favouring those provinces that had previously been discriminated against. For instance, Matabeleland North, which was the least well-served province in 1980, experienced the largest increase (98,5 per cent) between 1980 and 1985. Similarly, Mashonaland Central, the province ranking seventh out of eight in the number of centres available in 1980, received the second largest increase (75,1 per cent) during this period.

Given the unambiguous move toward equality, it is hard to detect any evidence of an ethnic bias in the distribution of rural health centres. It is true that Matabeleland South did not do particularly well in the provision of Centres; this province experienced a percentage increase below the national average even though the number of its centres was lower than the national average for 1985. However, Ministry of Health officials argue that the extremely low population density of this area (it is the least densely populated province in Zimbabwe, with only 7,8 people per km² compared with a national average of 19,3)[24] makes it impossible to site static centres in the same manner as in the rest of the country because it is often impossible to achieve the needed catchment populations around a fixed centre. Therefore, other solutions, such as mobile clinics to service the highly dispersed population, must be found. However, the massive increase in services experienced by Matabeleland North makes it impossible to argue that the Ndebele areas have been discriminated against in the provision of health services.

It is also extremely difficult to argue that any of the identifiable Shona sub-communities have been discriminated for or against in the government's allocation of centres. The Manyika in Manicaland experienced the lowest increase (37,3 per cent), but the number of centres already in this area was well above the national average. The Karanga in Masvingo have fewer centres than the national average for both 1980 and 1985, but since this province experienced an increase that was slightly above the national average, it would be difficult to find a bias. The Zezuru in Mashonaland Central received a large increase, but their region had been poorly served before, and this increase was certainly justified in equity terms. The statistics for Mashonaland West are just about at the national average and it received an increase in centres just below the national average. Mashonaland East also received a significant increase in services, although the number of centres in the province was already well above the national average. However, the Mashonaland East increase was only equal to the national average, and the less-definable Zezuru presence in this province once again makes it extremely difficult to attribute the allocation of centres to ethnic favouritism. Mashonaland East's statistics are also somewhat misleading, because even though the province had the highest

[24] Zimbabwe, *Main Demographic Features of the Population of Zimbabwe*, 43.

number of centres in 1980 (12,59 per cent), one district, Mutoko, had only two centres per 100 000 people. In five years the government managed to increase the availability of centres in Mutoko by 750 per cent to 15 per 100 000. The increase in Mutoko, one of six districts in Mashonaland East, was responsible for 48 per cent of the total increase for the province.

Explaining the Lack of Bias

Two factors are important in explaining the lack of bias in a political good as physically and symbolically important as health centres in a country where many have focused on ethnic factions as crucial actors in the political game. Firstly, the government was insulated from societal pressures because it used its structural autonomy — no one even questioned that the government alone would design the health-care system — to establish a decentralized decision-making process that allows provincial officials almost complete control over siting decisions. One PMD said in an interview, 'I've had pressure from politicians who want rural health centres built in their area, but in the end the PMD has the ultimate say'. A Mashonaland PMD confirmed this view and said that head office approves PMD decisions 'automatically' because it is the PMD who has the knowledge of the area in which the centre will be built. Civil servants in the Ministry of Health's head office confirm that the primacy of the PMD is not just theory. One official noted in an interview that

the PMD has a lot of muscle because the system has been decentralized. It is up to him and his team to determine where and how many centres to build. In the vast majority of cases we [in head office] just submit rural health centre requests to Treasury. Usually it is more a question of logistics — if we have supplies and engineers — as to when a centre actually gets built.

While PMDs uniformly complain that there has not been enough decentralization, it is clear that the selection of sites for rural health centres has been effectively devolved to the provincial level.

The decentralized decision-making process limits, if not eliminates, the possibility of significant ethnic influence on decisions about the distribution of centres. The devolution of power means that essentially all of the conflict for the political goods being allocated by the government rests at the provincial level, among each ethnic community, rather than at the national level, between ethnic communities. Ndebele compete against Ndebele for health centres at the Matabeleland North or Matabeleland South provincial office rather than against Shona in the head office of the

Ministry of Health. Thus, ethnic allegiances are not relevant in health care because the decision-making structure reduces the importance of these identities to leaders and communities whose primary concern is to convince the government to provide facilities for their village or area.

The same dynamics confront those who try to use ZANU(PF) to lobby health officials. Pressure to allocate heath centres is put on the provincial health bureaucracy by local-level party officials. However, because it is difficult for national officials to intervene in order to gain decisions favourable to a particular area, these demands are not transferred up the government bureaucracy. For instance, provincial medical officials report that local officials have at times attempted an 'end run' by trying to by-pass and go directly to the Ministry's head office with their requests for centres. This has not been a successful strategy. One PMD said: 'People have tried end runs on PMD decisions to head office; however, head office usually tells PMDs what is going on. If you are monitoring your district closely, you usually know ahead of time what is happening.' Similarly, the Ndebele population has not really been disadvantaged in the distribution of centres because ZANU(PF) is not popular in that region. Decisions on the siting of rural health centres are made at the provincial level between groups all of whom supported ZANU(PF) (in the Shona areas) or PF-ZAPU (in the Ndebele areas) rather than at the national level where claims endorsed with the ruling party's imprimatur might make more of an impact.

The decentralization of the health-care system is an unusual instance in Zimbabwe where power has actually been devolved away from the national government. In most cases — as noted in the studies of agricultural producer pricing, foreign investment, and minerals marketing policy — the new regime has made a conscious effort to centralize the decision-making process. The government was able to proceed with decentralization in health care because the health bureaucracy serving the rural areas was, essentially, an entirely new creation. The newness of the bureaucracy meant that it was automatically Africanized and that the government did not need to concern itself nearly as much with White influence — the chief motivation for moving the locus of decision-making upward — as it did in other areas.

The nature of the political good being allocated is also important in understanding the relative unimportance of ethnic influences on the decision-making process in this case. Local pressures and initiatives cannot force the Ministry of Health into building a rural health centre because the logistical and personnel requirements (e.g. nurses, drugs, equipment) can only be supplied by the Ministry. For instance, *The Herald* reported that

> parents in the Mashayamombe area of Mhondoro communal lands, Chegutu district, have raised $7 000 and moulded 30 000 bricks for building a clinic at Mutamba, but the project has hit a snag because the Ministry of Health decided that the clinic should be built at Chanakira . . . the parents would have no choice but to withdraw the funds if the Ministry insisted that the clinic be built at Chanakira, a long distance from Mutamba. They would then use the bricks for building more classrooms at Govamombe Primary School.[25]

In contrast to the case of squatters, where self-help enabled them to control the land immediately, communities are dependent upon government decision-making if they want a health centre in their area.

There does not appear to have been significant ethnic bias in the distribution of health centres because the institutional structure that the government has adopted forces the political conflict over centres to a level where ethnic allegiances are not important. Leaders and groups, therefore, have tried to influence provincial officials by using other, non-ethnic bases of power such as the personal prestige of local officials and the local councillor's standing in the ruling party. These attempts at influencing the health officials have not usually succeeded because the criteria for siting and the nature of the political good allow the PMD to make primary decisions on a technical basis.

Health Service Delivery to Commercial Farm-workers

Many studies have concentrated on the commercial farming sector in Zimbabwe because the 4 000 White farmers are responsible for Zimbabwe's almost unique status as an African country that, in most years, has a surplus of food. However, little attention has been given to the approximately 271 000 farm-workers on commercial farms who are at the same time the mainstay of the commercial agricultural sector and the largest single component (26,2 per cent) of Zimbabwe's formal labour force.[26] Since the farm-worker's wife (or wives) and children often work on the farm during peak working times (e.g. cotton-picking time), Blacks probably constitute an even larger percentage of the labour force than these figures suggest. The farm-workers and their families total approxim-

---

[25] *The Herald*, 26 Nov. 1986.

[26] Zimbabwe, *Statistical Yearbook, 1987*, 52.

ately 1,4 million people, and thus account for roughly 20 per cent of Zimbabwe's total population.[27]

A study of the demand for and the delivery of health services to commercial farm-workers and their families is important because they form a group that is defined by its relation to the means of production. Farm-workers are otherwise quite diverse because they come from all regions of the country and from several foreign countries. A group that can be clearly defined by its class nature is rare in Africa, because of the small size of the formal economy and the much greater importance of ethnic ties. There is probably no other group in Zimbabwe that is so clearly defined by its class characteristics.

Powerlessness of Commercial Farm-workers

The commercial farm-workers and their families face several barriers to making any effective demands for health or other services on either the farmer or the government. Firstly, the very nature of agriculture and the characteristics of Zimbabwe's farm-workers prevent them from being well organized. In Zimbabwe, commercial farm-workers are spread out over several thousand farms throughout the countryside. They seldom come into contact with workers on other farms, and on some ranches, such as the huge operations in Matabeleland, many may see even their fellow employees only infrequently. Secondly, in the rural areas of Zimbabwe, the commercial farm-workers must look to the farmer to provide all basic goods. Clarke has commented on 'the totality of employer control over workers':

The landowner is not only the sole employer of the worker's family, but is also the landlord of his worker-tenants. This imposes an additional constraint on employees. Loss of job means loss of right of tenure, loss of basic subsistence and a high degree of insecurity. Workers also rely extensively on employer-initiated welfare policies which often re-enforce dependency links. The provision of education, the supply of rudimentary medical aid, the hope of 'retainer status' after retirement, the prospect of gaining intermittent cash loans, and the *local* authority of the employer for discipline, order and obedience are dependent often on employer decision and inclination.[28]

While there have been some legislative changes in the status of farm-

[27] *The Sunday Mail*, 15 June 1986.

[28] D. G. Clarke, *Agricultural and Plantation Workers in Rhodesia* (Gwelo, Mambo Press, 1977), 51–2, emphasis in the original.

workers since Independence, especially in the area of job security, the
government has not defined what the farmer must actually provide the
labourer and his family. Even in independent Zimbabwe, farm-workers
and their families depend on the benevolence of the farmer to provide
them with decent living and working conditions and, of special interest
here, health services.

The nature of the farm-workers themselves also contributes to their
poor organization and powerlessness. Although exact figures are unavailable, it was estimated in the mid-1970s that approximately one third
of the commercial farm-workers in Zimbabwe were born in foreign
countries.[29] Almost all of these are from Malawi and Mozambique,
although they are usually married to Zimbabwean women. These workers, known in Malawi as *machona* (the lost ones),[30] are especially at the
mercy of the farmer because most have been in Zimbabwe for such a long
time that they have lost all connections with their home area, and thus
have nowhere to go if they are forced to leave the farm they are working
on. As a result of their dependence on the White farmers, one PMD
compared foreign workers' status to that of 'indentured servants'. While
they are officially viewed as having the same rights as Zimbabweans,
some people in the health bureaucracy argue that the government 'un-
consciously sees foreign workers as less of a problem' because they are not
Zimbabweans.

The commercial farm-workers are nominally organized at the national level and do have a union. However, the General Agricultural and
Plantation Workers Union of Zimbabwe (GAPWUZ) is extremely weak
and disorganized. GAPWUZ was formed in 1983 to replace the previous
agricultural workers' union (the Zimbabwe Agricultural and Plantation
Workers Union) whose leaders had been accused of corruption. The
Union has had trouble establishing any type of relationship with the
commercial farmers. For instance, it was not until three years after it was
established that GAPWUZ even met formally with its employers' body,
the CFU. GAPWUZ does not negotiate with the CFU, and seems to have
no appreciable effect on farmers' practices. Remarkably, GAPWUZ officials
report that they have only limited contact even with the government. No
health official ever mentioned GAPWUZ as even a minor player in the
effort to improve the lives of farm-workers.

Similarly, while there are supposed to be Workers' Committees on the

---

[29] Ibid., 31.   [30] Ibid., 79.

farms, they do not seem to be at all active or involved in the provision of health services.[31] One Matabeleland health official said, 'One wonders what the Workers' Committees are doing in regard to health'. Given their almost feudal relationship with the farmer, it is highly unlikely that farm-workers will make demands or engage in effective protest actions for better services. The large pool of unemployed and the shortage of land make it obvious to all that the farmer can easily replace the farm-workers, but that the farm-worker himself will have very few options to pursue if he loses his job.

Commercial farm-workers are also dramatically affected by the institutional structure of local government. In Zimbabwe the local-government structure is dichotomous: the peasant Communal Lands are governed by District Councils, while the commercial agricultural areas are administered by Rural Councils. The District Council areas are run by bodies that are elected by the local population, and these areas also have sub-district structures such as WADCOs and VIDCOs. In the communal areas, the District Councils have assumed responsibility for delivering many of the new services that the government has provided since Independence. In contrast, the Rural Councils are administered by councillors who are elected only by commercial farmers. The Black commercial farm-workers (who far outnumber the White farmers in the Rural Council areas) do not vote for the Rural Council officers and have essentially no voice in how the Council administers the area.

Zimbabwe's dual structure of local government is an inheritance from the previous regime. The District Councils are the successors to the old Native Councils (also called African Councils) which were each headed by a Native Commissioner during the colonial era.[32] The Rural Councils were first formed in the 1920s when they were known as road councils and had the single function of building and maintaining infrastructure in the White farming areas. For the next forty years these local authorities did little more than road work. Finally, in 1969, the local-government structures in the White farming areas began to take responsibility for health and housing, and consequently changed their name to Rural

---

[31] Poor worker committee organization is partially a reflection of the low guerrilla presence on most White farms during the war; see Ranger, *Peasant Consciousness and Guerrilla War in Zimbabwe*, 20.

[32] C. G. Karase and D. Sanders, 'The amalgamation of Rural and District Councils: Some issues and problems', *The District Council Journal* [Harare] (1985), II, 8.

Councils.[33] However, the maintenance of the infrastructure was still their major emphasis. Even in the Independence period a former Assistant Secretary in the Ministry of Local Government noted that many people still consider the Rural Councils to be no more than 'glorified road councils'.[34] Indeed, one Rural Council official admitted that 'roads were always our big love'.

As distinct, White-run local authorities, the Rural Councils have substantial autonomy from the rest of the government apparatus and can be an obstacle to providing health services to the Africans working on commercial farms. One study of provincial health care noted that

it appears as if there was no clear-cut communication between the Ministry of Health and Rural Councils as regards mutual planning of health services in the commercial farming areas. The Rural Councils appeared to be more responsible for the development and maintenance of road networks in their areas than for health and education.[35]

Indeed, some Rural Councils have actually resisted government's attempts to require them to provide better health care to Blacks working on White farms.

The result of the farm-workers' occupation and origin, of the problems of farm-worker representation at the national level, and of the current structure of local government in Zimbabwe is that Blacks on commercial farms are, at best, extremely poorly organized and lack anything which might be called 'political clout' — be it at the farm, district or national level. Rene Loewenson commented on commercial farm-workers' political position:

They have arrived at a position where they lack any political representation, whether in the Rural Councils . . . or in terms of an effective union. At central government level, therefore, they form a voiceless fifth of the Zimbabwean population.[36]

[33] A short history of Rural Councils is given by P. J. Field, 'The Association of Rural Councils', in *International Union of Local Authorities (Africa Region) Congress Programme* (Harare, IULA, 1986), 14.

[34] A. Sibanda, 'Socio-political organisation in the commercial farming areas', in *Report on the National Workshop on Health Services in the Commercial Farming Areas* (Kadoma, Ministry of Health?, 1986), 13.

[35] R. Loewenson, 'Evaluation of the Mashonaland Central Provincial Farm Health Worker Programme' (Harare, 1985, mimeo.), 10.

[36] *The Sunday Mail*, 15 June 1986.

While large portions of Zimbabwe's population face severe problems in transmitting their views to the government, no group is as lacking in power as the farm-workers.

Health Problems of the Farm-workers

The social and political weakness of the farm-workers and their families is reflected in their poor health. For instance,

a 1981 survey in Mashonaland Central [a very prosperous farming area] showed that farm-worker communities were living in overcrowded housing in fenced compounds. Their toilet system was the bush or in crowded pit-latrines, and the water supply came from communal taps and rivers in 67 per cent of the cases or more.[37]

These poor conditions cause an extremely high proportion of the Africans on commercial farms to suffer from environmental diseases common to the Third World; tuberculosis and water-borne diseases are especially prevalent. A 1986 survey of commercial farm-workers' children in Matabeleland, Mashonaland West and Mashonaland Central provinces also found that between 46 and 66 per cent were malnourished.[38] This is an extraordinary statistic in view of the fact that these children live where Zimbabwe's food surplus is being produced. An earlier study found that approximately 83 per cent of children on farms had not been immunized and 75 per cent of all farm families had never attended a clinic,[39] even though better facilities could have had a dramatic impact on the lives of these farm-workers. For instance, Save the Children (UK) estimated that 'seventy per cent of causes of death and disease on farms can be prevented by an effective primary health care programme within a framework of enhanced living conditions'.[40]

Government Efforts to Serve the Farm-workers

The new government recognized at its inception that commercial farm-workers and their families lived in exceptionally poor conditions and would need special attention; for instance, the 1980 election manifesto of ZANU(PF) singled out commercial farm-workers as a group in particular

---

[37] Ibid.   [38] Ibid.

[39] R. Loewenson, 'Health and farm-workers', *Journal of Social Change and Development* [Harare] (1983), IV, 7.

[40] *The Financial Gazette*, 29 Aug. 1986.

need.[41] However, after Independence in 1980 no immediate attention was devoted to farm-workers. One Mashonaland health administrator noted in an interview: 'At Independence communal areas were identified as the areas of greatest need. Commercial areas were kind of forgotten about. People did not pay close attention to commercial farming areas.'

Commercial farm-workers were initially ignored for several reasons. Firstly, the communal areas were ZANU(PF)'s prime constituency because it was the peasants who had provided the support for the guerrillas which proved instrumental in their winning the liberation struggle and in ZANU(PF)'s coming to power. In addition, the government felt in the first years of Independence that it should not intervene too actively in the provision of health care for commercial farm-workers because the welfare of Blacks on White farms was viewed as the responsibility of the farmers. One provincial health official noted, 'Commercial farmers were seen as responsible for Rural Councils, and government did not want to be seen as subsidizing commercial farmers in what was seen as their duty to their employees'. Unfortunately, by taking this stance the government inadvertently strengthened the feudalistic relationship between the farm-worker and the farmer.

At the same time, it was technically much easier for the Ministry of Health to deliver increased health services to peasants in the Communal Lands. It is often not possible for the government to build a static clinic in commercial farming areas because the low population within a feasible walking distance cannot justify the costs of the building. Therefore, the Ministry of Health had to find other ways to serve the farm-worker population, and this task took time, given all the other demands that were being placed on the health bureaucracy at Independence. Thus, the Ministry of Health's major planning document, *Planning for Equity in Health*, hardly mentions farm-workers or specific programmes designed to alleviate their plight.[42]

For these reasons, health provision to the farm-workers did not begin well in independent Zimbabwe. Table XVIII displays data on population, road development and clinics for Rural and District Councils. The Table clearly shows that, in every province except Masvingo, District Council areas are better served by health clinics than Rural Councils. Correspondingly, Loewenson found that the actual dollar amount per capita spent on

[41] Zimbabwe African National Union (Patriotic Front), *ZANU(PF) 1980 Election Manifesto*, 10.

[42] Zimbabwe, *Planning for Equity in Health*.

health care is 3,7 times greater in District Council than in Rural Council areas .[43]

From 1983, the government realized that it would have to intensify its efforts to promote the health of farm-workers and their families. This realization was brought about as a result of studies conducted by the Ministry of Health, Save the Children (UK), and the University of Zimbabwe's Medical School, which indicated that the health situation on

Table XVIII

POPULATION, ROADS AND HEALTH SERVICES
IN RURAL AND DISTRICT COUNCIL AREAS

Province	Population	Tarred roads per 100 km²	Population per clinic
	RC : DC	RC : DC	RC : DC
Manicaland	1 : 3,5	2,9 : 1	3,10 : 1
Mashonaland East	1 : 2,1	5,4 : 1	1,41 : 1
Mashonaland Central	1 : 1,5	2,4 : 1	3,55 : 1
Mashonaland West	1 : 0,8	10,8 : 1	1,74 : 1
Midlands	1 : 6,3	7,3 : 1	3,20 : 1
Masvingo	1 : 5,5	0,5 : 1	0,65 : 1
Matabeleland	1 : 4,8	1,8 : 1	1,19 : 1
Zimbabwe	1 : 2,9	3,4 : 1	1,84 : 1

Source: R. Loewenson, 'Rural Council Social Service Assessment', Tables 1a, 2a and 4.

commercial farms was not improving. The government responded to these reports in two ways. Firstly, the Ministry of Health, mainly through its provincial-level officials, sought to increase health facilities and provide better care to farm-workers by trying to convince Rural Councils to increase services and by attempting to persuade farmers to allow Farm Health Workers (whose wages would be paid by the farmers) on their farms. Secondly, it began a long-term effort to change the structure of local government in order to benefit farm-workers.

Provincial medical authorities admit that they have had mixed success in trying to convince Rural Councils to provide better health facilities.

[43] R. Loewenson, 'Rural Council Social Service Assessment' (Harare, 1985, mimeo.).

Some provincial authorities, especially those in the Mashonaland provinces, where a significant portion of the population is made up of
commercial farm-workers (see Table XVIII), have faced terrific resistance
by Rural Councils while trying to improve health facilities on commercial
farms or while implementing the Farm Health Worker Scheme. One
Mashonaland official said in an interview:

> While there has been pressure on Rural Councils and some progress has been
> made, there have been no breakthroughs. Rural Councils are still dedicated to
> building roads. Councils always say that they don't have money. Rural Councils
> have been seen as a sort of enemy and haven't been pushed enough to provide
> more services. We try to get farmers to do things voluntarily and the Commercial
> Farmers Union to adopt its own standards, but it is not clear how far it goes or how
> many farmers will actually follow standards.

A Matabeleland official reported similar obstructionism by Rural Councils and White farmers:

> Rural Councils present real problems. The PMD says you need a Farm Health
> Worker, we will train her, organize equipment, the farmer only needs to pay for
> a bicycle and an allowance of $36 a month. But then the farmer says, 'What if the
> labourer quits?' (even though the Farm Health Worker is usually the wife of a
> long-time worker), or [asks], 'Would she be acceptable to neighbouring farms?'
> (this could be taken care of). Farmers say that if they are paying $36 then they want
> hiring and firing privileges.

In general, provincial officials report that the greatest resistance to their
advocacy of better health care for farm-workers is in areas where Rural
Councils are well established and are a significant part of the province's
economy.

However, other provincial authorities report that Rural Councils and
farmers are generally helpful in their areas. In Masvingo, for instance,
officials report that Rural Councils have been very co-operative. Admittedly, this province is somewhat unusual because it is dominated by the
massive Hippo Valley and Triangle sugar estates owned by South African
multinationals. Officials report that these plantations have unusually
good health care for commercial agriculture in Zimbabwe. One official
said, 'It's lucky that we have the MNCs: they have several doctors and
clinics'. The large estates also have their own Farm Health Workers.
Masvingo, as noted in Table XVIII, has the best Rural Council to District
Council clinic ratio in the country and is the only province where
commercial agricultural areas are better served than peasant areas.

The reason for the relatively good co-operation between provincial authorities and Rural Councils in Masvingo can be found in the population and infrastructure figures presented in Table XVIII. Masvingo's economy is, relative to the rest of Zimbabwe, less dependent on commercial agriculture as a mainstay of the provincial economy. For instance, the province has the second lowest concentration of farm-workers in the nation. Similarly, it is the only province where there are more tarred roads in the District Council areas than in the Rural Council areas. As a result, the Rural Councils are not particularly well established and, therefore, lack the 'political clout' at the provincial level that Rural Councils in Mashonaland possess.

Similar co-operation between Rural Councils and health officials was reported in the Midlands Province. One official there reported that 'the majority of Councils are co-operative. On the whole we are doing fairly well, though doing less well in convincing individual farmers to put in water and sanitation.' Once again, provincial officials in the Midlands attribute some of their success to the relative unimportance of commercial agriculture in their province. Indeed, Table XVIII shows that the Midlands actually has the lowest concentration of farm-workers in the country. However, the Midlands provincial office also seems much more willing to confront the Rural Councils than PMDs in other parts of the country. One Midlands official said: 'In this province we do not recognize boundaries between District and Rural Councils; anywhere there are people it is our problem'. The official argued that it was possible to challenge the Rural Councils: 'If an official is willing to take risks and is politically sure of himself, then he can do a great deal.'

Government programmes for farm-workers, therefore, have a mixed record. In areas such as Masvingo and the Midlands, where the Rural Councils are not particularly strong, the health officials seem to have done fairly well, especially if they have taken the initiative and have actively pressured the Rural Councils. However, in those provinces where commercial agriculture dominates the economic life of the entire province (such as the three Mashonaland provinces) the PMD's office has generally not been successful in convincing Rural Councils and White farmers to improve health services to commercial farm-workers and their families.

Given the decentralized system of health care, it is not surprising that efforts to improve the lot of farm-workers vary according to the local positions of the Rural Councils and the personalities and forcefulness of the officials in the PMD's office. Since the national political leadership does not offer support, provincial health officials can only hope that their own prestige and initiative can triumph over the Rural Council's institutional resilience. In a very real sense, there is not one Zimbabwean government dealing with the commercial farm-worker problem but eight 'governments' confronting the problem in different ways and in varying circumstances.

The government's second effort to improve the health and welfare of commercial farm-workers and their families has been directed at institutional change. Since 1984 the government has sought the amalgamation of the Rural and District Councils so as to eliminate the anachronistic dichotomy in local-government structures and thereby remove some of the barriers that stand in the way of helping the Blacks on White farms. However, it was not until 1988 that Parliament finally passed the Rural–District Council Amalgamation Act. In view of the administrative problems involved, it will be several more years before the two local authorities are actually merged. For instance, the two types of Council are funded differently: Rural Councils gain their revenue by taxes on White farmers and from beer levies on beer halls in the commercial farming areas, while District Councils receive almost all of their money in grants from the central government. They also have different pay and pension schemes for their employees. Finally, the Rural Councils own considerable amounts of equipment (road-graders, for instance) and it is unclear what would happen to the title of this equipment, and the debts that were incurred by the Rural Councils when this equipment was acquired, if the local authorities merged.

However, it is uncertain even after the amalgamation Act has been passed what its impact will be. For instance, the Act does not give farm-workers the franchise in the area that they work in. The continued disenfranchisement of the commercial farm-workers may make it difficult for them to press their demands for better health care effectively, or at least in some way hold their leaders accountable for delivering better services. One PMD argued, therefore, 'If non-rate payers [i.e. farm-workers] continue not to have the vote, the Act will not change things fundamentally'. Rural Councils are also pressuring the government to reduce the impact of the amalgamation exercise in their areas. For instance, some Rural Councils have suggested that the old White government structures could become self-contained WADCOs under the newly merged Rural–District Councils, thereby allowing the Rural Councils to preserve their distinct administrative status.

It is important, therefore, to examine how much influence the Rural Councils have had on the government's consideration of the amalgamation process. In fact, it is unclear how much pressure Rural Councils have been able to bring to bear on government. For instance, the Association of Rural Councils — the organ of the Rural Councils that liaises with the government and which is supposed to play, in the words of one of its officials, 'a large part' in any Act or promulgation affecting Rural Councils — was not consulted about the draft amalgamation bill. One official in the Association reported that his organization 'had no idea what was going on [with amalgamation] until the draft Bill came out'. Rural Council officials say that there was very little opportunity to consult with government officials and that 'we had to fight like the blazes for a meeting with the Minister [of Local Government]'. While the Rural Councils did forward their suggestions to the government, most of these suggestions were ignored by national leaders. Officials in the Association report that they do not engage in an extensive lobbying effort and that they do not speak to Ministers other than the Minister of Local Government. However, the Association does work closely with one of the White members of Parliament: the MP, the Association reports, can do 'nothing' in Parliament, but does 'lobby people over cups of coffee'.

White political power at this point in time seems less important than the immense administrative problems caused by the amalgamation exercise. However, farmer power could become important during the implementation of the programme when those with technical skills will be at a premium. Therefore, it can be expected that, in such technical matters as the drawing of Rural Council boundaries, White political power could become quite influential in making the new structures more favourable to large-scale commercial agriculture.

Farm-workers and Institutional Failure

The new regime's response to the needs of commercial farm-workers and their families has been mixed at best. The government was late in focusing on the health needs of farm-workers and, given the speed at which the health-care system is developing in the communal areas, it appears that, even under the new order, the Blacks on White farms are the last in line for health services. However, even when the new regime began to attend to the welfare of commercial farm-workers, it was unable to devise an institutional response to a political good which gives a great advantage to the White farmers and their Rural Councils. The state, therefore, was not autonomous at either the structural or situational levels when trying to deliver more services to commercial farm-workers.

It is true that in some areas, primarily where commercial agriculture is not well established, the government has successfully pressured Rural Councils and White farmers to improve health services. However, because the decentralized institutional structure places the responsibility of increasing services on provincial authorities, the PMDs have often been unable to force Rural Councils to increase services significantly where commercial agriculture is strong. The government's role as advocate for the farm-workers cannot be reconciled with its decentralized health-care system because, given all the barriers to increasing on-farm health care, it takes more 'political clout' to guarantee better health services in commercial farming areas than most provincial health officials can muster.

Partly because it realizes that provincial pressure is not enough, the government is now engaged in an effort to remove the structural barrier posed by the Rural Councils and thereby drastically decrease the local power of White agriculture. However, the amalgamation exercise has not been fully implemented by the government. Even then, it is not clear how much the amalgamation exercise will help farm-workers and their families.

The state's institutional structure has served to make class characteristics quite significant in the case of health care. There is no organization or collective action among the farm-workers, so there is no question of class-based action and no need to ask whether the farm-workers are in some way class conscious. However, it is clear that the farm-workers' relationship to the mode of production is the chief characteristic which determines their receipt of health care. Class becomes important not because of the internal social characteristics of the farm-workers themselves but because of the state's institutional structure. While many have long recognized that institutions can have a determining effect on ethnic patterns, there has been far less recognition of the effect of government structures on class formation.

Conclusion

In the area of health care the state was able to act autonomously in the design of institutions and the siting of rural health centres, but it was often prevented by commercial farmers from being able to provide health services, and will probably be influenced by White farmers when trying to change the institutions governing the delivery of services to farm-workers. The area of health care is, therefore, a vivid demonstration of the impossibility of making global judgements about the autonomy of the state. Rather, state autonomy must be understood issue by issue because variations in institutions, issue-areas and interest groups will determine the location of the independent variables that explain political conflicts.

The impact of the state's institutional structure on state autonomy is particularly dramatic. The government's choice of a decentralized system for siting health centres gave it essential autonomy because PMDs were able to locate rural health centres on the basis of technical criteria. The usual image of a 'strong' state implies a high degree of centralization, but this case study indicates that, in certain circumstances, the state is more insulated from societal pressure when power is devolved away from the centre. In contrast, the inherited system of local government forced the government to be highly dependent upon White farmers to help it meet its goal of expanding health care to commercial farm-workers. Thus, the same decentralized system caused the government to be autonomous in one aspect of health policy but to be strongly influenced by society in another facet of its programme. If the government structure had been different, the politics of health care would probably have changed dramatically. For instance, a highly centralized health-care system might have enhanced the importance of ethnic groups which could bargain for more rural health centres in their regions but at the same time have made the Rural Councils irrelevant.

The area of health care in Zimbabwe also dramatically illustrates the potential for an issue-area to affect state autonomy. The nature of the rural health centres as a political good enhanced the prospects for government to act autonomously in the siting of the centres. However, the nature of health care in commercial agriculture reduced the prospects for state autonomy because it enhanced the power of the White farmers. The nature of the political good is the same in both: health care allows the provider to act autonomously because it requires supplies and know-how that cannot be controlled by patients. The divergence in outcomes is created by the simple fact that the government provides centres in the peasant areas, but farmers are responsible for health care in the commercial farming regions of Zimbabwe.

Locus of Decision-making

The very nature of health care forces power to flow to whatever level of government or society is actually providing the health care. The locus of decision-making, therefore, was clearly at the provincial level for the siting of centres and at the local level for the provision of health care to farm-workers. Health is particularly interesting in this regard because it is the only example in the seven cases examined in this study in which power actually devolved away from the national bureaucracy. Indeed, the decentralized nature of decision-making was a crucial factor in the evolution of health politics.

However, even though decision-making was decentralized, the ruling party did not play an important role in the decision-making process. ZANU(PF) officials did at times try to influence the siting of centres; however, the institutional procedures of the Ministry of Health and the nature of health centres as a political good made it impossible for them to pressure the civil service successfully. ZANU(PF) could not play the same role as it did with the squatters, because the complexities of health care require much more than simple control over the land. ZANU(PF) is not important in the commercial farm-worker controversy because it did not establish much of a presence on White farms during the war and is still exceptionally weak in commercial farming areas ten years after Independence. The party did not play a role in the national discussion of the plight of the commercial farm-worker because it is unable to participate in conflicts that require administrative and technical knowledge.

The delivery of appropriate health care has been one of Zimbabwe's biggest successes in the ten years since Independence. In going against the grain of most African political systems by decentralizing, the government enabled highly competent civil servants to create a system which will be of great benefit to millions of Zimbabweans, and has avoided the insidious ethnic influences that afflict so many distributional programmes in Africa. Unfortunately, the decentralized system has allowed the Rural Councils to play an important role in the provision of health services. The biggest challenge facing the health programme is to adapt the decentralized system so that it can provide the same benefits to farm-workers that it currently does to peasants in the Communal Lands.

Chapter Nine

National Minimum Wage Policy

The legacy of Rhodesia's labour reserve economy when Independence was achieved in 1980 was a large number of workers earning a wage that did not allow them to meet minimum subsistence needs. Soon after Independence the new government pledged to promote the welfare of Zimbabwe's workers by instituting a national minimum wage that would apply to all labourers in formal employment. However, although significant real wage increases were enacted for the first two years of Independence, the government's incomes policy has since failed to raise after-inflation income. Indeed, since 1982, many of Zimbabwe's workers have seen their after-inflation wage fall, and many earn less in real terms than they did in 1980. Studying decision-making in the area of wages is important because incomes policy is one of the most significant instruments available to the government in its quest to promote the welfare of the 1,1 million Africans employed in the formal labour sector. Furthermore, the wage-setting procedure has evolved into a formal bargaining process in which both business and labour seek to influence government policy. National minimum wage policy, therefore, provides another perspective into how the Zimbabwe government can be influenced by societal groups.

African Labour Unions in Rhodesia

The labour reserve economy was predicated on workers having no countervailing power to influence the setting of wages. The history of labour in Rhodesia, therefore, is a succession of attempts by Africans to organize themselves against the danger of being crushed by the overwhelming force of the colony's security apparatus. When a certain degree of worker organization became inevitable as a result of industrialization, labour legislation was designed in such a way that the government retained ultimate control over the wage-setting process. African workers did use other ways in which to resist, and these should not be ignored;[1] however, for the purpose of understanding post-1980 wage developments, the history of African unions in the country is very important.

White workers formed a labour union in Southern Rhodesia as early as 1916 (the Rhodesian Railway Workers Union), but it was not until 1927 that Black labourers organized. The Industrial and Commercial Workers Union (ICU) consisted of Black workers in the agricultural, domestic, construction, mining and manufacturing sectors. The Union tried to organize protests by workers and sought to establish links between labourers and the peasantry.[2] The threat posed by the ICU was quickly met by the colonial regime: 'the state responded to ICU campaigns with repression, imprisoning its leaders and banning its meetings'.[3] The colonial government's severe response, and internal organizational problems, caused the ICU to collapse.

During the 1930s the colonial regime institutionalized its African labour policy. The Industrial Conciliation Act of 1934 formally excluded Africans from the definition of 'employee'.[4] This definition gave the colonial regime control over Africans' efforts to organize because only 'employees' could form unions. The combination of the government's labour policy and the Great Depression caused a 30 per cent fall in the average monthly wages of workers in the early 1930s.[5]

After the Second World War the demands of the growing economy, especially the burgeoning manufacturing sector, forced the government to adopt a more sophisticated labour policy. With the emergence of a permanent workforce came the need to establish structures that enabled communication to, and control of, the workers. In the late 1950s, therefore, the labour legislation was reformed to allow some Africans to unionize. The Minister of Labour was quite clear about the government's perception of the role of these unions: 'It could be argued that to provide for these associations is nothing more than a control measure and, let me be

---

[1] See, especially, C. Van Onselen, *Chibaro: African Mine Labour in Southern Rhodesia, 1900–1933* (London, Pluto, 1976).

[2] Zimbabwe, *Labour and Economy: Report of the National Trade Unions Survey 1984* (Harare, Ministry of Labour, Manpower Planning and Social Welfare, 1987), I, 13.

[3] Ibid.

[4] International Labour Organization, *Labour Conditions and Discrimination in Southern Rhodesia (Zimbabwe)* (Geneva, ILO, 1978), 65.

[5] Phimister, 'Zimbabwe: The path of capitalist development', 280.

perfectly frank, it is'.[6] When workers did unite successfully, the state's repressive apparatus was able to crush any nascent activity. For instance, the Wankie Colliery strike of 1954, which involved 9 000 Black miners in an impressive collective action, was broken at gunpoint by the colonial regime.[7]

Continued industrialization allowed more Africans to unionize, but the colonial labour policy kept them under the effective control of the government. For instance, the reformed Industrial Conciliation Act allowed all White unions to negotiate with employers automatically, but African unions had to fulfil certain requirements in order to enter into collective bargaining.[8] The repressive legislation of the UDI period also effectively prevented any significant activity by African unionists. The right to strike was removed:

Successive legislative amendments to the Industrial Conciliation Act have had the effect of making a legal labour strike virtually impossible. After the deliberately drawn-out processes of negotiation, mediation and arbitration through which all disputes must go, it is still well within the administration's power to veto an intended strike action simply through presidential decree declaring the strike 'not to be in the national interest'.[9]

Between 1959 and 1980 there was not one legal strike by Black workers in Rhodesia.[10]

The Importance of the Minimum Wage

Although Zimbabwe is predominantly a rural society, a significant number of people are at least partially dependent on wage earnings because the appropriation of large tracts of land by the settlers foreclosed on the possibility of full-time cultivation for the majority of peasant households. (Table XIX shows the percentages of people employed in various sectors of the economy before and after Independence.) In independent Zimbabwe it is estimated that 50 per cent of the adult population (74 per cent of the men and 27 per cent of the women) participate to some

---

[6] Quoted in International Labour Organization, *Labour Conditions and Discrimination in Southern Rhodesia*, 65.

[7] Zimbabwe, *Labour and Economy*, 16.   [8] Ibid, 17.

[9] International Labour Organization, *Labour Conditions and Discrimination in Southern Rhodesia*, 23.

[10] Zimbabwe, *Labour and Economy*, 19.

degree in the labour force.[11] When the dependence of those who are too young or too old to work is considered, between 50 and 75 percent of the population is at least partially reliant on wage income.[12]

The particular economic system that developed in Rhodesia also had an effect on the pattern of remuneration. The labour reserve economy requires a large number of low- to non-skilled workers who receive the lowest level of wages. In 1981 it was estimated that 28,2 per cent of all

Table XIX

EMPLOYMENT BY SECTOR, 1975 AND 1983

	Share of labour force (%)	
Sector	1975	1983
Agriculture	34,6	26,2
Mining	6,0	5,3
Manufacturing	14,9	16,0
Electricity and water	0,6	0,7
Construction	5,8	4,4
Finance, insurance and real estate	1,2	1,5
Travel sector	7,4	7,7
Transport	4,3	4,8
Public administration	4,7	8,6
Education	3,4	8,1
Health	1,3	1,9

Source: Zimbabwe, *Statistical Yearbook, 1987* (Harare, Central Statistical Office, 1988), 52.

workers received the lowest possible wage (below $30 per month), although there were dramatic differences between sectors. For instance, in agriculture 90,4 per cent of all workers earned the absolute minimum while the skill requirements in the finance, insurance and real-estate sectors meant that only 1 per cent of workers in those areas earned below $30 a month. Another 25,7 per cent of all workers earned between $30 and $50, and 22,7 per cent received between $50 and $70.[13] Altogether, 76,6 per

[11] Zimbabwe, *Statistical Yearbook, 1987,* 46.

[12] Zimbabwe, *Report of the Commission of Inquiry into Incomes, Prices and Conditions of Service,* 53.

[13] Ibid., 55.

cent of all workers were, to all intents and purposes, at the bottom of the wage scale. The minimum wage, therefore, becomes crucial to a large number of workers:

> With scope for upward mobility limited by lack of opportunity to acquire skills on the job and little account being taken of length of service, the *basic rate* becomes of major importance for the bulk of workers in most sectors. In a wage structure that allows progression away from minima in the course of working life, wage minima are not so important. . . . *But in the absence of this type of progression, wage minima come to dominate the wage pattern.*[14]

Dilemmas of a National Minimum Wage

Soon after Independence the new government took emergency measures to establish a national minimum wage. The Minimum Wages Act (No. 4 of 1980) allowed the Minister of Labour to set base income levels for any employee. The Act clearly broke with the wage regime of the past because an 'employee' was defined as anyone receiving remuneration.[15] However, the government realized that it did not have a clear incomes or employment policy because it did not have any established criteria for setting wages. This lack of a concrete policy was particularly significant in view of the government's aspirations for dramatic socio-economic change and a rapid increase in workers' wages. Therefore, the new regime appointed a Commission of Inquiry, under the chairmanship of Roger Riddell, to make recommendations on all facets of Zimbabwe's labour policy.

In the best tradition of commissions of inquiry, Riddell and his colleagues produced innovative suggestions that were largely ignored by the government. Nevertheless, it is valuable to study the Commission's recommendations, because the government's response to them dramatically illustrates the fundamental problems in trying to implement a radical new incomes policy in Zimbabwe. The most important features of the Commission's report were its recommendations concerning the determination of the minimum wage. Specifically, the Commission strongly recommended that Zimbabwe's national minimum wage be set according to the poverty datum line (PDL). The poverty datum line, developed partly by Riddell in the 1970s, estimates the minimum wage

[14] Ibid, 55–6, emphasis in the original.
[15] Zimbabwe, Minimum Wages Act (No. 4 of 1980).

needed by a family if a basket of goods is to be purchased each month.[16] The value of the basket can be adjusted for inflation so that the PDL can provide an after-inflation indicator of minimum subsistence needs. The Commission wrote:

We recommend that, over a period of time, minimum wages should be targeted to the average PDL income level for a family of six people, a man, a wife, and four children. The target minimum should be 90 per cent of this PDL level and this minimum should be reached in a period of three-and-a-half years.[17]

The Commission calculated that the PDL in December 1980 was $128 per month.[18] If its recommendations were applied to the entire workforce, the lowest paid workers (those receiving below $30 per month) would receive a real wage increase of more than 380 per cent over four years while the segment of the workforce that earned between $30 and $70 a month would receive real raises of between 64 and 380 per cent. After the initial PDL target was met, the Riddell Commission recommended that wages be reviewed periodically in order to adjust workers' incomes for inflation.[19] Any link between wages and productivity or the type of work done was explicitly rejected by the Commission.[20] While recognizing the possibility that exemptions for certain businesses might be needed, the Commission argued that the 'onus should be on employer to *prove* his inability to pay'.[21]

While the government never explicitly rejected the wage-setting recommendations, it is fair to say that they were never seriously considered. Zimbabwe's leaders recognized very soon after Independence that their ambitious goal of massively increasing social services at the same time as retaining the structure of the economy required rapid growth to generate more resources and jobs. The *Transitional National Development Plan*, for instance, required that the economy grow at an annual rate of 8 per cent between 1983 and 1985 in order to achieve a 3 per cent annual growth in

---

[16] See V. S. Cubitt and R. C. Riddell, *The Urban Poverty Datum Line in Rhodesia: A Study of the Minimum Consumption Needs of Families* (Salisbury, Univ. of Rhodesia, Faculty of Social Studies, 1974), and V. S. Cubitt, *1979 Supplement to 'The Urban Poverty Datum Line in Rhodesia: A Study of the Minimum Consumption Needs of Families'* (Salisbury, Univ. of Rhodesia, Faculty of Social Studies, 1979).

[17] Zimbabwe, *Report of the Commission of Inquiry into Incomes, Prices and Conditions of Service*, 87.

[18] Ibid., 96.   [19] Ibid., 98.   [20] Ibid., 105.

[21] Ibid., 106, emphasis in the original.

employment.[22] The *First Five-Year National Development Plan* for 1986–1990 was less ambitious, but still assumed that the economy would grow at 5,1 per cent a year and produce a 2,7 per cent annual increase in employment.[23] Yet, even if this 2,7 per cent rate were achieved (a highly improbable prospect), only 10 per cent of the 300 000 school leavers in 1990 — as opposed to 29 per cent of the 95 000 school leavers in 1985 — would be employed.[24]

Despite the ambitious employment gains assumed by the two Development Plans, neither of the documents explicitly considered wage increases. The Riddell Commission's view that the highest priority be given to raising the wages of current workers went against the macroeconomic orientation of a government facing large increases in unemployment.

Political Conflict in the Wage-setting Process

There are three main actors in the political conflict over wages: the employers, labour and the government. The interests and structures of all the actors have changed markedly in the last eight years as employers and labour react to changes in government policy and everyone adjusts to Zimbabwe's changing economic fortunes.

For the purpose of bargaining on wages, as well as for certain other areas of labour policy, employers in Zimbabwe are now represented by the Employers' Confederation of Zimbabwe (EMCOZ). EMCOZ represents all the major employer groups: the African Labour Bureau (the Commercial Farmers Union's labour section), the Chamber of Mines, the Confederation of Zimbabwe Industries, and the Zimbabwe National Chamber of Commerce. EMCOZ was created recently — 1986 was the first year it was completely involved in wage bargaining — because the government wanted to negotiate with only one group of employers during the wage-setting process. EMCOZ is well organized, adequately funded, and quite sophisticated in its lobbying techniques. The director of EMCOZ, Dr David Chanaiwa, is a former Ministry of Labour official who was intimately involved in writing much of the current labour legislation. By 1989, the government was allowing management and labour through National Employment Councils to negotiate wage agree-

---

[22] Zimbabwe, *Transitional National Development Plan*, I, 29.

[23] Zimbabwe, *First Five-Year National Development Plan*, I.

[24] Zimbabwe, *Annual Economic Review of Zimbabwe, 1986*, 27.

ments within parameters set by the government after consultation with EMCOZ and the trade unions.[25]

Unlike during the colonial era, the unions, too, are given a formal place in wage negotiations. Organized labour has been able to increase its membership from 125 000 in 1980 to an estimated 250 000 in 1984.[26] However, unions in Zimbabwe still have severe organizational problems. A number of instances of incompetence or outright corruption by union leaders have seriously damaged labour's ability to mobilize workers. The Ministry of Labour's survey of trade unions noted that

unions had lost considerable credibility as worker-representatives in the eyes of non-unionized labour — i.e. potential union members. These workers were said to be feeling that there was no justification for joining unions if monies paid as subscriptions for trade union purposes benefited only a few officials of the movement.[27]

The unions also suffer institutional problems and their leaders require a large amount of training. The Riddell Commission noted:

Where unions do exist it is rare for them to have an organized structure reaching down to the grassroots; many union officials are ignorant of either the broad industrial legislation or the particular regulations or agreements under which their members work and, in addition, many appear to be ignorant of the structures of their own union.[28]

The Ministry of Labour's survey noted, for instance, that 36 per cent of all the unions that responded had faulty record-keeping.[29]

For the purpose of national minimum wage negotiations, workers in Zimbabwe are now represented by the Zimbabwe Congress of Trade Unions (ZCTU). The ZCTU is the only labour organization involved in the wage-setting process because, as with the employers, the government feels most comfortable dealing with one 'umbrella' organization that represents the whole of one side of the negotiations. The ZCTU is something of a worker success because it is a consolidation of the five national labour centres that existed at Independence. However, since

---

[25] 'Nkomo on labour matters', *Focus* [Magazine of the National Employment Council of the Financial, Distributive and Service Undertakings of Zimbabwe] (Nov. 1989), 5.

[26] Zimbabwe, *Labour and Economy*, 37–8.   [27] Ibid., 40.

[28] Zimbabwe, *Report of the Commission of Inquiry into Incomes, Prices and Conditions of Service*, 238.

[29] Zimbabwe, *Labour and Economy*, 70.

Independence it, too, has suffered from incompetence, favouritism and corruption and has had several leadership changes.[30] The ZCTU also has serious deficiencies in its ability to conduct research and analysis on economic issues, especially compared with the sectoral employer organizations and EMCOZ. For instance, it was not until 1986 that the ZCTU was able to hire an economist to help prepare labour's presentations to the government.

Government National Minimum Wage Decisions

For a proper understanding of the evolution of Zimbabwe's incomes policies, government wage decisions since 1980 have to be divided into three distinct periods. The first is marked by the economic boom of 1980 to 1982 when the economy grew at an unprecedented rate as a result of the war ending and sanctions being lifted. The second period occurred between 1982 and 1985, when the drought and the world recession caused a severe economic crisis. Finally, the uncertain recovery from 1985 onward distinguishes the third era of wage policy in post-Independence Zimbabwe. The chief reason for this demarcation is the radically different condition of the economy during these three periods, although there were also significant changes in government processes and in the political strengths of the major actors that coincided with, and were linked to, Zimbabwe's changing economic fortunes.

Boom Years: 1980–1982

With the euphoria of Independence came an economic boom that raised the expectations of the population and of government decision-makers. The lifting of sanctions, inflows of aid, decreases in defence outlays, and excellent weather allowed the country to experience an 11 per cent economic growth rate in 1980, which was followed by a 10,7 per cent rise in 1981.[31] The value of exports, for instance, increased from $798 million in 1979 to $1 042 million in 1980, and rose to $1 141 million by 1982 as Zimbabweans took advantage of unused capacity to export throughout the world.[32]

---

[30] These charges are detailed in ibid., 52–60.

[31] Zimbabwe, *Socio-Economic Review of Zimbabwe*, 2.

[32] Zimbabwe, *National Income and Expenditure Report* (Harare, Central Statistical Office, 1985), 11.

This initial economic boom allowed the government to post large increases in the national minimum wage in the first two years of Independence. The wage rates for 1980–2, shown in Table XX, meant significant increases in the incomes of most employees; Figure 2 displays wage and inflation indices for domestic and agricultural workers. After large increases in 1981 the wages of these workers were static for a year, but the

Table XX

STATUTORY MINIMUM WAGE RATES, 1980–1988

Year	Domestic service	Agriculture	Mining	Industry and commerce
		Dollars per month		
1980	30	30	43 + 27 *	70
1981	30	30	58 + 27 *	85
1982	50	50	105	105
1983	55	55	110	115
1984	65	65	120	125
1985	75	75	143,75	143,75
1986	85	85	158,13	158,13
1987	85	85	158,13	158,13
1988	100	100	181,85	181,85

* For the first two years of Independence miners were considered to receive $27 worth of in-kind benefits, mainly in the form of free or subsidized housing. After 1981, the miners received a higher cash income and paid for the benefits that they had previously received.

Sources: Zimbabwe, Socio-Economic Review of Zimbabwe, 1980–1985 (Harare, Ministry of Finance, Economic Planning and Development, 1986), 91, and Zimbabwe, Statutory Instrument No. 26B of 1988.

1982 increase brought them well above their real 1980 value. Figures 3 and 4 display similar real increases for miners and for workers in commerce and industry; both of these groups received real increases in wages in 1981 and 1982. For all groups of workers, the 1982 wage announcements marked the highest real wages of the post-Independence period.

The initial wage increases were not so much the first part of an overall wage policy as a reaction to the large number of strikes that erupted soon after Independence. Owing to a crisis of expectations — brought about to a large extent by the propaganda of the nationalist forces — thousands of

Figure 2: DOMESTIC AND FARM-WORKERS' INCOME

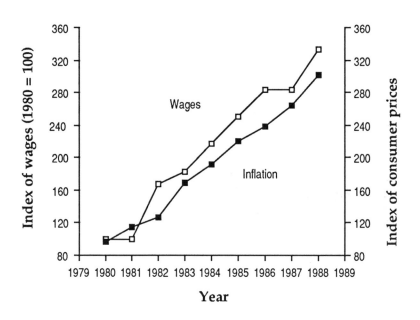

workers spontaneously went on strike, believing that the advent of a new government automatically entitled them to wage and salary increases. In the two weeks following the elections alone, 16 000 workers in forty-six firms went on wildcat strikes.[33] Lloyd Sachikonye lists a total of 178 enterprises that were affected by strikes between March 1980 and June 1981.[34] The strikes were not the result of formal union action; indeed, at Independence the Black unions were almost completely disorganized. Rather, workers took to the streets in an unstructured manner hoping to gain immediate benefits from the change in regimes.

In the light of these threatening and embarrassing strikes, the socialist government felt that it had to be seen to be doing something. In an interview, one former senior Ministry of Labour official argued that

[33] Astrow, *Zimbabwe: A Revolution That Lost Its Way?*, 175.

[34] L. M. Sachikonye, 'State, capital and trade unions', in I. Mandaza (ed.), *Zimbabwe: The Political Economy of Transition* (Dakar, CODESRIA, 1986), 268–72.

Figure 3: MINERS' INCOME

during the strikes the government appeared not to know 'where [the] nearest water pipe or toilet was'. He said that the minimum wage allowed the new regime to prove that it knew what it was doing'. Even Kumbirai Kangai, the first Minister of Labour, admitted that the initial wage legislation was a 'stop-gap . . . in view of the present industrial unrest'.[35]

All opinions suggest that the employers had very little influence on government actions in the early years of Independence. One former Ministry of Labour official described the early decision-making process: '[There was] one-way consultation with employers. We asked them questions but we did not tell them what we were going to do. We did not

---

[35] ZBC News, Radio 1, 1.15 p.m., 28 May 1984, cited in 'Government introduces minimum wage policy', *Foreign Broadcast Information Service: Daily Report: Near East and Africa*, 29 May 1980, U3.

Figure 4: INDUSTRIAL AND COMMERCIAL WORKERS' INCOME

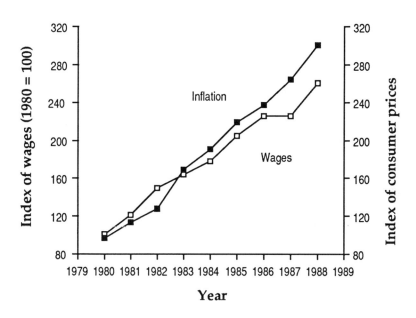

let the African Labour Bureau represent all of agriculture. . . . The setting of the minimum wage is held close to the purse.' The official said that it was fairly easy to set wages: 'We know in a few minutes the capability of industry. We can see what kind of production is going on and the value added. The idea was to let people free-float up while providing a minimum.' A Chamber of Mines official confirmed this description of the wage-setting process. He noted that before 1986 'the Ministry [of Labour] gets views [from industry] and then imposes wage settlements'. He said that there 'were no real negotiations' over wage increases during the first years of Independence. An African Labour Bureau official also agreed that there had been 'no consultation' over wages. Indeed, in the early years of Independence the government did not even have a formal structure or an institutionalized procedure for setting wages that could have attracted the lobbying efforts of employers.

Depression: 1982–1985

Just as the influence of the 'one-off' factors (such as the lifting of sanctions) that had caused the economic boom of 1980–2 were wearing off, Zimbabwe was suddenly confronted with a drought and the world recession. Annual economic growth dropped from the dramatic rates of the first two years of Independence to 1,4 per cent in 1982, a growth rate of –4,2 per cent in 1983, and then a positive rate of 2,6 per cent in 1984.[36] Owing to the drought's effects on export crops such as tobacco and cotton, Zimbabwe was faced with a deteriorating balance of payments and was forced to devalue its currency by 20 per cent in December 1982.[37] In January 1983 the government signed a standby agreement with the International Monetary Fund and therefore became subject to the IMF's 'high conditionality' recommendations.

The severe economic problems had an immediate impact on the country's wage policy. In a desperate effort to prevent lay-offs and keep threatened industries functioning, the government severely limited wage increases. Figures 3 and 4 show that between 1982 and 1983 the minimum wage after inflation for workers in mining, commerce and industry actually fell back below the 1980 level; real wages for domestic and agricultural workers (graphed in Figure 2) were still slightly above their 1980 level. It should also be noted that, in view of their low nominal wages, the fact that farm and domestic workers' real wages were still slightly above the 1980 level was no great achievement.

The setting of wages during this period was in dramatic contrast to that during the first two years of Independence. The government still had not established an institutionalized bargaining process, and employer groups say that they had no formal consultation with the government over wage levels. However, in many ways this was not necessary, given the country's bleak economic circumstances; the country's leaders were well aware that the nation could simply not afford large wage increases, and this sentiment was undoubtedly strengthened after consultation with business leaders on other aspects of the economy. In addition, the government was being pressured by the IMF to sharply reduce wage increases.

At the same time, the power of the workers was being sharply

---

[36] Zimbabwe, *Socio-Economic Review of Zimbabwe*, 2.

[37] Ibid., 62.

curtailed. The government made it clear that it was determined not to allow a repeat of the strikes that had occurred immediately after Independence. As early as May 1980 the government had shown impatience with the illegal work stoppages. Minister of Labour Kangai said, for instance, that he would take 'appropriate action in terms of the law against those who failed [to return to work]'. He warned: 'I will crack my whip if they do not go back to work. They must go back now.'[38] After eighteen months of Independence the entire government was committed to ending the spontaneous strikes. The Ministry of Labour, Manpower Planning and Social Welfare noted:

Towards the end of 1981 the Prime Minister himself was attacking striking teachers and nurses, calling them 'people with unrevolutionary minds who never experienced the hardships of the struggle for liberation'. Eventually the state did take action. During the Wankie strike of 1981, some of the strikers were charged in court for fermenting [sic] the strike, while a workers committee chairman was charged under the Law and Order Maintenance Act. In January 1982 several striking railwaymen were sent to jail.[39]

During the period of depression the government institutionalized its approach to strikes. In the Labour Relations Act, 1984 (No. 16 of 1985), Zimbabwe's major piece of labour legislation in the post-Independence period, those who want to strike have to give warning through a lengthy administrative procedure, and the Minister of Labour can make any strike illegal simply by declaring that the industry provides an essential service.[40] Like successive White regimes, the government has made it effectively impossible for unions to use strikes as a weapon against those who establish wages. One ZCTU official said in an interview that 'the [Labour Relations] Act gives the Minister draconian powers — he can do whatever he likes'. Strikes are formally discouraged because the present government, like the old White-dominated regimes, considers overall economic growth to be a more important goal than the creation of an environment in which workers can strive to increase their wages. As a result of government action, there have been no legal strikes in Zimbabwe since the enactment of the Labour Relations Act.

---

[38] *The Herald*, 30 May 1980.

[39] Zimbabwe, *Labour and Economy*, 24.

[40] Zimbabwe, Labour Relations Act, 1984 (No. 16 of 1985), section 118.

Uncertain Recovery: 1985–1988

In 1985 the three-year drought broke, and the world economic situation improved sufficiently to enable Zimbabwe's economy to grow again. Largely as a result of the recovery in agriculture, growth in GDP was 9,3 per cent that year.[41] Once the drought had broken, the government was able to post wage increases; however, as Figures 3 and 4 indicate, the real minimum wage for mining, industrial and commercial workers was still substantially below its 1980 level. The wages of agricultural and domestic workers, displayed in Figure 2, had also not risen substantially above their 1982 level, although they were still higher than they had been at Independence.

Even though the immediate worries caused by the long drought had largely disappeared, the government was, by 1985, fully aware of the fragility of the economy. This awareness, prompted by the severe depression between 1982 and 1985, was strengthened by what became known as the agro-industrial wage dispute. In 1985 the Minister of Labour, Dr Frederick Shava, suddenly announced an initiative whereby wages for all workers in 'agro-industry' would be immediately increased from $65 to $143,75 a month. The move was apparently designed to help workers in high value-added processing industries to achieve equity with industrial workers who received a minimum wage of $143,75. All the respondents interviewed reported that this initiative came from Minister Shava himself, apparently as a result of a campaign promise during the 1985 general elections, and was delivered with almost no warning. An official in the African Labour Bureau said, '[there was] no meaningful consultation. We felt shattered. We only found out about it [the agro-industrial wage] when it was announced.'

The wage initiative immediately encountered a host of problems. In the first place, it was not really clear what 'agro-industrial' meant, since this was a new classification in Zimbabwe. For instance, an official of the General Agricultural and Plantation Workers Union of Zimbabwe said, 'We don't understand what this 'agro-industrial' is all about. What is the difference between a man picking oranges and others?' The definition was fraught with contradictions; for instance, it apparently did not affect cotton and tobacco growers, even though significant on-farm processing is carried out these crops.

---

[41] Zimbabwe, *Socio-Economic Review of Zimbabwe*, 2.

In addition, the severe impact that the overnight doubling of wages would have on the viability of commercial enterprises immediately became an issue. At the height of the crisis it was estimated that many of the large plantation industries in the eastern province of Manicaland would go into a 'loss-making situation' if the new wages continued.[42] Applications for exemption, therefore, began to pour into the Ministry of Labour, and commercial agriculture applied pressure on the government to rescind the increases.

The government was, in fact, finally forced to grant widespread exemptions to farmers, and the agro-industrial wage initiative was dropped. There was, however, a large degree of labour unrest in the eastern region of the country when wage increases were suddenly announced and then withdrawn. In several instances workers went on strike or even kidnapped management personnel, demanding the wage that the government had seemingly promised them. Respondents in interviews indicated that in several cases the Zimbabwe Republic Police had to be called in to quell the unrest. For the government, these actions were an uncomfortably obvious replay of the times during the colonial era when the security forces had routinely crushed workers' protests.

The agro-industrial wage initiative can be seen as the last-ditch attempt by the government to radically increase the incomes of workers through *ad hoc* measures. After 1985 an institutionalized system of wage determination was established in the hope of avoiding the kind of problems caused by the informal system that had previously been in use. The Wages and Salary Review Board established in 1986 consists of senior civil servants from the major economic ministries and representatives of the labour and employer groups.[43] In the new wage-setting process EMCOZ and the ZCTU are first asked to submit papers to the Board. After considering the presentations from the two sides, the Board makes its own recommendations which are then submitted to the Ministry of Labour. The Ministry reviews these recommendations and then submits its own paper to the Ministerial Economic Co-ordinating Committee (MECC). MECC apparently makes its own suggestions to the Cabinet which then sets the final wages.

This institutionalization of the decision-making process fulfilled its desired intention of causing the setting of wages to be dominated by

---

[42] *The Herald*, 27 Nov. 1985.

[43] Zimbabwe, *Government Gazette*, 19 Dec. 1986, 1206.

technocratic considerations. Technocratic criteria, such as the effect increased wages would have on employment and on international competitiveness, replaced political considerations when bureaucrats in the Ministry of Finance, Economic Planning and Development began to exercise more influence over a process that had formally been supervised by politically-oriented officials in the Ministry of Labour. For instance, one official in the Ministry of Finance, Economic Planning and Development said in an interview:

Economic ministries try as much as possible to crystallize the process. We meet and see what has to be done. There is a realization that wages causes price spirals. We attempt to ask what effect increased wages will have on the economy. This is a more informed manner than just announcing wages.

In part, this shift was a victory for Minister Chidzero, whose patient, cautious technical advice became more attractive to the Cabinet after the fiasco of the agro-industrial wage dispute set off by Minister Shava's declaration. As one former Ministry of Labour official noted, 'Ministers poach on each others' territory; when there is a weakness, then they move in'.

The wage levels that were established in 1986 through the newly institutionalized system were a clear defeat for labour and a warning of poor times ahead for the workers. In its 1986 wage announcements the government accepted EMCOZ's recommendations that wage increases should be kept to half the inflation rate. Minister of Labour Shava called the raise a 'braking mechanism' on inflation. EMCOZ hailed the low raises because 'for the first time [government] consciously related wage and salary increments to employment creation, inflation and prices'.[44] However, the low wage increases led to an extraordinarily open conflict between the labour unions and the socialist government. The President of the ZCTU, Jeffrey Mutandare, after noting that inflation had increased by 20 per cent but that wages had risen by only half that, asked: 'Where do we get the other ten percent from?'[45] He recalled that the Riddell Commission had set the PDL at $191 a month five years earlier, 'but we are not even there five years after. That leaves us nowhere.' Mutandare explained the low wages by arguing that the employers had been able to influence the government on wages 'at the expense of the workers'.[46]

At the heart of the dispute between government and labour was, as

<hr>

[44] *The Herald*, 5 June 1986.   [45] *The Herald*, 30 June 1986.   [46] Ibid.

Mutandare correctly perceived, a shift in bargaining power to the employers. The establishment of a formal wage-setting process based on technocratic criteria, and the government's greater receptivity to employers' suggestions after the agro-industrial wage débâcle, gave the groups represented by EMCOZ much greater leverage in their discussion with the government. One agricultural representative said:

> In 1986 we see real consultation. [There was] pressure from the 'cock-up' over the agro-industrial wage and government didn't want to make the same mistakes. We feel free to go to the Minister with problems. Farming has big clout. It makes sense to lobby on wages but you have to be careful. People [in government] would appreciate having the information. We have access to most Ministers — more access than before. Now we have access to Minister of Labour. Labour was harder before.

Similarly, a Chamber of Mines official said: 'The first real participation [in wage negotiations] was in 1986'.

EMCOZ skillfully used the government's increased receptivity as an opportunity to present forcefully the employers' arguments against high wage increases. For instance, in the EMCOZ position paper submitted for the 1986 wage and salary review, the employers' confederation homed in on one of the government's greatest concerns: 'In the current world of recession, inflation and high unemployment among both adults and school leavers, it is impossible to raise wages and create jobs at the same time.'[47] The employers argued that large increases in the minimum wage would cause 'increases in producer and/or consumer prices which has the effect of wiping out the buying power of the workers in spite of the increases in wages and salaries'. It also warned of 'retrenchment of workers and/or hiring freezes which creates unemployment, especially now that we have an ever increasing number of unemployed school leavers'.[48]

EMCOZ was also able to 'piggy-back' on the pressure that international actors, mainly the IMF and World Bank, were putting on Zimbabwe to show wage restraint. For instance, the World Bank argued,

> there is little to no scope for further real increases in wages in the next few years. Increasing wages — for example, through raising the minimum wage — would

---

[47] Employers' Confederation of Zimbabwe, 'The Wages and Salaries Review of 1986: The EMCOZ Position Paper' (Harare, EMCOZ, 1986, mimeo.), 2.

[48] Ibid., 5.

have a prejudicial effect on the cost structures of actual and potential exporters; similarly, increasing the wages of public servants — teachers, for example — would tend to worsen the government deficit.[49]

EMCOZ reinforced this pressure by noting almost immediately in its position paper that 'the current world-wide formula for determining realistic wages and fight inflation at the same time has been one that keeps wages and salaries increments under 50 per cent of the national inflation rate'.[50]

In contrast to the growing receptivity that the employers' arguments enjoyed, representations from formal labour were becoming less and less convincing. Firstly, the government repeatedly expressed its impatience with trade union corruption, maladministration and disorganization.[51] There was also some direct criticism of the workers themselves; for instance, Prime Minister Mugabe noted in his 1987 New Year's address,

What we, however, find most disturbing is the great incidence of irresponsibility on the part of a large segment of workers which has shown itself by way of indiscipline at work, poor application, laziness, absenteeism, drunkenness, unpunctuality, et cetera.[52]

In contrast to what happened in 1980, the (smaller) wave of wildcat strikes after the 1985 general elections had no effect on government policy. In addition, the growing closeness of the employers and the government made the unions feel that they were being abandoned. One union official said:

The honeymoon between us and ZANU(PF) is over. Government doesn't give a damn about trade unions. At first government cared but now it only protects local and international capital. [The employers] have contacts, they can lobby. In the majority of cases employers get what they are asking for or close.

Labour's position was further weakened by its poor choice of bargaining tactics. For example, in its position paper for the 1986 wages and salary review the ZCTU based its demands totally on the poverty datum line.

---

[49] World Bank, *Zimbabwe: Country Economic Memorandum*, xvi.

[50] Employers' Confederation of Zimbabwe, 'The Wages and Salaries Review of 1986', 2.

[51] This was a major theme of the Ministry of Labour, Manpower Planning and Social Welfare's Trade Union Survey; see Zimbabwe, *Labour and Economy*.

[52] R. G. Mugabe, 'The Prime Minister's New Year message', *Zimbabwe News* (Jan. 1987), XVIII, ii, 10.

After accounting for inflation, the union representatives suggested a minimum wage of $250 for mining, industrial and commercial workers, $175 for agricultural workers, and $115 for domestic workers.[53] The ZCTU's requests amounted to increases of 174 per cent, 233 per cent and 153 per cent, respectively. No mention was made in the ZCTU paper of how these massive increases in wages would affect employment, despite repeated statements of concern by the government and the rhetoric of employers. This was a particularly serious deficiency as the agro-industrial wage controversy had made it clear to the government that it could not increase real wages quickly. One employer representative said: 'ZCTU became irrelevant as it can't answer the school-leaver problem'. The ZCTU was also unable to suggest how the increased wages would affect prices or Zimbabwe's export competitiveness.[54] Minister of Labour Shava publicly rebuked the ZCTU for its excessive demands:

The proposed increases by the ZCTU were unrealistic in the light of the economy which is just recovering from the recession and drought. Some of the proposed increases were 100 percent and in view of this, the government adopted what we regard as affordable in view of other constraints on the economy.[55]

The ZCTU's continued adherence to the Riddell Commission's PDL recommendations — even though the government had never adopted those guidelines — meant that its wage demands were so obviously extravagant that they made the employers' requests appear more attractive to the government. One EMCOZ official commented upon the ZCTU's position: 'ZCTU often loses because they become monolithic on inflation. When the employer says he is also facing inflation on raw materials, they do not have a response. Employers [therefore] seem to be more civic-minded.' Or as another employer representative said about the ZCTU: 'Starting off asking for the world is useless'. However, in view of their lack of skills in analysis and research, the ZCTU probably does not have the ability to make any case for increased wages other than by mechanistically adhering to the inflation-adjusted PDL.

Given Zimbabwe's continuing economic problems, it appears that the employers' arguments will continue to be persuasive to the government. In the 1987 wage review EMCOZ again asked for a wage increase that was

---

[53] Zimbabwe Congress of Trade Unions, 'Position Paper on Wages Review 1986' (Harare, ZCTU, 1986, mimeo.), 9.

[54] Ibid.   [55] *The Herald*, 1 July 1986.

less than 50 per cent of the inflation rate.[56] The Confederation wrote in its 1987 position paper:

As members of the [Wages and Salaries Review] Board know, currently the economy is generating only about 10 000 to 15 000 jobs a year. Realistically, we need to create more than 100 000 jobs a year in order to cope with school-leaver unemployment alone. . . . The question we are raising is: in the current atmosphere of the shortage of foreign currency, raw materials, and some consumer goods, as well as inflation and serious unemployment, can Zimbabwe afford to increase wages and salaries, and create at least 100 000 jobs at the same time.[57]

In contrast, the unions continued their unsuccessful negotiating posture. While EMCOZ was stressing the very real constraints imposed by the economy, the ZCTU said it would 'reject' a minimum wage below $277.[58]

The government eventually decided that, owing to another drought and the need to increase exports and investment, the nation could not afford a wage increase at all, and froze wages for 1987. Significantly, the decision to freeze wages, despite the fact that an informal agreement to raise wages by 10 per cent had already been made, was announced by Minister Chidzero, without EMCOZ, the ZNFU, or (apparently) Minister Shava being informed in advance.[59] A further dramatic demonstration of the primacy of technocratic considerations in the wage-setting process occurred in the 1988 Cabinet shuffle when Dr Shava was moved to the relatively unimportant position of Minister of State (Administration) in the President's Office, while Dr Chidzero became Senior Minister with responsibility for all the ministries dealing with economic affairs.

Empowering the Unions: The Dilemmas of Benevolent Paternalism

The government established the national minimum wage in 1980 because it thought, undoubtedly correctly, that the unions were too weak to engage in collective bargaining with employers. Unfortunately for the workers, however, the government's role in the wage-setting process, far from helping the unions, has actually prevented them from becoming

---

[56] Inflation was estimated at between 16 per cent and 20 per cent, *Financial Gazette*, 6 Mar. 1987.

[57] Quoted in ibid.

[58] *The Herald*, 24 May 1987.

[59] See B. T. G. Chidzero, 'Statement of the Minister of Finance, Economic Planning and Development on Incomes and State of Economy', in Zimbabwe, *Annual Economic Review of Zimbabwe, 1986*, 76.

stronger. Because government enacts wage increases for workers directly, the unions have severe mobilization problems because organized labour has little it can offer the workers. One union leader said:

The problem is that the government has been the trade union because all the benefits to the workers have come from the government and not the unions. So people now feel that the government runs the unions. The government has been spoon-feeding the unions . . .[60]

Similarly, one Ministry of Labour official noted in an interview:

[We] must look at the paternalistic logic of the state. Minimum wages started off as a very good initiative. [It was] not just a way of finding patronage among the workers. But now it weakens the labour movement. If the trade unions struggle with employers, they could start a process where the labour movement gains strength.

An employer representative agreed: 'The socialist state doesn't want to be on the wrong side of the *povo*. [But] we don't see unions being strong as long as we have the minimum wage.' The analysis by officials appears to gauge worker feelings correctly. For instance, in a survey of workers, 46,6 per cent of respondents rated the government first when asked which institution interested them the most, while only 28,6 per cent gave the best rating to the unions.[61]

In addition to weakening the unions, the government's takeover of the decision-making on wages has another effect on wage levels. Officials throughout the government and the private sector agree that the minimum wages announced by the government have now also become maximum wages. Jeffrey Mutandare, for instance, argues: 'Employers no longer increase wages according to the performance of their enterprises, but just wait for the government to announce new wage increases.'[62] EMCOZ has, in fact, admitted that 'employers are unlikely to make concessions to unions when they are uncertain how the concessions will be affected by government intervention'.[63] The minimum wage has, therefore, become a complete subversion of what the government originally intended: a minimum income has now become a wage ceiling.

[60] Quoted in Zimbabwe, *Labour and Economy*, 46.

[61] S. R. Shabalala, 'Private Enterprise System in Zimbabwe: An Environment Assessment Experience' (Harare, 1986, mimeo.), 44.

[62] 'Wage policies retrogressive — ZCTU', *Moto* (1986), XLVII, 3.

[63] *The Chronicle*, 6 June 1985.

However, the government faces severe risks if it follows its announced policy of trying to remove itself from the wage-setting process.[64] In the first place, after nearly a decade of Independence there are probably no more than a few unions that have the organizational, analytical and research capabilities to confront well-funded, sophisticated and knowledgeable employers. Workers may feel, therefore, that they have been abandoned by the government precisely because government took responsibility for setting the wages for most of the 1980s. Yet, removing itself from the wage-setting process is the only way in which the government will strengthen the unions in the long term. Secondly, if unions are to bargain collectively they must be given a right to strike that is not contingent upon ministerial approval. If the unions do not have the right to strike, they will have no leverage against employers. Yet, the government has been unwilling to allow strikes because it fears they will lead to a recurrence of the widespread disruptions that occurred in 1980 and 1981.

Institutions and Labour Power

The fundamental problem facing labour in Zimbabwe is the institutional structure that governs the political conflict over wages. Labour was at its most powerful in 1980–1 when spontaneous strikes forced the government into early establishment of minimum wages at levels that gave workers real increases in income. These strikes were possible because they were not dependent on the formal organizational skills of the unions; indeed, the confusion in the unions probably encouraged workers to act on their own. However, the government later closed off this avenue of protest by continuing the ban on strikes that had existed during the colonial era, and by threatening the use of physical force if workers persisted with their strike actions.

Since 1980 the transformation of the wage-setting process into a more formal bargaining structure has directly reduced the power of labour, because the formal structure of wage negotiations rewards the attributes in which labour is most lacking: analytic skills, co-ordinated bargaining approaches and organizational cohesion. The employers, in contrast, have a natural advantage when the process is based on technocratic considerations with which they are familiar. Indeed, the rejection by government of the Riddell Commission's recommendations is, with hindsight, significant, because only the adoption of an automatic wage-setting process could have prevented labour's loss of bargaining power in a setting where political conflict is institutionalized. If the wage-setting is not automatic, employers will have the advantage because of their greater organizational skills.

A committed government could possibly prevent the employers from being dominant in an institutionalized wage-setting process if it were able to match the employers' organizational and analytical skills. However, the government of Zimbabwe lacks the administrative ability and, to some extent, the willingness to guide a formalized process in such a way that it would favour workers. One Ministry of Labour official argued that the government could still help workers within the current structure, but that officials 'haven't developed a long-term incomes policy. We have responded on an *ad hoc* basis to the post-colonial state and after that to other conditions. . . . Incomes policy has been a failure.' For instance, one employer representative noted in an interview:

The argument that seems most persuasive is the big crisis in unemployment. EMCOZ emphasizes the fact that [the government] can't increase wages and employment at the same time. However, government doesn't monitor if, when the wage award is not high, there is an actual increase in employment.

As long as the government cannot match the capacity of the employers in analysis and research, bargaining power will inevitably shift to employers in the wage-setting process because it is they who will be able to set the terms of the debate. However, the prospect of the government developing a comprehensive labour strategy is faint as long as the ministry which takes the lead on wage policy is that of Finance, Economic Planning and Development, which focuses mainly on the performance of macroeconomic aggregates, rather than the Ministry of Labour.

An institutionalized structure of protest also has natural attractions for the government. The political conflict in the current wage-setting process, mainly in the form of contesting position papers, is much easier to manage than the highly embarrassing protests which occurred in the streets immediately after Independence. The similarities in the labour policy of successive colonial governments and that of the Independence government probably originate in the common desire to be able to manage conflict in an orderly manner through institutions. Just as the colonial regime allowed the establishment of unions when a permanent labour force began to emerge in the colony, the new government IMF has encouraged the creation of a federation of unions so that all communications with labour can be directed through one channel. When conflict is institutionalized in such a manner, labour is left, by design, with no other avenue of protest.

Some observers of the Zimbabwe experience have now come to the conclusion that labour can never be empowered if it engages in institutional co-operation with the state. For instance, a faction in the Confederation of South African Trade Unions (COSATU) does not want to endorse the aims of the African National Congress because 'they feared that by adopting the African National Congress political program, COSATU could become a tool of political groups and end up after majority rule without any real power, as happened in neighbouring Zimbabwe'.[65]

Conclusion

State autonomy in the area of national minimum-wage policy can once again be understood on two levels. At the structural level, the government did have the autonomy to design the rules according to which wages would be set. While the employers had been pressuring since Independence for a more formalized wage-setting process, it was the policy-makers' own decisions, especially after the agro-industrial wage dispute, that led to the institutionalization of the decision-making process. However, the type of structure that the government designed was particularly amenable to the political pressure that the employers had learned to exert and, as a result, the state has not been autonomous in specific decisions concerning the setting of minimum wages.

Once again, the government's choices concerning institutional structures had a determining effect on the pattern of distributional politics. The institutionalization of the wage-setting process, in combination with Zimbabwe's continuing economic crisis, has allowed employers to gradually gain the upper hand in bargaining over national minimum-wage levels. The structure of conflict — decision-making by civil servants based largely on highly technical information — has served over time to make the well-organized and sophisticated employers particularly powerful. The employers are further strengthened by World Bank and IMF exhortations to the government that real wage increases must be kept low.

---

[65] *New York Times*, 19 July 1987, 5.

Similarly, the structure of government decision-making penalizes the ZCTU because its analytical, research and organizational capabilities are poor. At the same time, the government's control of the entire wage process emasculates the unions and prevents them from developing more capable organizational structures because they now have no way in which to mobilize workers. Labour was strongest when there was no institutionalized procedure to set wages and when workers could pressure the government directly by taking to the streets.

Wage policy is another instance of the government's not strengthening itself by constructing elaborate, centralized institutions to consider every aspect of public policy. The government was much more autonomous, especially in its relations with the employers, when national minimum-wage policy was being made without formal procedures by a few civil servants who considered only some 'back-of-the-envelope' calculations.

It should be noted, too, that the nature of the issue-area itself also strengthened the employers' position relative to the state. Specifically, the fact that wage-setting is an iterated process conducted every year has, over time, led to a steady accretion of employer power. The employers were gradually able to learn government concerns and to structure their case so that it would be as persuasive as possible in wage negotiations. The employers also benefited from a subtle campaign conducted by businesses in Zimbabwe which, in all areas of public policy, has stressed the very real limits to the government's ability to change the economy radically. The unions could not benefit from this iterated process because they remained poorly organized: the ZCTU was still basing its case for higher wages on the poverty datum line, even though a recommendation by the Riddell Commission to use this indicator had been implicitly rejected by the government years before.

Locus of Decision-making

The locus of decision-making has been in a state of flux as far as national minimum-wage policy is concerned. During the early years of Independence the locus of decision-making was at the level of the national leadership; later, however, decision-making seems to be centred in the bureaucracy. This shift downward was the result of a deliberate decision by the government that, especially after the agro-industrial wage disaster, wage-setting should be done on a more technical basis and, therefore, would have to take account of far more factors than had been the case previously.

The national leadership could not possibly supervise as complex a decision-making process as wage-setting had become, so the bureaucracy naturally became much more important.

The ruling party has not played a major role in the setting of wages for several reasons. Firstly, the party's strength does not lie in the urban areas, where most employees live, because the party has never really expanded from the rural base it developed during the war. Indeed, championing wage increases for workers who were already better off than peasants may not have been particularly compelling to the leadership in view of its rural origins. Also, as has been the case in several areas examined in this study, ZANU(PF) has not developed the technical expertise necessary to become a significant player in the wage-setting process. One Ministry of Labour official noted in an interview: 'The party has no long-term perspective on wages. That comes much more from bureaucrats who can take economic issues and feed them to Ministers. The Politburo is more important on the purely political issues such as inter-party conflict.'

Finally, as in the conflict over the national distribution of land, the party does not have a clear enough ideology to enable it to establish general rules on wage levels that could be imposed on the bureaucracy. The party's ideology on wages at Independence was no more than a vague feeling that they should be raised, and very little effort has been dedicated to developing a more sophisticated stance. Without general principles that could be imposed on the bureaucracy, it was inevitable that, as the decision-making process became more complicated, the civil service would become more important. Ideological militants simply do not have the time or the ability to confront the bureaucracy on a case-by-case basis when wages are being determined.

Wage-setting will continue to be a contentious issue in Zimbabwe for the foreseeable future. However, it does not now appear that, unless there is a marked change in the country's economic circumstances, there will be any great shifts in who is ultimately powerful on this issue. The longer that technocratic wage-setting in an institutionalized context is the norm in Zimbabwe, the harder it will be for anyone to argue on a purely political basis —as was the case with the agro-industrial wage — that incomes for workers should be increased. Since employers will continue to dominate the decision-making that is done on a regular basis by the bureaucracy, workers cannot count on significant real wage increases being granted as a result of the wage-setting process in its present form.

Chapter Ten

The Evolution of Politics
in Zimbabwe since Independence

In the previous seven chapters, I have examined government decision-making in specific areas; however, these studies by themselves cannot provide an overall understanding of how the independent state of Zimbabwe has evolved. Case studies, by their very nature, provide an in-depth but very narrow perspective on only segments of the polity. It is now necessary to pick out the common strands in the case studies and look at the mosaic of politics so that Zimbabwe is treated as a country that is important in its own right and not just as a setting for a political investigation. Several aspects of the developing political system must be examined: the politics of reconciliation, the problems of designing economic policy, the role of ideology, the role of Robert Mugabe, and the implications of the unification of the two major political parties which was finally accomplished at the end of 1987. These over-arching political phenomena have been major issues in Zimbabwe's national politics since Independence, and they will continue to be so for the foreseeable future.

The Politics of Reconciliation

Undoubtedly the most striking development in independent Zimbabwe has been the reconciliation between Blacks and Whites. Although the country has a history of colonial repression, and many people of all races suffered greatly during the war, Blacks and Whites today live together peacefully and, for the most part, actively co-operate in government and business. It is true that half the White population left the country at Independence, but the fact that 100 000 Whites live peacefully in Zimbabwe means that reconciliation can be called Zimbabwe's greatest success. Indeed, many have based their hopes for a peaceful resolution of the problems in South Africa on the Zimbabwean precedent. Unfortunately, a proper understanding of the policy reconciliation makes it clear that the Zimbabwean experience is not transferable.

At Independence the Mugabe government, in effect, made a bargain with the remaining Whites. The bargain, which is never discussed but is generally understood, is basically that the Whites who are in independent Zimbabwe can stay, continue to operate their businesses and farms, and lead the 'colonial life style' that they are accustomed to for the rest of their lives. However, their children, in general, are discouraged from staying. The racial bargain has been implicitly signalled by a myriad of government actions and statements, and a general atmosphere which suggests that there is no economic future in Zimbabwe for most young Whites. It was relatively easy for the government to construct this bargain because of the role the state plays in every aspect of the economy: the possibility of lines of credit, government purchases, or tenders of public enterprises being biased against Whites is easy for all to imagine. For instance, foreign companies which sell their assets in Zimbabwe can have their funds remitted only if the purchasers are Black Zimbabweans, Black Zimbabwean co-operatives, or the government.[1] The racial bargain implies that Zimbabwe will not have to Africanize the economy by force because in a generation or so the White population will have dwindled into insignificance.

The implicit racial bargain appealed to the interests of both sides. For the Whites the bargain was certainly the best racial policy from a Black government that they could possibly have expected. Many Whites in Zimbabwe today continue to live a 'colonial' lifestyle with domestic workers, large gardens and tennis courts. Indeed, after the Rhodesian propaganda which painted Mugabe as a pathological maniac,[2] many Whites still seem surprised that they are allowed to live in Zimbabwe under a Black government in the style to which they are accustomed. While the foreclosure of economic opportunities for White children has meant separated families, there have been places for the young people to go. A large number, perhaps a majority, of young Whites have gone to South Africa, which readily accepts White immigrants. Many Whites also retained their British passports, and even those who had Zimbabwe passports could usually obtain residence in the United Kingdom through a family connection. As English-speakers, it was also possible for many young Whites to emigrate elsewhere. The Whites who did not fit into the

---

[1] *The Financial Gazette*, 10 Apr. 1987.

[2] See, for instance, J. Frederikse, *None but Ourselves: Masses vs. Media in the Making of Zimbabwe* (Harare, Zimbabwe Publishing House, 1982), 208.

government's long-term economic plans were therefore able to take, in Albert Hirschman's terminology, the exit option.[3]

For the Black government the bargain is also a sensible one. Having witnessed the chaos caused by the massive flight of Whites from Mozambique, the nationalist leaders understood the importance of discouraging the sudden emigration of those responsible for operating the economy. At the same time, the newly empowered Blacks obviously wanted to be assured that they would gain the skills necessary to operate and control the economy in the same way that the Whites did. By allowing Whites to stay, the new regime retains vitally-needed personnel until they can be replaced by trained Blacks. And, by discouraging White society from increasing its numbers, the government has the assurance that within a generation Blacks will, through attrition, gain control of the economy.

The racial bargain struck in Zimbabwe was possible because of the demographic and socio-economic characteristics of the White community. There have never been more than 270 000 Whites in the country, and they, at most, accounted for 5,6 per cent of the total population.[4] Although accurate statistics are unavailable, it is estimated that approximately half of the White population who stayed at Independence emigrated in the year or after, leaving a population of roughly 110 000. The Whites who stayed are also relatively old. In 1982 it was estimated that as much as 43,7 per cent of the White population was over forty years old; in contrast, only 16,4 per cent of the African population is over forty.[5] The White population is disproportionately old because many conscription-age males and their families left during the war, and older Whites who have accumulated non-remittable assets are more likely to stay in Zimbabwe than younger Whites who, in accordance with the racial bargain, leave because they still have their most productive economic years ahead of them.

The White population is small enough that, if the relatively few young people who remain were encouraged to leave, high mortality and low birth rates would guarantee that the settler presence would decrease so rapidly that they would quickly become insignificant as a threat to the Black government. Given present trends, within a generation the White population will probably be only one-fifth to one-tenth its current size.

---

[3] A. O. Hirschman, *Exit, Voice and Loyalty: Responses to Decline in Firms, Organizations and States* (Cambridge, Harvard Univ. Press, 1970), 21.

[4] The White population as a proportion of the total population apparently reached a peak in 1961, Zimbabwe, *Main Demographic Features of the Population of Zimbabwe*, 10.

[5] Zimbabwe, *Statistical Yearbook, 1987*, 18.

There will still be Whites in the country; however, they will be so few as to have lost the critical mass needed to be a political community. Zimbabwe, therefore, will become like Kenya or Zambia: a Black nation containing only a few scattered, but affluent, remnants from the colonial era. Demographic change and the government's pressure on young White people to leave means that Zimbabwe will not be a multiracial society for very long.

In addition to their being few in number, the socio-economic position of the Whites in Zimbabwe made reconciliation relatively easy. The Whites in Zimbabwe were colonists who came to the country when economic opportunity beckoned. The settlers, most of whom arrived after the Second World War,[6] were, by and large, well trained, and many were immediately able to advance to very high economic positions. In independent Zimbabwe, the White population occupies most of the highly-skilled positions in the economy. They are, therefore, not at present in direct competition with the vast majority of the Black population who are untrained. It was easy for Blacks to move into the lower-level positions formerly occupied by Whites, because many of the poorer Whites in those posts had already emigrated, and this will have occasioned no fall in the socio-economic position of the more affluent Whites. To take one example, the clerical positions in the Post Offices went from mainly White to almost completely Black within a very short time after Independence. Most of the Whites who worked in these positions were women who were earning additional family income and who did not need to work or could find employment elsewhere or decided to emigrate. What is important to note is that the absolute minimum requirement of the Black government — changing the racial nature of the state at the point where the public has the most contact with it — could be done easily without affecting the position of the Whites. The ease with which Blacks were able to move into many positions was one of the key factors in enabling reconciliation to succeed, because the economic positions occupied by most Whites did not require them to resist Black advancement.

This perspective on reconciliation is persuasive because it looks to the interests of the White and Black communities to explain political developments. Unfortunately, there has been little reconciliation of attitudes in Zimbabwe today. However, the government has structured a bargain so that the two communities can continue to work together for their common interests. The fact that there has been a reconciliation of interests but not

[6] See Chapter 2.

of attitudes was dramatically illustrated in the 1985 White election vote. The Whites had to elect twenty parliamentarians that year and were given the choice of backing Ian Smith's party or a group of White Zimbabweans who stood for much closer collaboration with the government. Smith's party, although they were perceived as representing past confrontational attitudes, won fifteen of the twenty seats. In addition, Zimbabwe's social life remains almost completely segregated; Blacks and Whites are generally not together unless they are at work. Zimbabwe is, to borrow W. Arthur Lewis's phrase, a society that is integrated by day but segregated by night.[7]

The Zimbabwean experience cannot be applied to South Africa because of the very different demographics of the two White populations. While they are a minority, the Whites in South Africa still number 4,6 million (eighteen times larger than the greatest number of Whites in Rhodesia) and comprise approximately 18 per cent of the country's population (three times the maximum White proportion of the population in Rhodesia).[8] The Whites in South Africa have a population large enough that they will reproduce themselves for the foreseeable future and the population simply will not disappear if some young people are encouraged to leave. Unlike that in Zimbabwe, the White community in South Africa must be viewed as a permanent feature of the political landscape. Any post-apartheid government committed to racial reconciliation, therefore, will be confronted with a much more complicated task than that which the new Black regime in Zimbabwe faced at Independence.

Furthermore, it is not nearly as easy for the Whites of South Africa to leave as it was for the young Rhodesians. In the first place, there is no other country that will serve as an assured place of emigration as South Africa did for the White Rhodesians. Secondly, the Afrikaners, who account for 57 per cent of White society[9] and are politically more significant than the English speakers, also cannot travel as freely because of language constraints. Finally, the Afrikaners have a very different relationship to the land from that which the British colonists had in Rhodesia. While the Whites arrived in Rhodesia only in 1890, with the bulk of the population

[7] W. A. Lewis, 'Black power and the American university', *University: A Princeton Quarterly* (1969), XL, 8.

[8] South Africa, *South African Statistics 1982* (Pretoria, Govt. Printer, 1982), section 1.4.

[9] Ibid., section 1.24.

coming after the Second World War, the Dutch ancestors of the Afrikaners first settled in South Africa during the mid-seventeenth century.
The Afrikaner republics, the Transvaal and the Orange Free State, were in
existence well before the BSA Company moved north of the Limpopo.
The Afrikaners are not only less able to take the exit option but are
probably less willing to do so. They are more likely, in Hirschman's
terminology, to stay within the nation and use their voice option to
fervently oppose change.[10]

Unfortunately, radical restructuring will also be exceptionally difficult
in South Africa because the White population is not only larger than
Zimbabwe's, it is also at much greater risk from Black competition. The
Afrikaners are not colonialists; they were in South Africa before economic
development began, and many are still in unskilled positions. In a free
labour market a substantial percentage of South African Whites, a percentage much greater than that of Zimbabwean Whites, would be replaced immediately by Blacks. Indeed, one of the major goals of the
apartheid system is to protect the large number of Whites (mainly
Afrikaners) who would be at risk from competition with Blacks. Reconciliation in South Africa will, therefore, be much more difficult because a
large number of Whites are likely to resist vociferously any possible Black
competition. For instance, many of the Whites who occupy clerical
positions in South African Post Offices will have no other means of
earning an income, and will therefore fight to retain their positions. Thus,
changing the racial composition of the state where it is most public will be
much more difficult in South Africa than it was in Zimbabwe.

Reconciliation in South Africa, if it is possible at all, will have to be on
much different terms from those on which it has taken place in Zimbabwe. A solution for South Africa similar to Zimbabwe's, in which the
White population is allowed to continue to dominate the country's
economy because it will virtually disappear within a generation, is not
possible. There will have to be a much more immediate and radical
restructuring of the economy in South Africa after the attainment of
majority rule because a Black government that seeks to replace the
apartheid system will not be able to count on Blacks gaining economic
dominance simply by allowing the White population to wither away.
Given the need for more radical and immediate socio-economic restructuring, reconciliation will be much harder, and the possibility of a

[10] Hirschman, *Exit, Voice and Loyalty*, 33.

long period of racial strife will be greater. Unlike Zimbabwe, South Africa faces the extraordinarily difficult task of building a multiracial society.

Socialism-for-the-Blacks and Economic Policy

Many studies have focused on the highly publicized transition from capitalism to socialism as the most important element of post-1980 politics. Unfortunately, the attraction or repulsion of the ideological labels has obscured what is actually happening in the political economy of Zimbabwe. The government has embarked on many new policies which it calls socialist: increased social services (e.g. health care), more access to basic resources (e.g. land), some insulation for workers from market forces (e.g, the minimum wage), and state operation of certain strategic business operations (e.g. the Minerals Marketing Corporation). However, as has been made clear throughout this study, the previous colonial governments engaged in all of these activities in order to aid the White population. Indeed, a persuasive argument can be made that, while there is a public commitment to socialism, market forces are stronger in post-Independence Zimbabwe than at any point in the country's history because the new government has removed the racial laws and practices which prevented Blacks from competing economically with Whites. This is most obvious in the case of agricultural producer prices where only since Independence has the price mechanism been allowed to function in the peasant areas. The Mugabe government's approach to serving its supporters is not very different from that of previous regimes; the major difference is in the size and the nature of the new government's constituency. Therein lies the problem not only for the transition to 'socialism' but for the government's entire macroeconomic strategy.

White Rhodesia was founded and operated on extravagance; the country was never rich enough to support the Western lifestyles of the White population. As noted in Chapter 2, even in the 1950s Whites were leading a material life similar to that in the United States although the country was only beginning to industrialize. The only way that the Whites were able to fund their 'colonial' life style was through the exploitation of the 95 per cent of the population which was Black. The labour reserve economy and complete control of the distribution of wealth allowed the Whites to have the best of all worlds; cheap labour operated their businesses and cleaned their homes while they allocated to themselves the capital necessary for a First World standard of living.

However, the underlying basis of Socialism-for-the-Whites cannot be duplicated in a Socialism-for-the-Blacks system because the labour system was a major grievance of the Black population. The new government, therefore, is faced with a dilemma. It cannot duplicate the extravagance of the Whites because its economic base cannot support lavish — or even substantially increased — expenditures for the *entire* population. However, if it works to expand the productive base of the economy (usually defined as the agricultural, mining and manufacturing sectors), it will not be able to establish, in the short to medium term, the kind of socialist programmes that it promised to the thousands who died in the liberation struggle and to the Black population in general. Also, the government is ambivalent about promoting economic growth, even though its social programmes are absolutely dependent on a high level of expansion, because the productive structures of the economy are still owned by Whites. The entire economic strategy of the government, therefore, can be understood as a series of responses to the dilemmas inherent in establishing Socialism-for-the-Blacks in an economy designed solely to provide a very small segment of the population with a Western standard of living.

The initial policy of the government after Independence was to try to duplicate the extravagance of the Whites. This is best exemplified by the goal in the *Transitional National Development Plan* of resettling 162 000 families in three years without any corresponding evaluation of the country's ability to support a programme of that scope; the productive base of the economy simply could not support the level of expenditure that the Plan demanded. The government's plans were probably unrealistic in an absolute sense, and the gap between its proposals and capabilities was enlarged by the new regime's poor record — best exemplified in the area of foreign investment — of increasing productive capabilities.

The new regime, therefore, had to endure the problems associated with spending beyond its capacity to generate income. For instance, the budget deficit, planned to be 5 per cent of Gross Domestic Product for 1983–5, increased from 8 per cent of GDP in 1981/2 to 12 per cent in the years following 1984 as the government's spending requirements outstripped its revenue.[11] For the fiscal year 1989/90, the deficit will be 9 per cent of GDP.[12] Even more ominously, foreign debt rose dramatically as the government for resources that could not be provided domestically. Debt repayment jumped from $152,4 million in 1981 to $577,3 million in

[11] Zimbabwe, *Socio-Economic Review of Zimbabwe 1980–1985*, 71–2.

[12] A. M. Hawkins, 'The price of a decade of missed opportunities', *Financial Times*, 21 Aug. 1989.

1985 and the debt-service ratio climbed from 15,7 per cent to 31,9 per cent,[13] though it did decline to 27 per cent in 1988 and is projected to be around 20 per cent in the 1990s.[14] The Ministry of Finance, Economic Planning and Development recognized the underlying problem facing the economy:

> The imbalance between material and non-material production, if continued, could have adverse effects on long-run growth performance of the economy and sustained development. The expansion of social services can only be sustained, in the medium and long term, through overall economic expansion at rates well above those attained in the previous five to six-year period.[15]

Zimbabwe has been affected by a number of adverse external shocks, especially the long drought and the world recession. However, these events should not have been completely unexpected,[16] and, in any case, even if the external environment had been friendlier, the economy still would not have been able to afford government's extravagant programme.

In the light of the country's economic problems, the government has tried to allocate more resources to the productive base of the economy while cutting back on its ambitious programmes. For instance, in the *First Five-Year National Development Plan* the government pledged to increase investment in the productive sectors of the economy from 40 per cent of total investment to 47 per cent.[17] However, this effort was fraught with contradictions: for instance, the government did not take the necessary steps (such as signing OPIC-type agreements) to expand investment in material production. The government did manage, as the discussion of wage policy in Chapter 9 makes clear, to achieve cutbacks in consumption, even though this meant a significant political cost in the alienation of the workers. Ten years after Independence, therefore, the government is in the throes of its central dilemma: it has reduced its ambitious social programme but has not sufficiently expanded the productive base of the economy to be able to afford even the existing programmes.

[13] Zimbabwe, *Socio-Economic Review of Zimbabwe 1980–1985*, 61. The debt-service ratio is the amount of total debt repayment divided by total goods and services exported.

[14] Hawkins, 'The price of a decade of missed opportunities'.

[15] Zimbabwe, *Socio-Economic Review of Zimbabwe 1980–1985*, 22.

[16] For instance, the semi-arid nature of Zimbabwe's ecology makes a drought every several years almost inevitable.

[17] Zimbabwe, *First Five-Year National Development Plan*, I, 13.

Since, from the government's perspective, further cutbacks in consumption are undesirable, it will take a major effort to be able to increase production to get the country out of its current economic problems. However, the conflict between a programme that seeks major expansion in the productive sectors and the political objectives of the regime is so great that this option may not be feasible. Zimbabwe, therefore, finds itself in a 'Catch-22' situation: the structure of the economy has disabled the government's political programme, while at the same time the government's political project has severely retarded economic growth. Until this contradiction is somehow resolved, the project of developing Socialism-for-the-Blacks will go nowhere.

The Role of Ideology

The significance of ideology in the formulation of public policy in Zimbabwe is difficult to determine. On the one hand, the new regime has self-consciously portrayed itself as a Marxist state; on the other, it has often adopted economic policies which are far from radical. In fact, the direction that ideology has taken since 1980 has largely been affected by factional politics within the party and government. While a comprehensive examination of the divisions within the national leadership is beyond the scope of this study, the course of factional rivalries, and the consequent evolution of ideology, is very important for an effective analysis of the country's political development.

The strength of pressure on the government to pursue a Marxist-oriented line of policy — even if this orientation is ill defined — fluctuates, but the undercurrent is always present as a result of the radicalization of a large number of people during the liberation war, and because of the presence of committed ideologues in all sectors of the government. In some cases, however, Marxist ideology has not been able to penetrate policy decisions. The government has, for example, publicly declared that it will not seize land or nationalize businesses, preferring to follow a moderate line because of Zimbabwe's inability to afford the radical alternative, or as a result of real doubts as to the ultimate efficacy of certain Marxist policies — particularly in the light of the experience of other African countries. In other instances, there has not been an ideological conflict because ideologues and technocrats have pursued the same goal: this was the case in the provision of preventive care through rural health centres.

Ministers and officials with a relatively technocratic background have gradually come to occupy areas in which ideology is less important. This has happened both for positive reasons (because they were seen to be the most suitable occupant for the post) and for negative reasons (because of the failure of non-technocratic appointees). For example, Dr Bernard Chidzero, the Minister of Finance, Economic Planning and Development and chief economic policy maker, was a natural choice for that portfolio owing to his experience as an international civil servant dealing with development issues. His replacement of Enos Nkala, a ZANU(PF) partisan with no economic background, is an example of government's conscious decision to place technocrats in ministries which require particularly complex economic judgements. Chidzero gradually expanded his influence when, as in the case of the agro-industrial wage dispute, the ideologically-motivated policies of others failed. By 1988, Chidzero had become the Senior Minister responsible for economic affairs, while Nkala had moved first to Home Affairs, then to the Ministry of Defence, and finally resigned after being implicated in the 'Willowgate' car scandal.

While rising in government, Chidzero has made clear his technocratic approach to policy issues. When asked about his personal ideology, he answered simply:

I suppose realism, that's all. To be realistic is to be an optimist and a pessimist at the same time. Seriously speaking, I believe in the gradual evolution of the national order, as well as the international order, toward better and more equitable forms of government and distribution of income.[18]

His approach, therefore, differs dramatically from others in the government who are committed to forcing changes to bring about a transition to socialism. While Chidzero claims that 'there is no inherent contradiction between socialism and market forces',[19] neither he, nor anyone else in Zimbabwe, has made any attempt to explain how to resolve that apparent contradiction.

Ideology also does not play a major role in the ministries dealing with technical issues because ZANU(PF), viewed by everyone as the body responsible for furthering ideology, has neither the organization nor the formulated plans to make a significant impact on technocratic decision-making. Ministers such as Enos Nkala consistently said that the 'highest

[18] Quoted in C. L. Morna, 'Bernard Chidzero: Toward a durable strategy', *Africa Report* (Sept.–Oct. 1988), 46.

[19] Quoted in A. Meldrum, 'Zimbabwe goodbye to socialism with new business code', *Weekly Mail* [Braamfontein, Johannesburg], 12 May 1989.

organs' of ZANU(PF) must be involved in the planning and formation of economic policy.[20] However, in such areas as the national distribution of land, agricultural producer prices, health, and national minimum wages, the party was simply not able to influence policy-makers. The possibility of these programmes being seriously affected by the current ideology is limited because no other organization in Zimbabwe can provide the impetus for a radical approach to public policy. Similarly, after almost a decade of Independence, no theorist has really attempted to outline a Zimbabwean form of socialism which would be relevant to public policy. For instance, President Mugabe, in his introduction to former-President Banana's book on socialism, admits that Banana's call for socialism falls short of suggesting which particular ideology should be adopted.[21]

Where ideology does play a strong role is in non-distributional issues that allow Zimbabwe to make high-profile statements with little actual cost. In particular, this has meant that the government has been at its most ideological when dealing with foreigners. Foreigners have a special position in Zimbabwe's demonology because, since the founding of the colony by the BSA Company, the White population has been associated with foreign capital. Many Black leaders also attribute the staying power of the Rhodesians during UDI to hidden or — as in the case of the US Byrd Amendment allowing Rhodesian chromium imports despite UN sanctions — open collaboration with Western nations. Thus, in the case studies examined, it was the government's approach towards new foreign investment that was most influenced by ideology because of the symbolism that foreign investment possessed and because of the desire of government leaders to reiterate their ideological stance. Similarly, of all the public policy issues in Zimbabwe, it is in foreign policy that ideology has played the greatest part. Zimbabwe's determined effort to develop a significant voice in foreign affairs, most notably in its decision to accept leadership of the Non-Aligned Movement and in its conflicts with the United States,[22] stems from the desire to have an ideological

[20] *The Herald*, 14 Sept. 1985.

[21] R. G. Mugabe, 'Foreword', in C. S. Banana, *Towards a Socialist Ethos* (Harare, College Press, 1987), x.

[22] Although the United States initially promised a large amount of aid to Zimbabwe at Independence, this assistance was eventually cut off in 1986 after former President Carter walked out of a US Embassy Fourth-of-July reception when a Zimbabwean junior minister delivered a long speech criticizing US policy in Southern Africa. This incident had been preceded by several cuts in US aid as a protest against Zimbabwe's criticism of American foreign policy. Aid was resumed in 1988.

basis for at least some part of its public policy. Ibbo Mandaza notes perceptively that

> it is in the field of foreign policy that the government is most keen to project the impression of independence of action, even though it should be obvious that *international relations* by definition prescribe and proscribe the limits of that 'independent' action on the part of the individual state.[23]

The reason that ideology plays such an important role in Zimbabwe's foreign policy is precisely because the country is so constrained in other areas: an ideological foreign policy is the easiest way of maintaining the image of a radical state without indulging in risky policy measures. It turned out that Zimbabwe probably paid a higher price for its foreign policy than it had originally expected, especially in view of the cut-off of aid by the United States. However, there are few signs that the government would have been deterred even if it had been able to predict how the US would act.

Many of the radical members of the government have shaped those areas in which ideology can influence policy. They are not only attracted to areas where they can leave their imprint but are put there as a way to keep more technical economic matters from being influenced by ideology. For instance, Nathan Shamuyarira, the former Minister of Information, Posts and Telecommunications and probably the most outspoken radical in the Cabinet, used the 'information' function of his portfolio to become the major radical voice in foreign policy; he was eventually appointed Foreign Minister in 1988. Also in the 1988 Cabinet reshuffle, Dr Herbert Ushewokunze and Dr Frederick Shava, two of the more radical voices in the leadership, were moved to the President's Office in order to help strengthen the structure and operations of ZANU(PF).

Therefore, Zimbabwe can have a public policy that is essentially dichotomous: technocrats handle economic matters such as exchange rates or the placement of clinics, while the more ideologically committed attend to symbolic politics, especially in foreign policy, which allows Zimbabwe to claim that it is a bona fide radical state. It follows that most factional conflict will occur where economic issues and political symbolism collide. In fact, for many years the government had refused to sign the OPIC-type agreements which would have made Zimbabwe more attractive to foreign investors. However, the new investment guidelines do not

---

[23] I. Mandaza, 'The State and politics in post-White settler colonial situation', in his (ed.), *Zimbabwe: The Political Economy of Transition*, 63, emphasis in the original.

represent a sudden reversal of socialist policy because the government's socialist ideology had never become developed enough to mould policy in the first place. The changes in the foreign-investment regulations represent not so much a changed ideology as a change in the division of labour among politicians and technocrats: owing to the unemployment crisis, foreign investment is now seen as an issue that needs to be handled by technocrats rather than one that is appropriate for symbolic politics. Zimbabwe found that allowing ideology to influence foreign-investment policy was too expensive, and therefore decided, as it has in many issues, that its pronounced ideology should no longer play a substantial part in this area.

Ideology does have a role in Zimbabwe but that role is limited by the realities of the state's capabilities and by the judgements of the nation's leaders. Marxism is not absent from policy discussions and, contrary to what some believe, the national leadership has not undergone a sudden ideological transformation; there is too much bitterness against the previous regime for that ever to happen. Therefore, because so many areas of public policy have been exempted from ideological influence, in those area — such as foreign policy — in which Zimbabwe can display its ideological commitment at low cost, it does so enthusiastically. Zimbabwe is neither 'radical' nor 'conservative' but a country where there is a constant conflict between ideological and technocratic advice and where both of these influences are allowed to affect public policy.

The Role of Robert Mugabe

The complexity of the role of ideology in Zimbabwe is to some degree a reflection of the different facets of the personality of, and the many different roles played by, Robert Mugabe. It is, of course, always extremely difficult to explain a leader's contribution successfully while he is still in power. Without Mugabe, Zimbabwe would still have gained its Independence and the country would have evolved under a different leader, but given Mugabe's pre-eminent political role it is difficult to imagine how it would have evolved. This section can only provide the most general evaluation of Mugabe from the evidence gathered in the case studies; a fuller assessment will have to be the task of other scholars. Yet Zimbabwe's first leader is too important and too interesting to ignore.

Unlike most revolutionaries who come to power, Robert Mugabe has both the temperament and the intellect to lead his country successfully in peacetime. In striking contrast to his friend, Samora Machel, Mugabe has been able to temper his strongly-felt revolutionary beliefs with the realities of the present. For instance, even during the war, when moderation was hardly being rewarded, Mugabe said: 'We also have to examine the theory [socialism] in the light of our history and the environment of our country. Only in this way can we evolve, from the pure ideology of socialism, a workable practical ideology for Zimbabwe.'[24] While Cabinet discussions are confidential, those who interact with Mugabe usually place him with the more ideological camp on most policy issues. As one former senior civil servant said, 'Mugabe is oriented toward the *povo* [the people]. He always has to be brought down [to less radical positions].' Similarly, it is widely believed that Mugabe was ready in 1986 and 1987 to impose sanctions on South Africa but that he was convinced by other Ministers that such a move would be an economic disaster for Zimbabwe. Unlike in the domestic arena, where constraints abound, Mugabe has been able to follow his radical instincts in foreign policy, both at the bilateral level (except for the sanctions issue) and in his capacity as Chairman of the Non-Aligned Movement from 1986 to 1989. In many ways Mugabe is the embodiment of the conflict between the technocratic advice and ideological imperatives that confront the whole regime on almost every policy.

In contrast to many African leaders, Robert Mugabe is not closely associated with many specific aspects of public policy. Despite frequent Cabinet reshuffles, Zimbabwe's leadership is collegial, and Ministers are usually seen as being responsible for policy measures that fall under their portfolio. For instance, there are very few countries in Africa where the Finance Minister is seen to have such an important and prominent role in decision-making as Chidzero does in Zimbabwe. Indeed, at times it appears that Mugabe stands back from the policy-making process, intervening only when there is scandal (as in the case of the badly managed parastatals,[25] or in the internecine leadership battle that revolved around charges of tribalism in 1986) or when a policy clearly is not working (as with the agro-industrial wage dispute). This detachment is occasioned partly by the amount of work demanded by a system which forces most

[24] Quoted in 'The early life and work of President Robert Gabriel Mugabe', *Zimbabwe News* (December 1987), XVIII, 18.

[25] I have discussed the parastatal crisis and Zimbabwe's problems in restructuring its public sector in J. Herbst, 'Political impediments to economic rationality: Explaining Zimbabwe's failure to reform its public sector', *Journal of Modern African Studies* (1988), XXVII, 67–84.

decisions to Cabinet-level, but it is also a reflection of the disposition of a leader confident enough of his own position not to need to develop the kind of ostentatious personality cult found in many other parts of Africa. To take a small but significant example, Robert Mugabe is one of the few leaders in East and Southern Africa who does not have his portrait on the nation's currency.

Other than foreign policy, the issue that Mugabe has been most closely associated with is reconciliation. It was Mugabe's personal appeals to many of the Whites after the 1980 election that led to a reduction of tensions and allowed the country to progress in the early months of Independence. He was perhaps most eloquent on Independence night: 'If yesterday, I fought you as an enemy, today you have become a friend. If yesterday you hated me, today you cannot avoid the love that binds you to me and me to you.'[26] In subsequent years, when racial tensions threatened to increase, Mugabe repeatedly intervened to promote domestic tranquillity. As has been noted above, reconciliation is based on several very hard political bargains, but not all leaders would have been creative enough to reach a *modus operandi* with the White population and then work to make sure that the political arrangements survived.

Therefore, although Robert Mugabe is involved in a great number of policy decisions — indeed, there are very few issues discussed in this book in which he was not a participant at some level — there are also few issues that are clearly his alone. This position allows him to concentrate on broad issues, such as reconciliation or foreign policy, that interest him and are clearly of great importance to the nation. However, it also means that many issues in Zimbabwe are left unresolved when neither the technocratic nor the more ideological factions within the regime are able to assert themselves, and Mugabe does not often become involved enough in specific policies to be an effective arbiter. There are also risks when a leader detaches himself from the actual decision-making process. Indeed, the dangers posed by Mugabe's distance from the policy process first became evident when the Army was allowed to run amok in Matabeleland. His distance from the cut and thrust of the policy process will become even more significant in the 1990s when the country is faced with many hard choices while adjusting the structure of the economy in order to provide employment for the large number of school-leavers. There is a danger that, without firm leadership on the many individual

---

[26] 'The early life and work of President Robert Gabriel Mugabe', 28–9.

decisions that will have to be made, the ideological split within Zimbabwe's Cabinet as well as sheer inertia will prevent the adoption of the new measures that will have to be taken if the country is to avoid economic stagnation and potentially great social upheaval. Unfortunately, there are few indications so far that Mugabe will be able to transfer his grand vision of where the country is heading to concrete policy decisions in order to prevent Zimbabwe from continuing to stagnate because of the indecision of its leaders.

The Drive for a One-party State

With the announcement of a successful end to the unity talks between ZANU(PF) and PF-ZAPU in December 1987, Zimbabwe took the most important step toward the creation of a one-party state. In the 1990 general elections, the government will have the right to prevent other parties from contesting parliamentary seats. If this step is taken, party competition in Zimbabwe will come to an end.

Unfortunately, much of the analysis concerning the proposed consolidation of the parties is ahistorical. As the outline of Zimbabwe's history in Chapter 2 makes clear, Rhodesia always had a *de facto* one-party system. Indeed, after examining the country's history, it becomes clear that it is the present period of multi-party competition that is the aberration rather than the new government's desire for a one-party state. For the same reasons that the Rhodesian Front had a monopoly on political representation — enormous ethnic (in the case of the Smith regime, racial) support and the ability to determine access to power almost completely — the new government is moving towards a one-party state. The interesting question is not whether a one-party state will come (or, rather, return) to Zimbabwe but what this evolution of the electoral system will mean, if anything, for the distribution of power and benefits.

The first step in the drive to a one-party state occurred mid-1987 when the twenty seats in Parliament that were reserved for Whites were abolished. In the most concrete demonstration of reconciliation yet, the government then announced almost immediately that it was voluntarily appointing eleven Whites to the parliament so that the settler community could retain a public voice in Zimbabwe. However, even if there were no White presence in Zimbabwe's Parliament, the effect on overall politics in Zimbabwe would have been minimal. While many people in Zimbabwe think that the provision in the Lancaster House Constitution which gave the Whites the ability to veto constitutional changes has had a restraining effect on the government in such areas as land seizure, the procedural veto is not actually crucial to government actions. The history of Africa over the last twenty-five years is replete with Constitutions that have been abandoned almost immediately after Independence; if the government had truly thought it in its interest to violate the Constitution, the procedural requirements would have been ignored. Rather, the Lancaster House Constitution was so successful because the economic bargain between the Whites and Blacks in Zimbabwe allowed the government to fully respect the constitutional provisions which safeguarded White property. For instance, once the government had decided that, rather than attempt to institute dramatic change in the racial composition of the private sector, it would simply let the White population wither away, it was relatively easy to respect the constitutional prohibition against seizing businesses. If the underlying economic bargain between Whites and Blacks had not been present at that time, no matter how well constructed the Constitution was, it would have failed because the new government would have soon found the guarantees of the rights of Whites impossible to live with in view of the political exigencies of instituting a dramatic redistributive programme. It is the government's overall strategy on economic transition, and not procedural safeguards, that preserves the Whites' property and position in society. Indeed, it is probably in the Whites' best interests that their Parliamentary seats were abolished, because the disproportionate representation served only as a source of racial friction.

Similarly, the elimination of the reserved Parliamentary seats does not mean that the Whites' political voice will be lost. This study has repeatedly demonstrated that groups that represent Whites' interests have developed alternative lines of communication with the government which bypass Parliament completely. Representations to the government by the CFU, CZI, Chamber of Mines and other interest groups are much more important than mediocre speeches by White parliamentarians. Of all the White interest groups studied, only the Association of Rural Councils mentioned White parliamentarians as a significant source of help in pressuring government, and they did not seem to be particularly successful in this endeavour. In an area such as agricultural producer pricing, where communication between commercial farmers and the government is crucial, Whites will continue to transmit their views through their representative federations which have become the major avenue of communication between the Black government and the settlers.

It is also doubtful whether the merging of ZANU(PF) and PF-ZAPU will have an impact on distributional politics. MPs would probably interfere in the political process now if they could benefit politically by securing more political goods (e.g. clinics or land) for their areas. However, ZANU(PF) already has a strong majority in Parliament and unquestioned control of the government so there was actually very little competition between candidates in the 1980 and 1985 elections. Where ZANU(PF) won (in six of the eight provinces of Zimbabwe) it had overwhelming support, and where it lost (in Matabeleland) its candidates appeared to have no chance of winning. The Midlands Province, the only area of the country that had even some electoral competition in 1980 (ZANU(PF) won 'only' 59,7 per cent of the vote), became another ruling-party stronghold in 1985 when Robert Mugabe's party won 82,9 per cent of the vote.[27] The incentive for MPs to try to intervene in bureaucratic decisions, therefore, is low because the outcome of almost all electoral conflicts in Zimbabwe is clear ahead of time. One official in the Ministry of Lands confirmed this portrait:

MPs do not play a role. MPs are hand-picked from the centre. They don't really represent the people. All MPs have to sing a song given from the centre. Many don't know what is happening in the rural areas.

Indeed, this respondent noted that many MPs do not come from the areas they now represent. Of all the decisions examined in this study, only groundnut pricing was affected by the political rivalry between the two main parties, and that in only one year. Therefore, an end to the multi-party system should bring no real differences in the way in which the government makes basic allocation decisions.

The one area where unification of the parties has made a difference is in Matabeleland, where tensions decreased noticeably after the unity pact was announced. As was noted in Chapter 8, electoral competition between the parties had aggravated ethnic tensions because of the clear association of PF-ZAPU and ZANU(PF), respectively, with the Ndebele and Shona groups. Unity has also meant that PF-ZAPU's supporters can no longer be suspected by the government of being potential sympathizers with South Africa's attempts to destabilize Zimbabwe. The decrease in suspicion, combined with the noticeable drop in dissident activity after the amnesty following the announcement of the unity pact, means that

[27] See Table XVI, p. 170.

the kind of ethnic violence that erupted in the mid-1980s will probably not occur again.

A further question remains concerning the role of the ZANU(PF) in a one-party system. It now appears that the party, even if it gains a monopoly on electoral representation in Parliament, will not play a significant role in decision-making on most allocation issues at the national level. As the case studies have repeatedly suggested, the party has not developed a middle-level cadre of technical experts who could intervene when issues are being considered by the bureaucracy. Indeed, respondents were often surprised that I even asked whether the party played a significant role in decision-making. The party is, however, the locus of decision-making on some purely political issues. For instance, it was repeatedly suggested in interviews that the Politburo would make the ultimate decision concerning the unification of the parties; but this is naturally a party issue.

Another indication that the party will not play a significant role in decision-making in the near future can be found in the increasing importance of the Cabinet. One of the clearest strands of Zimbabwean politics since Independence has been the upward movement of decision-making. In many of the case studies examined (e.g. agricultural producer prices, foreign investment) what had previously been decided by the bureaucracy is now considered at the ministerial level. However, when the government shifted the locus of decision-making, it chose to enhance the role of Cabinet and not the party. Cabinet leaders are (with the important exception of Chidzero) also the top members of the party, but the fact that the new centres of decision-making were formally kept inside the traditional government structure suggests that ZANU(PF) will not become part of the state apparatus. Indeed, the initial absence of Chidzero from the Politburo, and his lack of responsibility for economic matters in his later appointment to that body, suggest that the party, despite the rhetoric, is not meant to have an important role in the policy process.

Many in ZANU(PF) have suggested that the party's presence at grass-roots level should be used to allow local grievances to be transmitted to the government leadership without having to go through the bureaucracy. However, this development would seem unlikely because of the party's poor organizational structure. The party does not have nearly as strong a structure as the Rhodesian Front had (see Chapter 2), mainly because the RF was representing only a few thousand people while ZANU(PF) tries to be the spokesman for several million peasants often in isolated areas. For instance, in the case of the squatters, ZANU(PF) encouraged land seizures, but it was the government's own procedures, rather than the party, which gave the illegal settlers access to the national leadership. It would require a complete restructuring of the ruling party and a massive increase in the size and competence of its middle-level cadres to allow local grievances to be transmitted directly to the national leadership.

A role for the ruling party in strengthening local-level demands also seems unlikely, given the predominance of the bureaucracy in allocation decisions. The case studies of health and land clearly show that the nature of the issue-areas and the government's own decisions on the structuring of institutions have made the civil service the key element involved in the issues of most concern to people in the rural areas. The national leadership is important on issues such as foreign-investment policy, but this kind of policy would never be affected by the views of those at the village level. Of the issues studied, only in the area of agricultural producer prices would it be appropriate to have a structure that is able to transmit local-level concerns to the national leadership. The party could conceivably play a role in the setting of producer prices, because this issue affects every peasant who grows crops and the Cabinet has seized control of the price-setting process. However, ZANU(PF) has yet to show any interest in this issue and, once again, has not developed the technical expertise necessary to become a significant player in the setting of farm product prices. Indeed, in a rather ironic reflection of the role ZANU(PF) is not playing, there is already a group doing an excellent job in transmitting grass-root concerns about prices to the national leadership: the Commercial Cotton Growers Association.

The establishment of a multi-party system in Zimbabwe was primarily a British device to reassure Whites that they could continue to live in the country under Black rule. Now that the government has made its overall policy clear, such a constitutional reassurance is no longer necessary. Neither will the abolition of inter-party competition among Blacks cause significant changes in Zimbabwe, because actual electoral conflict was rare due to the overwhelming strength of each party in its respective ethnic homeland. Therefore, elimination of party competition will not affect the distribution of political goods because MPs even in the 1980s had very little incentive to interfere with bureaucratic decision-making. However, once inter-party competition is abolished, it is unlikely that ZANU(PF) will use its monopoly on political representation to become a significant actor in the decision-making process. It lacks the structure, the personnel, and a defined political agenda to perform such a role, and the government's own institutional procedures make significant party intervention unlikely.

Conclusion

Zimbabwe's political system has undergone tremendous changes since 1980. Reconciliation, the drive for socialism, and the attempt to consolidate the parties have had and still have the potential to have a major effect on the nature of politics in the young country. With such dramatic changes occurring in the economy and in the polity, it is only natural that some would use to labels to try to describe the evolution of politics in Zimbabwe. In every country, of course, labels do matter because they are an important element of political symbolism, but, especially for the outsider, these labels have to be understood in context. Thus, in Zimbabwe, reconciliation has meant a compromise of interests, not a change in human nature; the transition to socialism is more a struggle to expand the existing system than an attempt to overturn the current arrangements; the radical ideology espoused during the war has neither been abandoned nor fully adopted; and the consolidation of parties into a one-party state is a return to the historic norm rather than a striking new goal. Only by understanding what these developments truly mean in the light of the country's history and current politics can we hope to comprehend the actions Zimbabweans will take as they approach their second decade of Independence.

Chapter Eleven

Understanding State Autonomy
and the Locus of Decision-making

In Chapters 3–9, I have surveyed a variety of cases that can be used to theorize constructively about the nature of the African state. After discussing the empirical foundation, I will return in this chapter to the central problem of the study: understanding the autonomy of the state and the locus of decision-making. In keeping with the analysis developed in Chapter 1, the conclusions will focus on developing middle-level generalizations in order to understand better where the independent variables for explaining politics reside and which parts of the state are the most important in resource-allocation decisions.

Range of Issues Studied

Since countries do not design their politics to fit social scientists' matrices, it is almost impossible to design a study that encompasses a perfect range of issues. Similarly, it is possible to study only a limited number of cases if in-depth research is to be undertaken. However, within the constraints of time and access, the cases examined in this study do cover a very broad range of institutions, issue-areas and interest groups.

The variety of institutions considered in this study can be seen in Table XXI. The structures range from the old agricultural price-setting bureaucracy to the institutions to distribute land that the government is still trying to establish at the local level. In between these extremes are new national structures (such as the Minerals Marketing Corporation and the Wages and Salaries Review Board), new provincial structures (such as the Provincial Medical Directors) and old local structures (such as the Rural Councils). The age of the institution is very important in Zimbabwe because institutions created before Independence will tend to be White-dominated. In contrast, institutions established after Independence have none of the problems reviewed in Chapter 2 concerning the trustworthiness of the state apparatus because these new structures had been designed and staffed by the new government. The ability of Zimbabwe's

Table XXI

RANGE OF INSTITUTIONS STUDIED

Issue	Level	Age	Test of institutional capabilities
Land (White farmers vs. government)	National/Bureaucracy	New	Moderate
Land (Squatters vs. government)	Local	New	Extreme
Agricultural producer prices	National/Cabinet	Old	Slight
Foreign investment			
A) Existing	National/Cabinet	Old	Slight
B) New	National/Cabinet	New	Slight
Minerals marketing	National/Permanent Secretary	New	Slight/Moderate
Health			
A) Rural health centre siting	Provincial	New	Slight/Moderate
B) Commercial farm-workers	Provincial/Local	Old	Extreme
National minimum wage	National/Bureaucracy	New	Moderate

leaders to create viable institutions also differed considerably from case to case. For instance, the government had little difficulty establishing the Foreign Investment Committee or changing the nature of the agricultural producer price process because both of these reforms could be achieved by executive fiat. A more difficult test of state capabilities was the establishment of the national minimum wage machinery, because the government did not have the requisite technical expertise to set wages in a coherent manner. At the far end of the scale, establishing structures to distribute land or provide adequate care for farm-workers was extremely difficult for the government, because both of these issues required the creation of strong local institutions where none had existed before, or involved extreme administrative burdens which threatened to over-whelm the new regime.

A similarly broad array is found in the issue-areas studied (see Table XXII). Firstly, the issue-areas vary in the number of decisions that have to be taken at any one time. For instance, resource allocation in some of the issues (such as land acquisition) requires many complex decisions to be made and demands a minimum level of technocratic expertise. In con-trast, other issue-areas (such as minerals marketing and foreign invest-ment) involve relatively few decisions which can be easily controlled by national leaders. Secondly, issue-areas also vary in the number of de-cisions taken *over* time. At one end of the continuum are issues that require only one set of decisions (such as the creation of the MMCZ) which allow the use of 'blitzkrieg' tactics by the government. At the other end is the yearly process of setting farm product prices and national minimum wages, the iterated nature of which has allowed the interest groups trying to influence the government to learn from their experience. Some of the issues studied also involve political goods which give a strong advantage to the central government (such as in the siting of health centres) or to interest groups (as in the cases of the squatters and of commercial farmers in the area of health care).

Thirdly, the type of interest group studied varies dramatically. The interest groups first differ by race: there are White groups that try to pressure the government individually (foreign investors, mining com-panies), White groups that united with Black groups (the CFU–NFAZ–ZNFU alliance on farm product pricing), and Black groups that lobby the government by themselves (squatters). The case studies have also exam-ined groups that are highly organized (the CFU), well organized (the Chamber of Mines), poorly organized (the ZCTU) and not organized at all

Table XXII

RANGE OF ISSUE-AREAS STUDIED

Issue	Number of decisions at any one time	Number of decisions over a period of time	Nature of political good favours . . .
Land (White farmers vs. government)	Many	Many	
Land (Squatters vs. government)	Many	Many	Squatters
Agricultural producer prices	Few	Annually	
Foreign investment			
A) Existing	Few	Many	
B) New	Few	Many	
Minerals marketing	One	One-time	
Health			
A) Rural health centre siting	Few	Many	Government
B) Commercial farm-workers	Many	Many	Rural Councils
National minimum wage	Few	Annually	

(commercial farm-workers). Finally, these groups vary in the legitimacy they hold in the eyes of government: from high (Black communal farmers demanding more land) to low (foreign mining companies) with the others arrayed in between. Some of these groups have also gained or lost legitimacy since Independence. The CFU, for instance, has sought to improve the government's view of White farmers through its alliance on pricing policy with Black farmers, while the unions have lost some of their standing because of Zimbabwe's poor economic circumstances and their continually unrealistic demands. Once again, there is an almost infinite variety of societal groups, but the range depicted in Table XXIII does capture the major elements of diversity among groups that seek to pressure the African state.

Interaction of Institutions, Issue-Areas and Interest Groups

One of the clearest findings of this study is that neither state autonomy nor the locus of decision-making can be understood — or, even more importantly, predicted — from an examination of institutions, interest groups or issue-areas in isolation. For instance, the squatters would never have been powerful except that the structure of the resettlement bureaucracy gave them an exceptionally valuable entrée to the national leadership and the nature of land itself allowed them to easily control the political good being allocated. Similarly, because the institutionalization of the wage-setting process rewards the organizational attributes of the employers, workers were actually much more powerful when they were striking in an unco-ordinated manner than when they were formally represented by a national organization. The effect of the interaction between institutions, interest groups and issue-areas demands that certain elements of African politics be viewed in a different light.

The Power of Institutions

Over recent years, an increasing number of scholars have denigrated the role that institutions play in African politics. For instance, Jackson and Rosberg begin their influential book on personal rule by arguing that 'politics in most Black African states do not conform to an institutionalized system'.[1] They make this claim because

most African states have *abstract* constitutions and institutions in the Rawlsian sense but very few have them in fact: the formal rules of the political game do not

---

[1] Jackson and Rosberg, *Personal Rule in Black Africa*, 1.

Table XXIII

RANGE OF INTEREST GROUPS STUDIED

Issue	Interest group/Race	Organizational ability	Legitimacy
Land (White farmers vs. government)	CFU–White NFAZ–Black	Good Poor	Low/Medium High
Land (Squatters vs. government)	Squatters–Black NFAZ–Black	None Poor	Low High
Agricultural producer prices	CFU–White NFAZ/ZNFU–Black	Good Good	High High
Foreign investment A) Existing B) New	Foreign–White Foreign–White	Medium Medium/Poor	Low Very low
Minerals marketing	Chamber of Mines–White	Medium	Very low
Health A) Rural health centre siting B) Commercial farm-workers	Ethnic groups–Black Farm-workers–Black Rural Councils–White	Poor None Good	Low Medium Low
National minimum wage	EMCOZ–White ZCTU–Black	Good Low	Low first, then medium High first, then medium

effectively govern the conduct of rulers and others political leaders in most places most of the time.[2]

It is clearly true that very few countries in Africa have managed to institutionalize political order through parliaments and courts. However, it is a major mistake to argue that, simply because most African countries lack strong national structures, institutions play an insignificant role in influencing the pattern of resource-allocation politics. As this examination of Zimbabwe's politics has shown repeatedly, institutions — even weak institutions — structure state decision-making and have a determining effect on the kind of interest group that will benefit from allocation processes. For instance, the decentralized system in health care played an important role in reducing the influence of ethnic groups, while at the same time it enabled the Rural Councils to be exceptionally important in the delivery of services to commercial farm-workers. Similarly, the government was able to establish new procedures or institutions in the areas of agricultural producer pricing, foreign investment (up to 1989) and minerals marketing that greatly influenced the nature and relative bargaining positions of the major actors. In all these cases, institutions have played a major role, even though Zimbabwe can hardly be classified as a strongly institutionalized country. Indeed, there are always plans to change the Constitution, and the national leadership has had to adopt a whole series of informal decision-making rules because it does not trust a large part of the state apparatus.

It is important that a distinction is drawn between overarching political formations such as constitutions and courts, which are not usually institutionalized in Africa, and the everyday battle over resources, which is always shaped by the nature of institutions whether they are strong in the traditional sense or very weak. This point becomes clear, however, only when institutions are examined as part of a complex process of decision-making that also involves interest groups and issue-areas. Scholars are misled into thinking that African institutions do not play a significant role in the political process because they judge African state structures in a vacuum and come to the conclusion that they are either weak or non-existent. Jackson and Rosberg, for instance, conclude that in countries such as Ghana and Zaïre the government is 'more nominal than

---

[2] Ibid., 11, emphasis in the original.

real'.[3] The usual assumption is, therefore, that state structures in Africa are not important in resource allocation. However, the significance of institutions lies in the way in which they influence the nature of the decision-making process, rather than in how strong they are in themselves. Institutions, then, are the templates of resource-allocation politics.

The Poverty of Organization

One of the most common assumptions in the analysis of politics in the Third World (and in richer countries) is that interest groups gain power as they increase their organizational skills. Huntington, for instance, wrote that, especially in the Third World where public institutions are not strong, 'organization is the road to political power'.[4] However, in the cases studied, interest groups that at first glance seem strong because of their organizational prowess often fared poorly in government decision-making, while those which seem powerless sometimes did well. By far the best example is that of the Chamber of Mines, which appears to be extraordinarily powerful because it is composed of five or six of the largest and most politically sophisticated multinational corporations in the world which dominate a strategic sector of Zimbabwe's economy. Yet the mining houses lost in their conflict with the government over the Minerals Marketing Corporation because of the juridical power lodged in state institutions. Similarly, groups that were not well organized occasionally succeeded in benefiting from allocation decisions. For instance, the mhunga and rapoko farmers were favoured by the introduction of peasant welfare considerations into the price-setting process, and the squatters were able to acquire land because government procedures gave them direct access to the national leadership.

However, this does not imply that a group which is seeking resources from the state cannot expect to benefit from good organization. For instance, the well-organized employers' confederation did influence the government on wages — but only after an institutional structure was adopted which enhanced their particular strengths. Similarly, the unorganized commercial farm-workers, as might be expected, fared poorly in government decisions, though their fate was aggravated by the nature

---

[3] R. H. Jackson and C. G. Rosberg, 'The marginality of African states', in G. M. Carter and P. O'Meara (eds.), *African Independence: The First Twenty-Five Years* (Bloomington, Indiana Univ. Press, 1986), 59.

[4] Huntington, *Political Order in Changing Societies*, 461.

of Zimbabwe's local-government system. The interaction of institutions and interest groups means that organizational strength is only partly a predictor of group power. It is not sufficient, therefore, to say simply that organizational strength will cause societal groups to be 'relatively powerful' when influencing the state: the important task is to identify the factors which make organizational strength significant when those groups try to influence the state.

State Autonomy

The complexities of the dynamics of state autonomy have constantly been illustrated by the seven case studies of government decision-making in Zimbabwe. Given the dramatic differences in state autonomy revealed in the case studies, it has become clear that global judgements as to whether the state is or is not autonomous are simplistic and misleading. It is possible to say that the state is or is not always autonomous only with a tremendous loss of analytic rigour and with a grave risk of simply being wrong. To truly understand state autonomy, a much more complicated and subtle analytical strategy will have to be developed.

The first step in developing a more sophisticated perspective on state autonomy is to break down the concept. It was shown explicitly in the case studies that states can be seen to be making two types of decisions: those concerning the structure of the decision-making process (involving structural autonomy), and those concerning actual resource allocations within the institutional structures of the state (involving situational autonomy). The second type of decision is much more common than the first because states seldom redesign institutions in fundamental ways. States can be autonomous when designing decision-making processes, but not when allocating resources within those structures. For instance, the Zimbabwe government could be structurally autonomous when reforming the mechanism for setting prices for farm products but, by design, be susceptible to societal pressures when the actual price decisions were being made. Similarly, the structure that the government decided upon when it institutionalized the wage-setting process rewarded the organizational capabilities of EMCOZ and gave the employers much greater leverage in bargaining over national minimum wages. The reverse is also occasionally true: for example, Zimbabwe sacrificed structural autonomy in the area of land acquisition in order to gain more freedom of action in the provision of services to its population and in its relationship with South Africa. By breaking down the concept of state autonomy, it is possible to draw more sophisticated conclusions about societal pressures against the state, and eliminates the danger of making a single, generalized judgement.

Structural Autonomy

Given that institutions are so important in the actual decision-making process, it is crucial to examine the state's structural autonomy. However, because scholars have generally failed to discern the role of institutions in African states, they have usually not discussed explicitly the concept of autonomy in the design of state structures. This is unfortunate because many have asked what difference formal independence has made for weak African countries that are then at the mercy of the international economy and are often still economically linked to their former colonizer. A study of a state's structural autonomy highlights the area in which Independence should make the most difference because, if nothing else, formal control over the state apparatus gives leaders the capacity to change the nature of decision-making processes. A study of structural autonomy, therefore, examines the most basic level of state power.

Situational Autonomy

It is equally important to understand situational autonomy, because, as this study has repeatedly demonstrated, there is room within many institutional arrangements for interest groups to influence states successfully — but only if the societal groups choose the correct tactics. For instance, in the case of agricultural producer pricing it was essential to understand the tactics of the commodity groups because the different strategies they adopted allowed them different degrees of influence on the state's decisions. Similarly, while the employers were favoured by the bargaining structure which the government adopted to determine wages, they still had to present their case persuasively by focusing on the issues that were of greatest concern to the government. A study of the state's situational autonomy also enables an understanding of how the issue-area affects state–society relations. For instance, it is only when examining the iterated nature of the process of setting agricultural producer prices that it becomes clear how the characteristics of this particular issue-area allowed the various farmer groups to devise a viable strategy for negotiations with the government.

Determinants of State Autonomy

This study of decision-making in Zimbabwe makes it clear that the first thing that must be considered when trying to understand either the state's structural or situational autonomy is the 'match-up' between interest groups and state institutional structures. By 'match-up' I mean an interest group directly confronting the particular part of the state that is making the allocation decision in such a way as to cause political conflict. If the organizational structure of the interest group cannot match up against the institutional structure of the state, the state will be autonomous. For instance, in Zimbabwe, ethnic groups could not match up against the government structure dealing with the siting of rural health centres because these groups are able to join forces only when national decisions are being made between regions; therefore, the state was effectively insulated from societal pressure in determining the location of health centres. Similarly, the NFAZ could not match up against government institutions on the land issue because the communal farmers' organization had no access to the officials making the actual decisions and, as a result, were unable to debate with them the technical issues involved; therefore, there was no political conflict and the state was autonomous.

The key to being able to identify the factors which enable an interest group's nominal economic power or organizational cohesion to be translated into real influence over the state lies in the way in which the interest group relates to the state's institutional structure. Unless a pressure group can match up to state structures, thereby causing an actual conflict, the characteristics of the group will be irrelevant. Therefore, it is the relationship between state institutions and interest groups that will determine whether the organizational abilities of the societal group are to play an important role in conflicts over allocation decisions.

The match-up of interest groups and state structures is particularly important in Africa because there is seldom any other system (such as a voting system) through which society's views can be presented to the state. In other types of political systems it is possible that the match-up between societal groups and institutions will not be as crucial because there are alternative ways in which to pressure the state. For example, tax reform in many parts of the United States (e.g. Proposition 13 in California) has been enacted mainly as a result of voter-sponsored referenda rather than by interest groups lobbying for reductions in taxes. However, in Africa, this sort of approach is not usually possible, so, if an interest group cannot match up to the state's structures, it will not be able to influence allocation decisions in its favour.

If the interest group can match up against the state structure, then other factors will determine whether the state can be autonomous in the face of societal demands. The second issue that must be examined, therefore, is to what extent the state is capable of carrying out its intended action. There is a much greater likelihood that a state will be autonomous if the execution of the policy contemplated derives from the state's juridical power rather than from its administrative or organizational expertise. For instance, the government of Zimbabwe could act autonomously in the establishment of the Foreign Investment Committee and the Wages and Salaries Review Board and in the revision of the price-setting mechanism for farm produce, because all these bodies could be created or reformed by legal fiat. The Minerals Marketing Corporation could also be established by fiat, though the implementation of the functions of that organization also involved skillful manœuvring by the government. However, in complicated exercises that require extended capabilities — such as in the distribution of land through a new bureaucracy or in the amalgamation of Rural and District Councils — it is likely that the state will be open to societal pressures. Policies that stretch state capabilities will result in porous institutions that leave policy-makers exposed to societal demands (as in the case of the squatters) or in a bureaucracy so dependent on outside actors for expertise that the government may become compromised (as was the case with Rural Councils).

As far as many states are concerned, it would be quite difficult to say just what kind of policies involve extended state capabilities, as states differ widely in their abilities and organization. However, because African states in general are poor and have weak organizational and administrative capabilities, any policy which does not originate from the state's juridical powers will leave the state open to societal pressures (other factors are also involved and are discussed below). Simply because a policy requires extended capabilities does not mean that the state will automatically lose its autonomy; however, the only actions of the African state whose outcome, when there is a political conflict, is likely to be determined by internal factors will be those originating from the state's juridical power.

It is possible to go still further in determining the autonomy of the state, even when interest groups do match up against state institutions and when the policy does involve extended state capabilities: the next level of analysis is that of the nature of the political good. If the state's capabilities are already stretched on an issue in which there is political conflict, a political good that provides a decisive advantage to the societal interest group can have a determining effect on the state's autonomy. The best example of such a political good is land, as demonstrated in the conflict between squatters and communal farmers in Zimbabwe. The characteristics of land gave the illegal settlers an overwhelming advantage against the weak bureaucracy that they were matched up against. In a similar way, the nature of health care on commercial farms gave the White farmers a major advantage in the conflict over the provision of health care to farm-workers. On the other hand, the nature of the political good may also reinforce state autonomy, as was the case with the siting of rural health centres.

In issues where there is political conflict, where state capabilities are stretched, and where the nature of the political good does not give either side an overwhelming advantage, the interaction between the attributes of the interest group and the nature of the issue-area will have a significant effect on state autonomy. It is clearly possible that groups involved in recurring issues will have an advantage in influencing the state because they can learn which lobbying techniques work best. However, there is no simple relationship between recurring issues and state autonomy. The ZCTU and the CFU, to take a comparison of extremes, have had contrasting experiences in their relationship with the government, even though both lobby on an issue that recurs annually. The key to determining whether an interest group will be able to take advantage of an iterated process is in its organizational ability. For instance, while the CFU and the ZCTU faced exactly the same kind of issue in terms of the number of decisions to be made, the CFU had the organizational wherewithal to take advantage of the iterated process of producer price setting and to learn how to influence the government. In contrast, the ZCTU's ability to learn was so poor that the iterated process of minimum wage setting actually weakened it because its demands were continually viewed by the government as being unrealistic. An iterated process, therefore, will probably lead to a loss of state autonomy when the lobbying group has the organizational capability to learn better pressure tactics.

The schematic diagram in Figure 5 displays the determinants of state autonomy in a serial pattern. Each of the middle-level hypotheses developed here is listed in a central box and examples of cases in which the state was or was not autonomous are cited in the boxes on the right-hand

Figure 5: THE DETERMINANTS OF STATE AUTONOMY

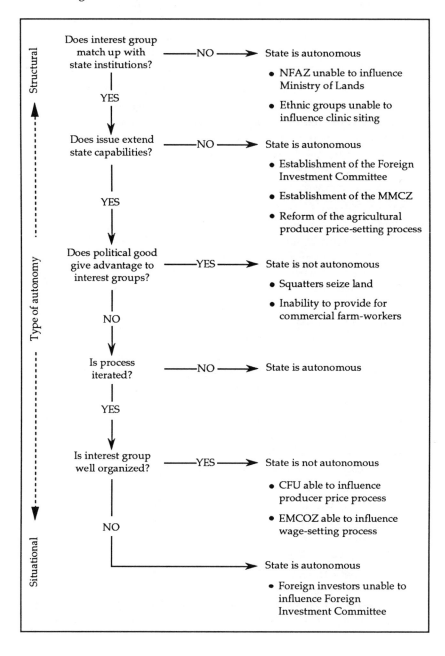

side. The schematic vividly displays the effects of interaction which play such an important part in understanding state autonomy. For instance, the answer to the question whether there is a match-up between institutions and interest groups has an immediate effect on whether further questions even need to be asked about the potential for state autonomy. Similarly, the different effects that the organization of the interest group can have even within the same type of iterated process is clearly demonstrated by the different branches of the schematic.

The display of the issues in the schematic also confirms the utility of the distinction between structural and situational autonomy. While both can be determined by asking the same questions, the issues eventually fall into very different categories. For instance, the propensity of African states to have more autonomy at the structural level is shown by the fact that conflicts regarding the nature of the decision-making process (such as those of the MMCZ and the FIC) appear at the top of the schematic because they are determined mainly by the juridical power of the state rather than by administrative or technical expertise. On the other hand, questions of situational autonomy, in which there is a clash between the state and societal groups within an institutional structure, tend (the exception is when there is no match-up between state structures and interest groups) to be decided further down the schematic, because situational autonomy is more dependent on such factors as the nature of the political good, the pressure group's legitimacy in the eyes of the state, and the ability of the interest group to choose appropriate tactics. As the schematic demonstrates, the African state is far less likely to be autonomous in these issues. For instance, the Zimbabwean state was autonomous in reforming the producer price setting process (a structural issue) but was not in many of its negotiations with the CFU over prices (a situational question). Similarly, factors occurring within the state probably explain the changes in the structure of institutions regulating foreign investment (thus structural autonomy) which led the state to design a process whereby it would be much more open to the pressure of foreign investors on a day-to-day basis.

This analysis of state autonomy provides a clear set of guidelines for understanding how insulated the state can be from pressure from societal groups. As general theories have clearly failed to address the question of volition in African politics, the series of middle-level propositions described above presents an attractive alternative to current theories. While these propositions may lack the elegance of grand theories, they are much less likely to be wrong than scholarly treatises which seek to describe every aspect of African politics. At the very least, these propositions form a set of testable propositions that can be used to examine other cases of government decision-making in the Third World.

Locus of Decision-making

The attention given to the locus of decision-making in this study was well rewarded. The new regime's clear response to the problem of the trustworthiness of the inherited state apparatus was to move the locus of decision-making upwards. Only in the cases (such as health) where a new bureaucracy was created — which would not arouse the suspicions that the bureaucratic structures inherited from the White regime would — was the decision-making process allowed to devolve to a lower level of government. In the case of land, it was certainly not the intention of the leadership that the bureaucracy should play such an important role in the decision-making process. In the case of foreign investment, the government first moved the locus of decision-making up and away from the white-dominated Reserve Bank, and only later moved it back to the bureaucracy whose racial nature, at least, would now be more acceptable.

The shift upwards in the locus of decision-making has had ramifications for the entire governmental system. The changes in formal and informal government procedures have resulted in a dramatic slowing down of the decision-making process as there is now a 'log-jam' at the Cabinet level because so many issues that were once decided in individual ministries are now debated by the national leadership. As a result, the government has been consistently late in making its policy decisions and this delay has resulted in confusion and considerable inefficiency. For instance, for the last several years President Mugabe has not been able to announce the national minimum wage increases on May Day, as he is supposed to, because of the slowness of the wage-setting process. Similarly, the decision in 1986 to discriminate against White maize growers was taken so late that it led to considerable confusion because farmers had already prepared their fields.

Determinants of the Locus of Decision-making

The locus of decision-making for a given issue is most clearly determined by the number of decisions that have to be taken at any one time, although other aspects of state operations will also have an effect. Issues that could be acted upon in a definitive, quick manner could be decided by Zimbabwe's leadership because they had neither the liberty nor the ability to solve the kind of problem that required many technical decisions to be taken over a period of time. In contrast, for those issues that require a large number of decisions the locus of decision-making will usually be the bureaucracy. The most dramatic example of this phenomenon was in the case of land. The bureaucracy dominated the process of land acquisition, but Ministers were able to intervene in land seizures because an instant decision could be made that would give land to a large number of people. Indeed, their frustration at the bureaucracy's control over the land-acquisition process may have made Ministers even more willing to intervene on the side of the squatters.

The relationship between the locus of decision-making and the number of decisions that have to be taken at any one time and becomes blurred when institutions are created with the specific intention of preventing the bureaucracy from gaining control of an issue. For instance, the creation of the Foreign Investment Committee, a distinct body that had sole respons-ibility for approving investment proposals, allowed Ministers to retain control of the decision-making process that regulated new capital inflows. When Ministers did not have the time to review the complexities of an investment proposal, investors simply had to wait, because no one outside the FIC had the authority to approve their proposal. Without such an institution, the locus of decision-making could have shifted to the bureaucracy, which was more capable of handling the complex decisions involved in many potential investments. Following the changes in the foreign investment regulations in 1989, the Cabinet was formally re-moved from the decision-making process by the creation of a new institution which will eventually be completely outside ministerial con-trol, thereby preventing ministers from interfering with investment decisions.

The Role of the Party

The attention to the locus of decision-making has also clarified the role of the ruling party, ZANU(PF), in government decision-making. The only area of government decision-making in which ZANU(PF) was involved was that of land seizures. The ruling party was able to become involved in this issue because the locus of decision-making was at the local level where the party was strong and because the action taken involved the physical seizure of an asset rather than long debates about a technical issue. ZANU(PF) has shown a marked inability to develop the kind of technical expertise that would allow it to become at least an actor in the other issues discussed in this study. It could be argued that, since the Cabinet is almost synonymous with the leadership of the party, ZANU(PF), in the final analysis, is intimately involved with all government decisions. However, the analysis in the case studies repeatedly made it clear that Ministers received their information from the government bureaucracy rather than from the party and that the party was not seen to be important in government decision-making. When the party and the government become indistinguishable at the pinnacle of the state, it is ZANU(PF) that loses its identity.

The key to the party playing — or, as is the case in Zimbabwe, not playing — a major role in decision-making is the party's ability, in the same way as a lobbying group's, to match up to state institutions. The party places demands on the state in the same way as other interest groups do, and it will be effective only if it can engage in a political dialogue with state institutions. If the party cannot address the civil servants on their own institutional and technical terms, then, as the case studies have shown, the party will not be a significant political actor. When the party does have a presence at the level of the state where decisions are being made, it is possible for it to play a role in the decision-making process, as ZANU(PF) did in the case of the squatters. For the party to play a role in the state, therefore, it is not a question of ideologues versus technocrats (or 'reds' versus 'experts'). Rather, the appropriate question is: do the ideologues need to be technocrats, and, if so, do they have the structural and organizational abilities to match up with the relevant part of the state apparatus. This explanation is persuasive in Zimbabwe's case because it suggests why even a party such as ZANU(PF), which played a much more powerful role over a longer period of time in the gaining of Independence than was the case for most parties in Africa, has become irrelevant in so many of Zimbabwe's decision-making processes in the post-Independence era.

Conclusion

African states are extraordinarily weak by world standards. Their administrative and organizational capabilities are hampered by a lack of resources and continual shortages in trained manpower. Their economies are continually affected by fluctuations in world commodity markets; poor transport and communications infrastructure often prevents them from establishing a significant presence in large parts of their country;

some, such as Zimbabwe, are also threatened by their neighbours. This seeming powerlessness has often led scholars to develop theories which do not comprehensively investigate whether the state can be an important actor in its own right in the conflict over resources. However, this study of decision-making in Zimbabwe suggests that, even in a country that faces many constraints, the state does have a degree of freedom to act in response to its environment. In the formation of institutions, in the design of decision-making processes, and in the everyday allocation of resources, the very real choices made by the state will have a determining effect on the course of politics in Africa.

Bibliography

Material Relating to Zimbabwe

Government Documents

AGRICULTURAL MARKETING AUTHORITY *Economic Review of the Agricultural Industry in Zimbabwe* (Harare, The Authority, various years).

COTTON MARKETING BOARD *Report and Accounts for the Year Ended 28 February 1985* (Harare, The Board, 1985).

GRAIN MARKETING BOARD *Report and Accounts* (Harare, The Board, various years).

MINERALS MARKETING CORPORATION OF ZIMBABWE *Annual Report 1983* (Harare, The Corporation, 1984).

ZIMBABWE *Air Zimbabwe Corporation: Interim Report of the Committee of Inquiry into Parastatals* [Chairman: L. G. Smith] (Harare, Govt. Printer, 1986).

ZIMBABWE *Annual Economic Review of Zimbabwe, 1986* (Harare, Ministry of Finance, Economic Planning and Development, 1987).

ZIMBABWE *Budget Statement 1987* (Harare, Ministry of Finance, Economic Planning and Development, 1987).

ZIMBABWE *Delineation of Village and Ward Development Committees in District Council Areas of Zimbabwe* (Harare, Ministry of Local Government and Town Planning, 1985).

ZIMBABWE *First Five-Year National Development Plan 1986–1990* (Harare, Ministry of Finance, Economic Planning and Development, 2 vols., 1986).

ZIMBABWE *Foreign Investment: Policy, Guidelines and Procedures* (Harare, Govt. Printer, 1982).

ZIMBABWE *Intensive Resettlement Programme: Planning and Management Perspectives* (Harare, Department of Rural Development, 1983).

ZIMBABWE *Intensive Resettlement Programme: Policies and Procedures* (Harare, Department of Rural Development), 1985).

ZIMBABWE *Intensive Resettlement: Policies and Procedures* (Salisbury, Ministry of Lands, Resettlement and Rural Development, 1981).

ZIMBABWE *Labour and Economy: Report of the National Trade Unions Survey 1984* (Harare, Ministry of Labour, Manpower Planning and Social Welfare, Department of Research and Planning, 1987).

Zimbabwe *Main Demographic Features of the Population of Zimbabwe: An Advance Report Based on a Ten per cent Sample* (Harare, Central Statistical Office, 1985).

Zimbabwe *National Income and Expenditure Report* (Harare, Central Statistical Office, 1985).

Zimbabwe *National Manpower Survey* (Harare, Ministry of Manpower Planning and Development, 3 vols., 1983).

Zimbabwe *Planning for Equity in Health: A Sectoral Review and Policy Statement* (Harare, Ministry of Health, 1984).

Zimbabwe *The Promotion of Investment: Policy and Regulations* (Harare, Govt. Printer, 1989).

Zimbabwe *Report of the Commission of Inquiry into Incomes, Prices and Conditions of Service* [Chairman: R. C. Riddell] (Harare, Govt. Printer, 1981).

Zimbabwe *Report of the Commission of Inquiry into the Agricultural Industry* [Chairman: G. L. Chavunduka] (Harare, Govt. Printer, 1982).

Zimbabwe *Report of the Commission of Inquiry into the Distribution of Motor Vehicles* [Chairman: W. R. Sandura] (Harare, Govt. Printer, 1989).

Zimbabwe *Socio-Economic Review of Zimbabwe 1980–1985* (Harare, Ministry of Finance, Economic Planning and Development, 1986).

Zimbabwe *Statistical Yearbook* (Harare, Central Statistical Office, various years).

Zimbabwe *Transitional National Development Plan 1982/83–1984/85* (Harare, Ministry of Economic Planning and Development, 2 vols., 1982).

Zimbabwe *Zimbabwe 'Health for All' Action Plan* (Harare, Ministry of Health, 1985).

Other Works

Arrighi, G. *The Political Economy of Rhodesia* (The Hague, Mouton, 1967).

Astrow, A. *Zimbabwe: A Revolution That Lost Its Way?* (London, Zed, 1983).

Beach, D. N. *War and Politics in Zimbabwe 1840–1900* (Gweru, Mambo Press, 1986).

Blake, R. *A History of Rhodesia* (London, Eyre Methuen, 1977).

Bourdillon, M. F. C. *The Shona Peoples* (Gweru, Mambo Press, 2nd edn., 1982).

Bowman, L. W. *Politics in Rhodesia: White Power in an African State* (Cambridge, Harvard Univ. Press, 1973).

BRADBURY, J. and WORBY, E. 'The mining industry in Zimbabwe: Labour, capital and the state', *Africa Development* (1985), X, 143–69.

BRATTON, M. 'Development in Zimbabwe: Strategy and tactics', *Journal of Modern African Studies* (1981), XIX, 447–76.

BRATTON, M. 'Settler state, guerrilla war, and underdevelopment in Rhodesia', *Rural Africana* (1979), IV–V, 115–30.

BRATTON, M. 'Structural transformation in Zimbabwe: Comparative notes from the neo-colonisation of Kenya', *Journal of Modern African Studies* (1977), XV, 591–612.

BRATTON, M. 'The public service in Zimbabwe', *Political Science Quarterly* (1980), XCV, 441–64.

BRATTON, M. 'The comrades in the countryside: The politics of agricultural policy in Zimbabwe', *World Politics* (1987), XLIX, 174–202.

CHEATER, A. P. *Idioms of Accumulation: Rural Development and Class Formation among Freeholders in Zimbabwe* (Gweru, Mambo Press, 1984).

CHIVIYA, E. M. 'Land Reform in Zimbabwe: Policy and Implementation' (Bloomington, Indiana Univ., Ph.D. thesis, 1982).

CLARKE, D. G. *Agricultural and Plantation Workers in Rhodesia* (Gwelo, Mambo Press, 1977).

CLARKE, D. G. *Foreign Companies and International Investment in Zimbabwe* (Gwelo, Mambo Press, 1980).

CLIFFE, L. 'Zimbabwe's political inheritance', in C. Stoneman (ed.), *Zimbabwe's Inheritance* (Harare, College Press; New York, St Martin's Press, 1981), 8–35.

COKORINOS, L. 'The political economy of state and party formation in Zimbabwe', in M. G. Schatzberg (ed.), *The Political Economy of Zimbabwe* (New York, Praeger, 1984), 8–54.

CRONJE, S. *et al. Lonrho: Portrait of a Multinational* (London, J. Friedmann, 1976).

CUBITT, V. S. *1979 Supplement to 'The Urban Poverty Datum Line in Rhodesia: A Study of the Minimum Consumption Needs of Families'* (Salisbury, Univ. of Rhodesia, Faculty of Social Studies, 1979).

CUBITT, V. S. and RIDDELL, R. C. *The Urban Poverty Datum Line in Rhodesia: A Study of the Minimum Consumption Needs of Families* (Salisbury, Univ. of Rhodesia, Faculty of Social Studies, 1974).

DAVIDOW, J. *A Peace in Southern Africa: The Lancaster House Conference on Rhodesia, 1979* (Boulder, Westview, 1984).

DAY, J. 'The insignificance of tribe in the African politics of Zimbabwe Rhodesia', in W. H. Morris-Jones (ed.), *From Rhodesia to Zimbabwe: Behind and beyond Lancaster House* (London, Cass, 1980), 85–109.

ECONOMIST INTELLIGENCE UNIT *Zimbabwe's First Five Years* (London, The Unit, EIU Special Report 111, 1981).

ECONOMIST INTELLIGENCE UNIT *Zimbabwe 1988–1989* (London, The Unit, 1988).

FLOWER, K. *Serving secretly* (Harare, Quest; London, Murray, 1987).

FREDERIKSE, J. *None but Ourselves: Masses vs. Media in the Making of Zimbabwe* (Harare, Zimbabwe Publishing House, 1982).

GAIDZANWA, R. B. 'Promised Land: Towards a Land Policy for Zimbabwe' (The Hague, Institute of Social Studies, M.Dev.Stud. thesis, 1981).

GANN, L. H. and GELFAND, M. *Huggins of Rhodesia* (London, Allen and Unwin, 1964).

GILMURRAY, J. *et al.*, *The Struggle for Health* (Gwelo, Mambo Press, 1979).

GREEN, R. H. and THOMPSON, C. B. 'Political economies in conflict: SADCC, South Africa and sanctions', in P. Johnson and D. Martin (eds.), *Destructive Engagement: Southern Africa at War* (Harare, Zimbabwe Publishing House, 1986), 245–80.

GREGORY, C. 'The impact of ruling-party ideology on Zimbabwe's post-Independence domestic development', *Journal of Social, Political and Economic Studies* (1987), XII, 115–56.

HANCOCK, I. *White Liberals, Moderates and Radicals in Rhodesia* (New York, St Martin's Press; London, Croom Helm, 1984).

HAWKINS, A. M. *Economic Growth, Structural Change and Economic Policy in Rhodesia 1965–1975* (Salisbury, Whitsun Foundation, 1976).

HAWKINS, A. M. *et al. Formal Sector Employment Demand Conditions in Zimbabwe* (Harare, Univ. of Zimbabwe Publications, 1988).

HAZLEWOOD, A. 'Kenyan land-transfer programmes and their relevance for Zimbabwe', *Journal of Modern African Studies* (1985), XXIII, 445–62.

HERBST, J. 'Political impediments to economic rationality: Explaining Zimbabwe's failure to reform its public sector', *Journal of Modern African Studies* (1988), XXVII, 67–84.

HODDER-WILLIAMS, R. *Conflict in Zimbabwe: The Matabeleland Problem* (London, Institute for the Study of Conflict, Conflict Studies 151, 1984).

INTERNATIONAL LABOUR ORGANIZATION *Labour Conditions and Discrimination in Southern Rhodesia (Zimbabwe)* (Geneva, ILO, 1978).

JORDAN, J. D. 'The land question in Zimbabwe', *Zimbabwe Journal of Economics* (1979), I, 129–38.

KINSEY, B. H. 'Emerging policy issues in Zimbabwe's land resettlement programmes', *Development Policy Review* (1983), I, 163–96.

KINSEY, B. H. 'Forever gained: Resettlement and land policy in the context of national development in Zimbabwe', in J. D. Y. Peel and T. Ranger (eds.), *Past and Present in Zimbabwe* (Manchester, Manchester Univ. Press, 1983), 92–113.

LAN, D. *Guns and Rain: Guerrillas and Spirit Mediums in Zimbabwe* (Harare, Zimbabwe Publishing House; Berkeley and Los Angeles, Univ. of California Press, 1985).

LANNING, G. *Africa Undermined: Mining Companies and the Underdevelopment of Africa* (Harmondsworth, Penguin, 1979).

LAWYERS COMMITTEE FOR HUMAN RIGHTS *Zimbabwe: Wages of War* (New York, The Committee, 1986).

LEYS, C. *European Politics in Southern Rhodesia* (Oxford, Clarendon, 1959).

LIBBY, R. T. 'Development strategies and political divisions within the Zimbabwean state', in M. G. Schatzberg (ed.), *The Political Economy of Zimbabwe* (New York, Praeger, 1984), 144–63.

MACHINGAIDZE, V. 'Company rule and agricultural development: The case of the BSA Company in Southern Rhodesia 1908–1923', in *The Societies of Southern Africa in the 19th and 20th Centuries: Volume 9* (London, Univ. of London, Institute of Commonwealth Studies, Collected Seminar Papers 24, 1981), 49–62.

MANDAZA, I. 'The state and politics in post-White settler colonial situation', in his (ed.) *Zimbabwe: The Political Economy of Transition 1980–1986* (Dakar, CODESRIA, 1986), 21–74.

MANDAZA, I. (ed.) *Zimbabwe: The Political Economy of Transition 1980–1986* (Dakar, CODESRIA, 1986).

MORRIS-JONES, W. H. (ed.) *From Rhodesia to Zimbabwe: Behind and beyond Lancaster House* (London, Cass, 1980).

MOYANA, H. V. *The Political Economy of Land in Zimbabwe* (Gweru, Mambo Press, 1984).

MUNSLOW, B. 'Prospects for the socialist transition of agriculture in Zimbabwe', *World Development* (1985), XIII, 41–58.

MUNSLOW, B. *Mozambique: The Revolution and Its Origins* (New York and London, Longman, 1983).

MURAPA, R. 'Race and the public service in Zimbabwe, 1890–1983', in M. G. Schatzberg (ed.), *The Political Economy of Zimbabwe* (New York, Praeger, 1984), 55–80.

MURRAY, D. J. *The Governmental System in Southern Rhodesia* (Oxford, Clarendon, 1970).

MUTAMBARA, J. G. 'Africans and Land Policies: British Colonial Policy in Zimbabwe, 1890–1965' (Cincinnati, Univ. of Cincinnati, Ph.D. thesis, 1981).

MUTIMBA, J. W. 'A Case Study of the Victoria Association of Master Farmers' Clubs with Specific Reference to the Role of Provincial Committees' (Harare, Univ. of Zimbabwe, B.Ed. thesis, 1981).

NICOLLE, W. H. H. 'The development of the subsistence sector in Rhodesia', *Rhodesian Journal of Economics* (1971), V, iv, 1–8.

PALLEY, C. *The Constitutional History and Law of Southern Rhodesia 1880–1965 with Special Reference to Imperial Control* (Oxford, Clarendon Press, 1966).

PALMER, R. H. 'The agricultural history of Rhodesia', in R. H. Palmer and N. Parsons (eds.), *The Roots of Rural Poverty in Central and Southern Africa* (London, Heinemann, 1977), 221–54.

PHIMISTER, I. R. 'Zimbabwe: The path of capitalist development', in D. Birmingham and P. M. Martin (eds.), *History of Central Africa* (New York and London, Longman, 2 vols., 1983), II, 251–90.

PHIMISTER, I. R. *An Economic and Social History of Zimbabwe, 1890–1948: Capital Accumulation and Class Struggle* (London, Longman, 1988).

RANGER, T. 'Matabeleland now', *African Affairs* (1989), LXXXVIII, 161–74.

RANGER, T. *Peasant Consciousness and Guerrilla War in Zimbabwe* (Harare, Zimbabwe Publishing House; Berkeley and Los Angeles, Univ. of California Press, 1985).

RANGER, T. *The Invention of Tribalism in Zimbabwe* (Gweru, Mambo Press, 1985).

RIDDELL, R. C. 'Zimbabwe's experience of foreign investment policy', in *Papers and Proceedings of the Seminar on Foreign Investment: Policies and Prospects* (London, Commonwealth Secretariat, 1985).

RIDDELL, R. C. 'Zimbabwe's land problem: The central issue', in W. H. Morris-Jones (ed.), *From Rhodesia to Zimbabwe: Behind and beyond Lancaster House* (London, Cass, 1980), 1–13.

RIDDELL, R. C. *The Land Question in Rhodesia* (Gwelo, Mambo Press, 1978).

RIFKIND, M. L. 'The Politics of Land in Rhodesia' (Edinburgh, Univ. of Edinburgh, M.Sc. thesis, 1968).

SACHIKONYE, L. M. 'State, capital and trade unions', in I. Mandaza (ed.), *Zimbabwe: The Political Economy of Transition* (Dakar, CODESRIA, 1986), 243–73.

SANDERS, D. 'A study of health services in Zimbabwe', in United Nations Conference on Trade and Development, *Zimbabwe: Towards a New Order: An Economic and Social Survey: Working Papers* (n.p., United Nations, UNDP/UNCTAD Project PAF/78/010, 2 vols., 1980), II, 401–58.

SCHATZBERG, M. G. (ed.) *The Political Economy of Zimbabwe* (New York, Praeger, 1984).

SCHNEIDER-BARTHOLD, W. 'Determinants and forms of external and internal dependence in Rhodesia and Namibia: Possible solutions to the problem of twofold dependence', in German Development Institute, *Perspectives of Independent Development in Southern Africa: The Cases of Zimbabwe and Namibia* (Berlin, The Institute, Occasional Paper 62, 1980), 1–31.

SEIDMAN, A. 'A development strategy for Zimbabwe', *Zambezia* (1982), X, 13–40.

SIBANDA, A. 'Socio-political organisation in the commercial farming areas', in *Report on the National Workshop on Health Services in the Commercial Farming Areas* (Kadoma, Ministry of Health?, 1986).

SMILEY, X. 'Zimbabwe, Southern Africa and the rise of Robert Mugabe', *Foreign Affairs* (1980), LVIII, 1060–83.

STONEMAN, C. 'Foreign capital and the prospects for Zimbabwe', *World Development* (1976), IV, 25–58.

STONEMAN, C. (ed.) *Zimbabwe's Inheritance* (Harare, College Press; New York, St Martin's Press, 1981).

STONEMAN, C. (ed.) *Zimbabwe's Prospects* (London, Macmillan, 1988).

STONEMAN, C. and DAVIES, R. 'The economy: An overview', in C. Stoneman (ed.), *Zimbabwe's Inheritance* (Harare, College Press; New York, St Martin's Press, 1981), 95–125.

SYLVESTER, C. 'Continuity and discontinuity in Zimbabwe's development history', *African Studies Review* (1985), XXVIII, 19–44.

UNITED NATIONS INDUSTRIAL DEVELOPMENT ORGANIZATION *Study of the Manufacturing Sector in Zimbabwe* (Vienna, Unido, DP/ID/SER.A/631, 3 vols., 1985).

VAN ONSELEN, C. *Chibaro: African Mine Labour in Southern Rhodesia, 1900–1933* (London, Pluto, 1976).

VERRIER, A. *The Road to Zimbabwe* (London, Cape, 1986).

WEINER, D. 'Land and agricultural development', in C. Stoneman (ed.), *Zimbabwe's Prospects* (London, Macmillan, 1988), 63–89.

WEST, R. *River of Tears* (London, Earth Island, 1972).

WHITESIDE, A. W. *Investment Opportunities in Southern Africa: The Business Climate in SADCC States* (Braamfontein, The South African Institute of International Affairs, 1987).

WHITSUN FOUNDATION *Trade and Investment in Zimbabwe: Volume II: Investment* (Harare, The Foundation, 1983).

WHITSUN FOUNDATION *Land Reform in Zimbabwe* (Harare, The Foundation, 1983).

WORLD BANK *Zimbabwe: Country Economic Memorandum* (Washington, World Bank, 1985).

ZAMBIA *Report of the Special International Commission on the Assassination of Herbert Wiltshire Chitepo* (Lusaka, Govt. Printer, 1976).

ZIMBABWE AFRICAN NATIONAL UNION (PATRIOTIC FRONT) *ZANU(PF) 1980 Election Manifesto* (Salisbury, ZANU(PF), 1979).

ZIMBABWE NATIONAL FARMERS' UNION *Settlement of Qualified Farmers in Resettlement Areas* (Harare, The Union, 1987).

General Works

BACHRACH, P. and BARATZ, M. S. 'Two faces of power', *American Political Science Review* (1962), LVI, 947–52.

BATES, R. H. 'The nature and origins of agricultural policies in Africa', in his *Essays on the Political Economy of Rural Africa* (Cambridge, Cambridge Univ. Press, 1983),107–33.

BATES, R. H. *Markets and States in Tropical Africa* (Berkeley and Los Angeles, Univ. of California Press, 1981).

BIENEN, H. 'State and revolution: The work of Amilcar Cabral', *Journal of Modern African Studies* (1977), XV, 555–68.

BIERSTEKER, T. J. *Multinationals, the State and Control of the Nigerian Economy* (Princeton, Princeton Univ. Press, 1987).

CALLAGHY, T. M. *The State–Society Struggle: Zaire in Comparative Perspective* (New York, Columbia Univ. Press, 1984).

CARTER, G. M. and O'MEARA, P. (eds.) *African Independence: The First Twenty-Five Years* (Bloomington, Indiana Univ. Press, 1986).

DAHL, R. A. 'A critique of the ruling elite model', *American Political Science Review* (1958), LII, 463–9.

ELLIS, F. *et al. Agricultural Pricing Policy in Mozambique, Tanzania, Zambia and Zimbabwe* (The Hague, Institute of Development Studies, 1985).

FREY, F. W. 'On issues and nonissues in the study of power', *American Political Science Review* (1971), LXV, 1081–101.

GOULBOURNE, H. 'Some problems of analysis of the political in backward capitalist social formations', in his *Politics and the State in the Third World* (London, Macmillan, 1979), 11–32.

HIGGOT, R. A. 'The state in Africa', in T. M. Shaw and O. Aluko (eds.), *Africa Projected: From Recession to Renaissance by the Year 2000?* (London, Macmillan, 1985), 14–42.

HINZEN, E. 'External dependence and structural underdevelopment in Liberia', in E. Hinzen and R. Kappel (eds.), *Dependence, Underdevelopment and Persistent Conflict: On the Political Economy of Liberia* (Bremen, Ubersee Museum, 1980), 320–40.

HIRSCHMAN, A. O. *Exit, Voice and Loyalty: Responses to Decline in Firms, Organizations and States* (Cambridge, Harvard Univ. Press, 1970).

HODDER-WILLIAMS, R. *An Introduction to the Politics of Tropical Africa* (London, Allen and Unwin, 1984).

HUNTINGTON, S. P. *Political Order in Changing Societies* (New Haven, Yale Univ. Press, 1968).

HYDEN, G. *No Shortcuts to Progress* (London, Heinemann, 1983).

JACKSON, R. H. and ROSBERG, C. G. 'The marginality of African states', in G. M. Carter and P. O'Meara (eds.), *African Independence: The First Twenty-Five Years* (Bloomington, Indiana Univ. Press, 1986), 45–70.

JACKSON, R. H. and ROSBERG, C. G. *Personal Rule in Black Africa* (Berkeley and Los Angeles, Univ. of California Press, 1982).

KITCHING, G. 'Local political studies in Tanzania and the wider context', *African Affairs* (1972), LXXI, 282–92.

LECA, J. and VATIN, J-C. *L'Algérie politique: Institution et régime* (Paris, Presses de la Fondation Nationale des Sciences Politiques, 1975).

LEYS, C. 'Capital accumulation, class formation and dependency: The significance of the Kenyan case', in R. Miliband and J. Saville (eds.), *The Socialist Register 1978* (London, Merlin Press, 1978), 250–3.

LEYS, C. *Underdevelopment in Kenya: The Political Economy of Neo-colonialism* (Berkeley and Los Angeles, Univ. of California Press; London, Heinemann, 1975).

LONSDALE, J. 'States and social processes in Africa: An historiographical survey', *African Studies Review* (1981), XXIV, 139–226.

MLIMUKA, A. K. L. J. and KABUDI, P. J. A. M. 'The state and the party', in I. G. Shivji (ed.), *The State and the Working People in Tanzania* (Dakar, CODESRIA, 1985), 57–86.

OUGAARD, M. 'Some remarks concerning peripheral capitalism and the peripheral state', *Science and Society* (1982–3), XLVI, 385–404.

ROTHCHILD, D. and CURRY, R. L. *Scarcity, Choice and Public Policy in Middle Africa* (Berkeley and Los Angeles, Univ. of California Press, 1978).

SAMOFF, J. 'Class, class conflict and the state in Africa', *Political Science Quarterly* (1982), XCVII, 105–28.

SCHAZTBERG, M. G. *The Dialectics of Oppression in Zaire* (Bloomington, Indiana Univ. Press, 1988).

SCOTT, I. 'Party and administration under the one-party state', in W. Tordoff (ed.), *Administration in Zambia* (Manchester, Manchester Univ. Press, 1980), 139–61.

SHIVJI, I. G. 'The state in the dominated social formations of Africa: Some theoretical issues', *International Social Science Journal* (1980), XXXII, 730–42.

SKOCPOL, T. *States and Social Revolutions: A Comparative Analysis of France, Russia and China* (Cambridge, Cambridge Univ. Press, 1979).

WORLD BANK *Accelerated Development in Sub-Saharan Africa: An Agenda for Action* (Washington World Bank, 1981).

WORLD BANK *World Development Report, 1989* (New York, Oxford Univ. Press, 1989).

WRONG, D. H. *Power: Its Forms, Bases and Abuses* (New York, Harper and Row, 1980).

YOUNG, C. and TURNER, T. *The Rise and Decline of the Zairian State* (Madison, Univ. of Wisconsin Press, 1985).

Magazines and Newpapers

Africa Economic Digest	London
Africa Report	New York
African Business	London
The Chronicle	Bulawayo
District Council Journal	Harare
The Financial Gazette	Harare
The Financial Times	London
Focus	Harare
The Herald	Harare
Journal of Social Change and Development	Harare
Moto	Gweru
New York Times	New York
The Sunday Mail	Harare
Weekly Mail	Johannesburg
Zimbabwe News	Harare

Index